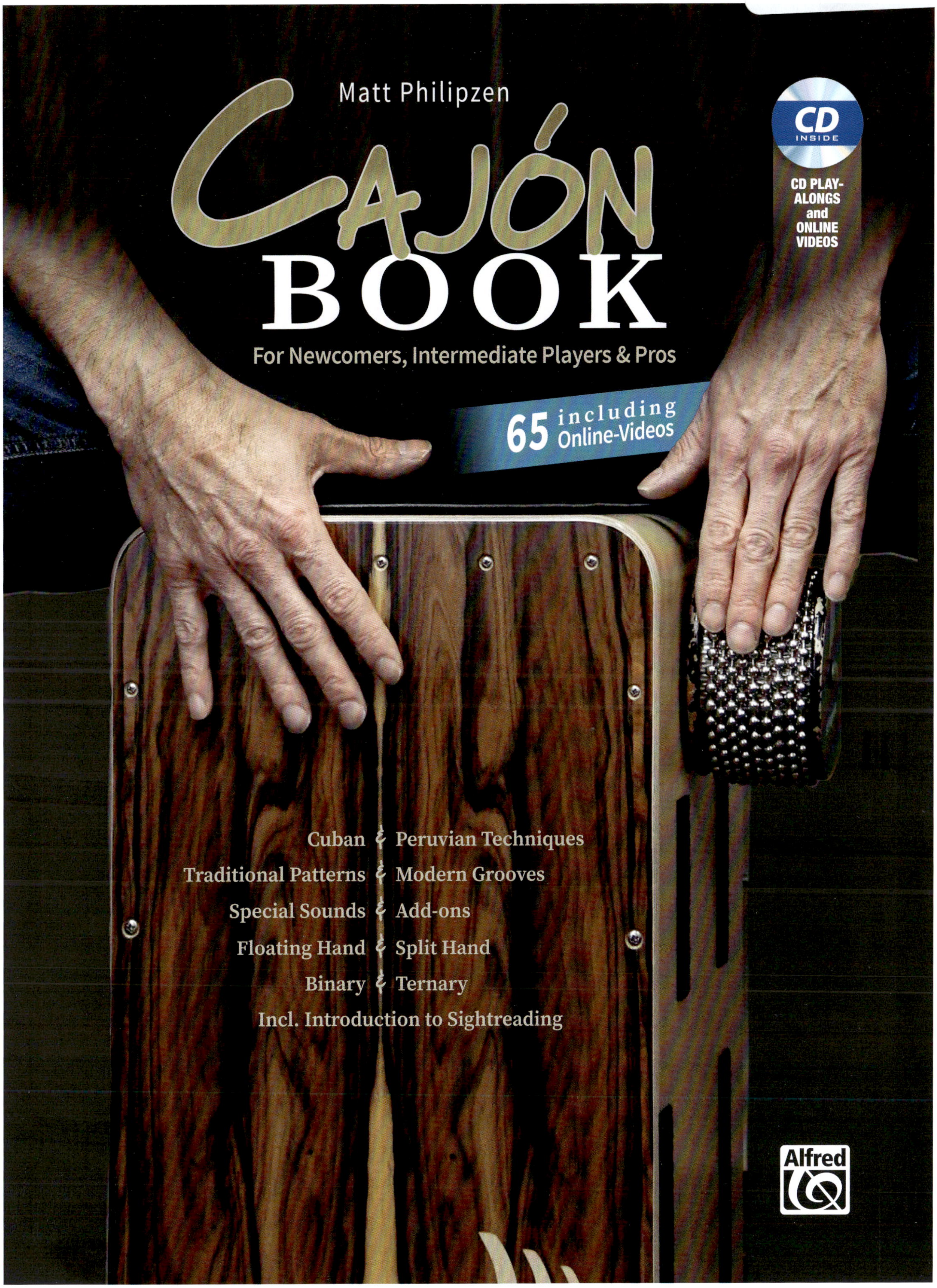

Matt Philipzen

CAJÓN BOOK

For Newcomers, Intermediate Players & Pros

CD INSIDE

CD PLAY-ALONGS and ONLINE VIDEOS

65 including Online-Videos

Cuban & Peruvian Techniques

Traditional Patterns & Modern Grooves

Special Sounds & Add-ons

Floating Hand & Split Hand

Binary & Ternary

Incl. Introduction to Sightreading

Alfred

Matthias Philipzen
CAJÓN BOOK

IMPRINT

THANKS

I dedicate this book to my wife Silke Al-Taie with Marius, Hannah, and Alex.

My special thanks to:
- my parents **Hanns** and **Else Philipzen** for their constant support.
- my brother **Peter Philipzen** for his wonderful music that completes my book again.
- **Rob Collomb** for inspiration, commitment and creativity in the creation of the first recordings and videos.
- **Thomas Petzold** from **Alfred Music** for his never ending input, his editing, his structure and the endurance.
- **Sven Peks** for the video production: audiolodge.de.
- **Christine Schröder** for years of friendship and the special photos: schroeder-foto.de
- **Manfred Feser-Lampe** for the detailed photos: manfredlampe.de

Many thanks for the instruments to:
- **Marianne** and **Gerhard Priel** for the unique **Schlagwerk** instruments: schlagwerk.com
- **Christian Wenzel** from **Paiste** for the best cymbals: paiste.com
- **Reiner Hartfil** from **Audiopro** for the **AKG Mikrophones** audiopro.de

www.matthias-philipzen.de

Alfred Music
LEARN • TEACH • PLAY

© 2021 by **Alfred** Music Publishing GmbH
info@alfredverlag.de
alfredmusic.de | alfred.com | alfredUK.com

All Rights Reserved.
Printed in Germany.

Coverdesign by Matthias Bielecke
Artwork & engravings by Thomas Petzold
Translation by Leonie McCaughren
Editing by Thomas Petzold, Matthias Bielecke
Item-#: 20296US (Book & CD & Online Videos)
ISBN 10: 3-947998-35-X
ISBN 13: 978-3-947998-35-7

Note:

*Matthias Philipzen's CAJÓN BOOK comes with a CD as well as links to video recordings on **youtube.com**.*

*The enclosed CD is a **Play-Along CD** containing two versions of each title:*

*1. **Demo track:** full version with cajón;*
*2. **Play-Along:** without cajón but incl. click track.*

*Demo tracks and play-alongs are marked with a **CD symbol** in the book.*

If you do not have a CD player, you can download the corresponding MP3 files from our website:

alfredmusic.de/downloads: Your password: 3947998341

*The entire work is protected by copyright in all its parts. By purchasing this product, the buyer receives the rights on the book and the associated digital data **for personal use only.** Any form of use outside the narrow limits of copyright law requires the prior written consent of the publisher. This applies in particular to reproductions like photocopies, printing, storage and processing in electronic media as well as translation into another language or dialect. **Any form of commercial, non-private use is strictly prohibited!***

Photos:
© by Manfred Feser-Lampe (cover photo)
© by Christine Schroeder (p. 3, backcover): schroeder-foto.de
© by Manfred Feser-Lampe: manfredlampe.de
(pp. 6, 11, 24, 25, 66–70, 97, 128)
© by Schlagwerk (p. 65): schlagwerk.com
Recordings: Peter and Matthias Philipzen
Video productions: Sven Peks: audiolodge.de

2

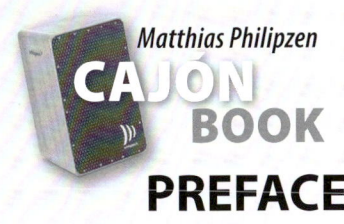

PREFACE

Dear reader,

*Welcome to the **CAJÓN BOOK**, my method for drummers new to the cajón , intermediate players, and pros!*

I have tried to meet the demands of the percussionists as well as the drummers and to show numerous facets of this wonderful percussion instrument.

In the course of my countless workshops over the last few years I have got to know different ways of playing, playing techniques, possible uses and rhythms, which have largely flowed into this book. There is a special focus on the cajón as a replacement for the drum set. Among others you'll find answers to the following burning questions:

- *How do I transfer drum rhythms to the cajón?*
- *How do I transfer traditional and modern patterns to the cajón to use in my music?*
- *Which stroke techniques for playing dynamically?*
- *How can I accompany songs on the cajón?*
- *What kind of add-ons are helpful for improving my playing with additional sounds and playing options to sound interesting and authentic?*

The **CAJÓN BOOK** covers *five* major subjects:

- *Basics*
- *Sounds & Movements*
- *Grooves & Styles*
- *Special Sounds & Add-Ons*
- *Techniques and Phrasing*

My fascination for this nearly 200 year old instrument may also infect you and show you that authentic rhythms from Peru, Brazil and Cuba, for example, have not lost any of their appeal and can be used just as well as modern grooves in current pop music.

I wish you a lot of fun while discovering, practicing and trying out my **CAJÓN BOOK**.

Matthias Philipzen
CAJÓN BOOK

CONTENT

First Basics and Tips

Sitting Position

Tilt your cajón slightly backwards. This will help take the strain off your back and make it easier to reach the playing surface. If this is difficult for you at the beginning, place a piece of wood under the front edge of the cajón so it is stable.

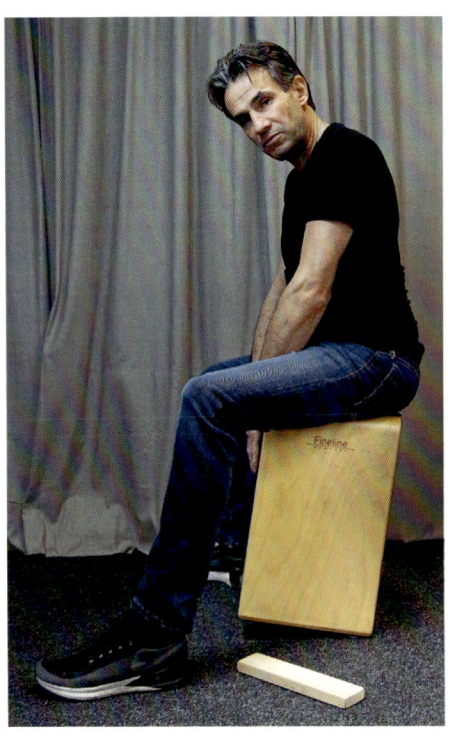

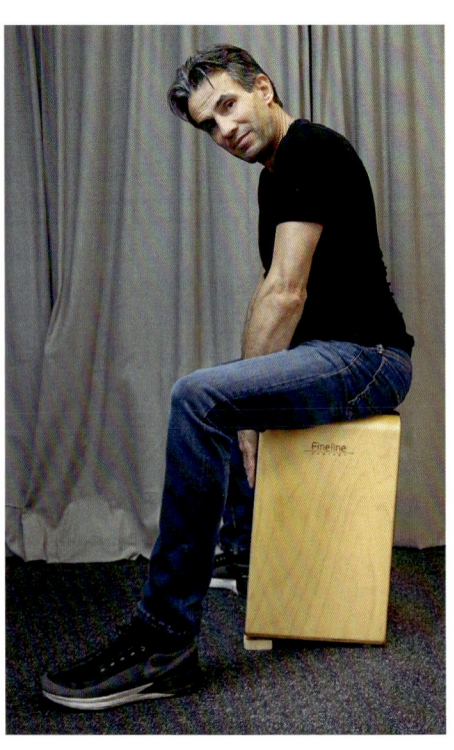

To tilt it, place a piece of wood ...   *... under the front edge of your cajón.*

Always try to practice in front of a *mirror* in order to be able to correct your hand position and the position on the instrument. You will find that after a while your hands will automatically find the right position, you can almost 'feel' the tone and its position.

Then the cajon will sound and you'll be able to elicit all its different timbres and colours.

The Sound Characteristics of the Cajón

The *cajón* is very different from a *conga* or a *snare drum* in terms of sound development. While the latter two instruments 'radiate' upwards—i.e. every nuance of the instrument is perceived directly by the player—the cajón develops its volume through the resonance hole on the back and thus emits its sound pressure to the rear (from the player's point of view). Take advantage of this characteristic.

Practicing Cajón in your Flat

If you want to practice in your apartment without disturbing the neighbors, cover up the resonance hole with a pillow and put a towel inside the cajón. This way the high and low tones of the instrument will still be audible and you can practice as usual without being concerned about the volume.

Playing Cajón on Stage

When you play with amplified instruments on stage, be sure to create a reflection. Sit about eight inches in front of a smooth wall or place a wooden board at the same distance behind you. This will enable you to hear the basses and nuances much better, you will play in a more relaxed way and you do not run the risk of compensating for a lack of volume with strength.

> **IMPORTANT:**
>
> *I recorded the exercises as a **left-hander**, for **right-handers** it appears **like in a mirror**.*
>
> *Use the rhythms beyond stylistic boundaries and you will see that this can be very exciting. The presented rhythms are only the basics that should stimulate your creativity and experimentation.*

Play-Along CD

The enclosed CD is a **Play-Along CD**. The 18 pieces are marked in the book with the CD symbol on the right. When you insert the CD you can select a total of 36 tracks. So I have recorded each piece in two versions as:

1. Demo Track where you can hear the band arrangement including the cajón. So you get an impression of how the cajón should sound.

2. Play-Along Track on which you can listen to the band arrangement as a play-along without cajón—including a click track only. In contrast to the demo tracks, a play-along can fit to several examples of the same style. The play-alongs will help you to play tracks that reflect the styles as authentically as possible.

If you don't have a CD player, you can download the corresponding MP3 files from our website: **alfredmusic.de/downloads**. You will find the password required on *page 2*.

Online Videos

I have recorded **small videos** for many of the examples in this book, where I show you exactly how the individual techniques work. Each video is marked with a **QR-Code** that links to the **YouTube channel** of **Alfred Music**. If you scan the QR code shown here with your cell phone or tablet, you will be taken directly to the complete playlist on *YouTube*. You will also find a QR code *for each individual film* at the corresponding place in the book.

Notation Symbols

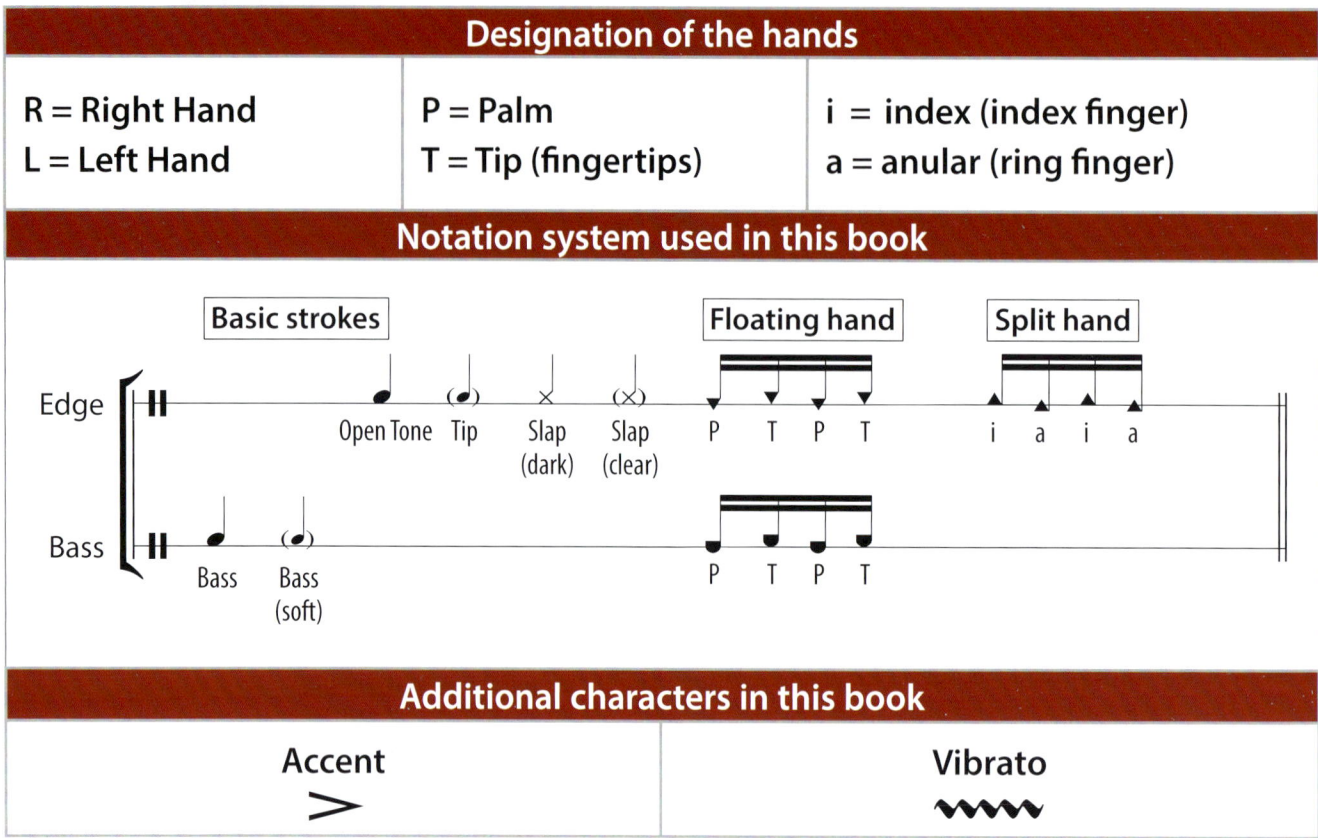

Designation of the hands

| R = Right Hand L = Left Hand | P = Palm T = Tip (fingertips) | i = index (index finger) a = anular (ring finger) |

Notation system used in this book

Basic strokes · Floating hand · Split hand

Edge: Open Tone, Tip, Slap (dark), Slap (clear), P T P T, i a i a

Bass: Bass, Bass (soft), P T P T

Additional characters in this book

Accent	Vibrato
>	∿∿∿

Counting or Rhythmic Language?

In my clinics I use the *basic idea* of the centuries-old Indian rhythm language *Konnakol*, which works with syllables for certain rhythmic figures. However, my version is simplified, since I use it only as a methodical tool to quickly grasp rhythms. I also do not claim to have correctly executed this complex topic, nor to have developed it further. It's important, that ...

1. you enjoy speaking the syllables,
2. the syllables help you to understand rhythms,
3. you manage them quickly—in all conceivable variations and situations—without any effort,
4. they simply 'roll!'

However, the syllable language is not ideal for the cognitive understanding of note values and their relationship to each other. For this, the mathematical method of counting is more useful which is why I include both methods in this book:

The classical counting method for the introduction of new note values, which are based on a mathematical understanding.

The syllable language for the development of rhythm patterns or rhythm sequences, in which the focus is on automation and internalization

This book is not explicitly aimed at cajón beginners, however, I decided to include some 'beginner's knowledge' regarding music notation. This is for the newcomers, intermediate players and pros who do not consider reading music notation as one of their strengths which, in my experience, is quite a few players.

Syllable Language Chart

The following chart shows at first sight, which kind of syllables and countings will be used in this book:

Note values	Syllables	Countings	Abbreviation
	Ta	1 (2 3 4)	4ths (quarter notes)
	Ta - ki	1 and (2 and 3 and 4 and)	8ths (eighth notes)
	Ta - ki - di also for groups of 3	tri - pa - let tri - pa - let ...	3plets (eighth-note triplets)
	Ta - ki - di - mi	1 e + a (2 e + a ...)	16ths (sixteenth notes)
	Ta - di - mi sustain 1st syllable!	1 + a... (2 + a ...) sustain 1st count!	8th + two 16ths (rhythm figure 1)
	Ta - ki Ta sustain last syllable!	1e e +... (2 e + ...) sustain last count!	Two 16ths + 8th (rhythm figure 2)
	Ta - ki - (di) - mi leave out (di)!	1 e (+) a leave out (+)!	16th+8th+16th (rhythm figure 3)
	Ta-ki-di-Ta-ki-di	six - tup - let six - tup - let ... counting is not very practicable!	6-tuplets (sixtuplets)
	Ta - ki - di - mi for groups of 4	1 e + a (2 e + a ...) 2 beats per syllable!	32nds (thirtysecond notes)

PART 1: SOUNDS & MOVEMENTS

PART 1 deals with the most important aspect of cajón playing for me, the **sound**. Every player will develop his or her own sound, his or her own personal touch, after intensive practice.

There are certain basics that you should master which will allow you to create different nuances of sound on your instrument faster. Please be sure to check out the *online videos* on how to do this!

Cajón translates as 'box,' and this should NOT be associated with this instrument when playing and listening to it. A more appropriate description would be a drum set substitute with a very unique wooden sound.

There are **four basic strokes** commonly used on the cajón:

Basic strokes (commonly known)			
BASS	OPEN TONE	TIP	SLAP

These four strokes are applicable if you want to get a quick overview of how to play the cajón. However, they are a rough abbreviation. Since *my focus is on the sound*, I prefer a more differentiated approach considering that all four basic strokes are derived from two different, regional ways of playing:

The two different ways of playing	
Cuban style	Peruvian style

Both differ primarily in their **volume**. The sound depends not only on the **strength of the stroke**, but also on the **position** and **execution** of the stroke, i.e. where the stroke is struck and which parts of the hand or fingers hit the surface.

The Cuban Way of Playing

Let's start with the *Cuban style*, which can also be called the *loud way of playing*. We owe this playing technique to the national instrument of the Cubans, *the conga*, and it can be transferred easily to the cajón. A distinction is made between the *bass stroke* and the *beat on the edge* of the cajón, which corresponds to the open tone.

BASS STROKE (Cuban)		EDGE STROKE (Cuban)	
When you hit the **bass stroke**, your hand is slightly hyperextended and your wrist is stiff. You play with the whole arm.	Online video 01	You hit the **edge** below the base of your finger and stretch your thumb away.	Online video 02

You perform both bass and edge stroke in a *elastic, bouncy* manner. Think out of the cajón surface as you would when *rebounding* the sticks on the drum kit.

On the following page you will find a *detailed overview* of both strokes played the Cuban way.

BASS STROKE — Cuban way of playing

 Full-size notehead **on the bottom line** of the staff

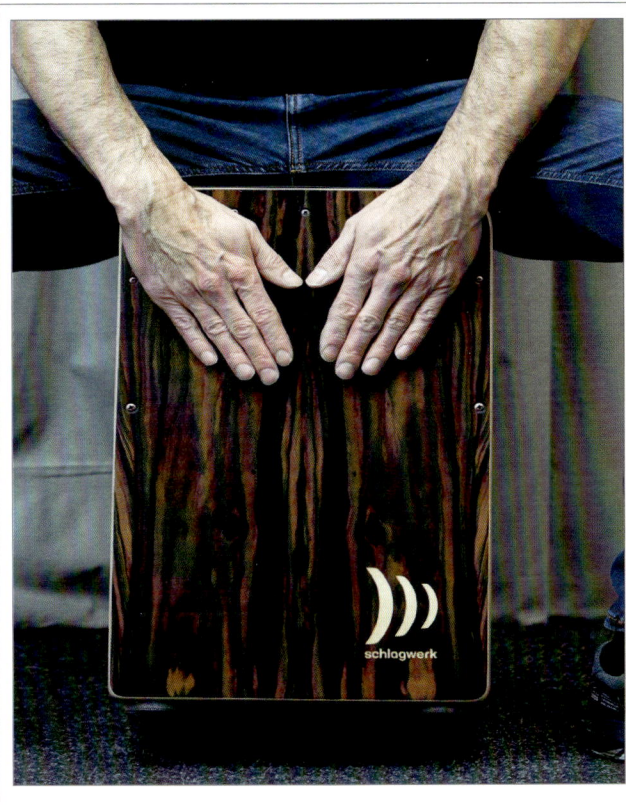

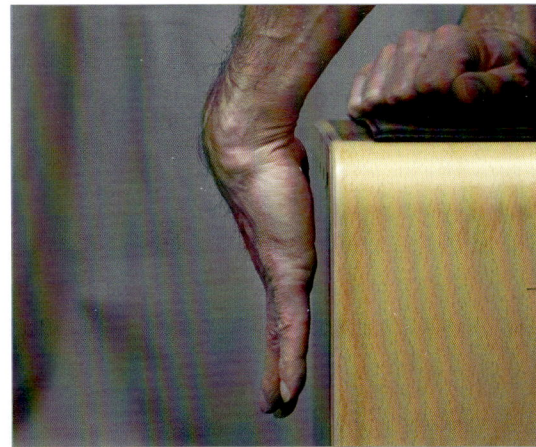

Position: Central, just above the center of the cajón face.

Execution: With a slightly overstretched hand, a stiff wrist and closed fingers, you strike with the flat of your hand from the whole arm. Only the palm of the finger and the upper palm of the hand hit the cajón face.

Sound: deep, warm, muffled, bassy

Function: bass drum

EDGE STROKE (Open Tone) — Cuban way of playing

 Full-size notehead **on the top line** of the staff

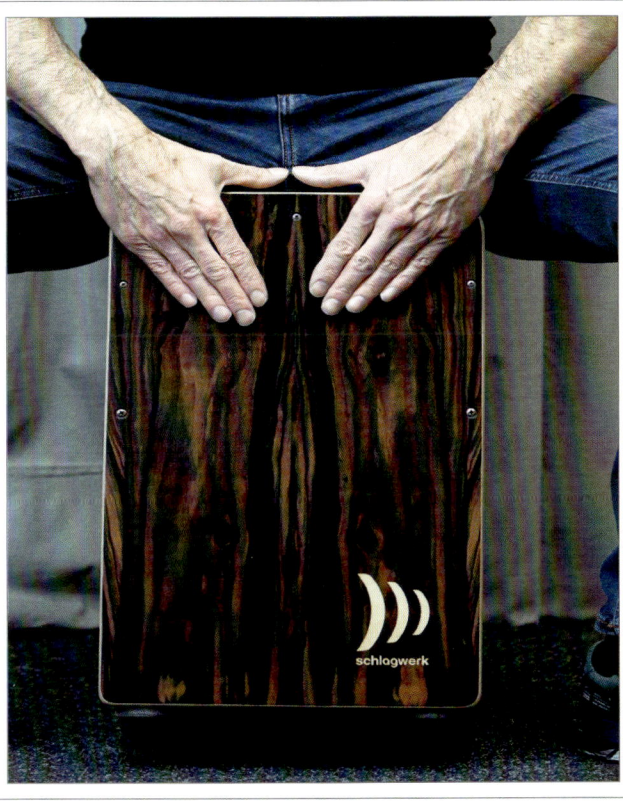

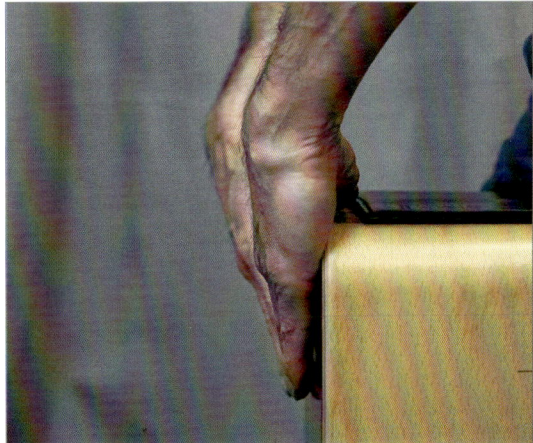

Position: Hit on the top edge to the side of the center (RH: right of center, LH: left of center).

Execution: Hit with stretched, but loose arched fingers. The thumb is straightened to the side. The front phalanges and the wrist hit the cajón face.

Sound: short, bright, open (quieter than the slap, *see p. 30*)

Function: snare drum

11

IMPORTANT:

*Watch the **videos** and choose a **slow tempo** (**60 bpm** = **60 beats per minute**). You can set the tempo exactly on a mechanical or electronic metronome (also available online as an app).*

You can practice both basic *Cuban strokes* in the following exercises to get used to the notation. In the **upper** system **the edge stroke** and in the **lower system** the **bass stroke**.

The first example only contains *quarter notes* and *quarter rests*. Repeat each line three times. The $\frac{4}{4}$ time signature at the beginning of the first line means: *Four quarter notes* are included in each bar.

Quarter note	Quarter rest
 ♩	 𝄽
Time signature	**Repeat sign**
 $\frac{4}{4}$	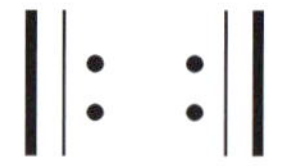 ‖: :‖

Count: *1 2 3 4* or **speak:** *Ta Ta Ta Ta.*

Pay attention to the correct execution of the strokes and count aloud!

Online video 03

Exercises with quarter notes (bass & edge)

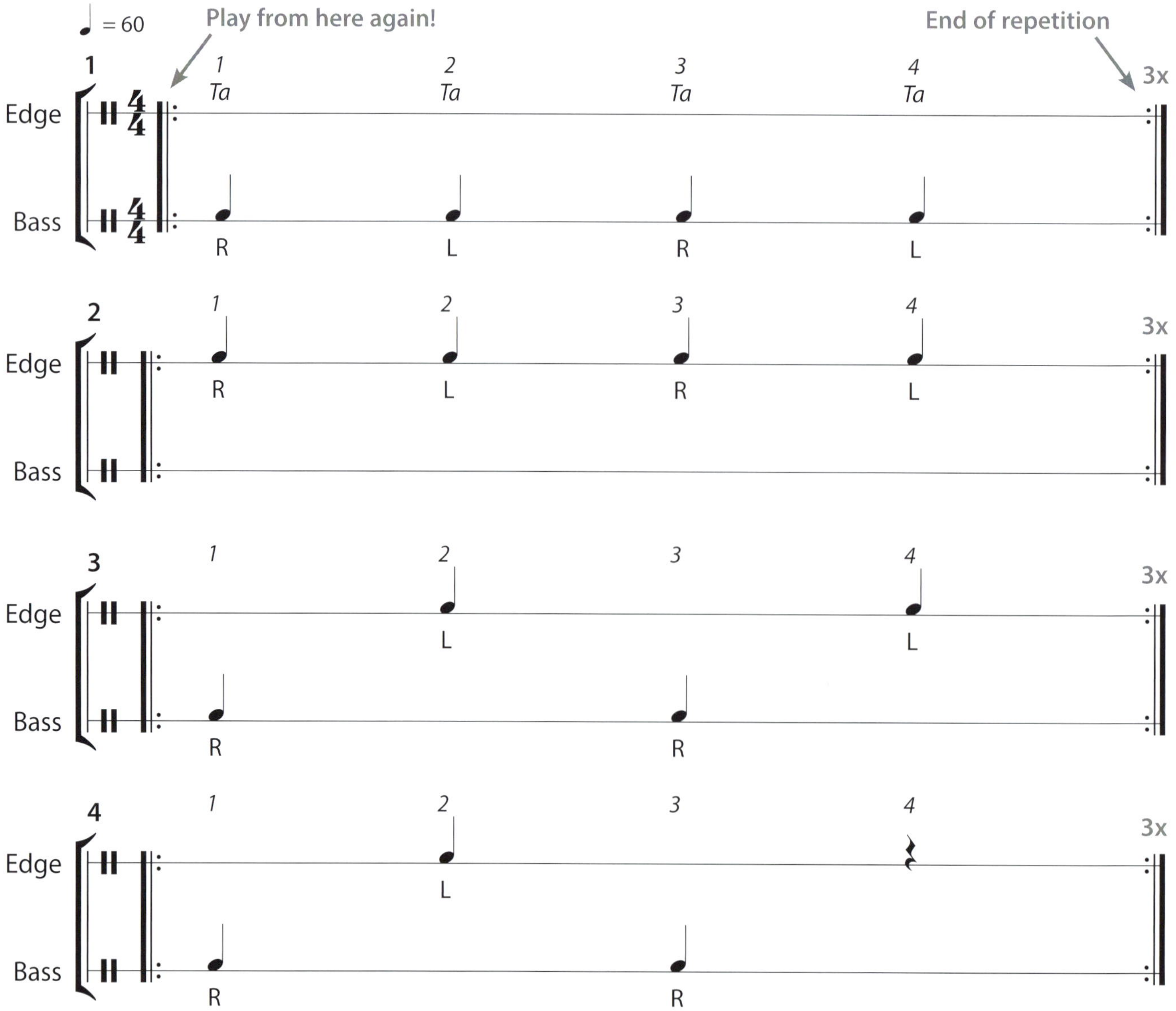

Play from here again! · End of repetition

The next exercise contains *eighth notes* and *quarter rests* only. Two eighth notes are just as long as a quarter note. *Eight* eighth notes fit into one $\frac{4}{4}$ bar.

Count aloud: *1*   +   *2*   +   *3*   +   *4*   +
                  (One and two and three and four and)

Speak aloud: *Ta*   *ki*   *Ta*   *ki*   *Ta*   *ki*   *Ta*   *ki.*

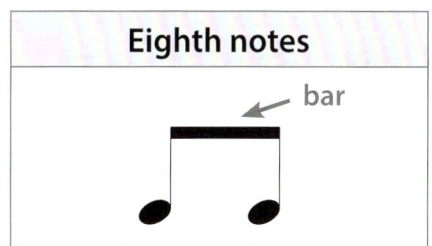

Eighth notes

bar

Sequential eighth notes are interconnected with a bar.

The focus here is on clean execution of the two strokes as well as rhythmic evenness.

Again, repeat each line—as indicated by the repeat signs.

Online video 04

Exercises with eighth notes (bass & edge)

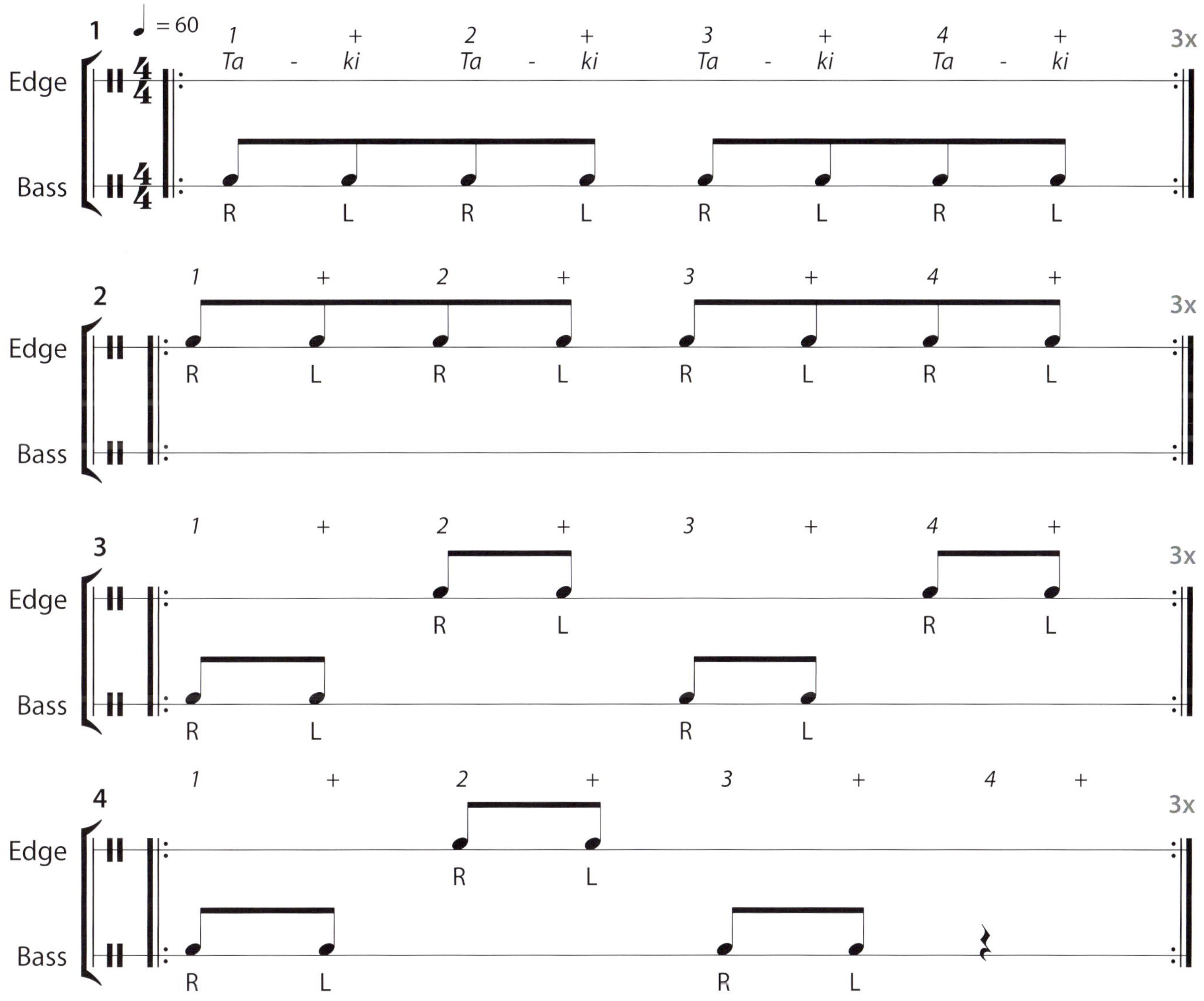

Single eighth note notation image:

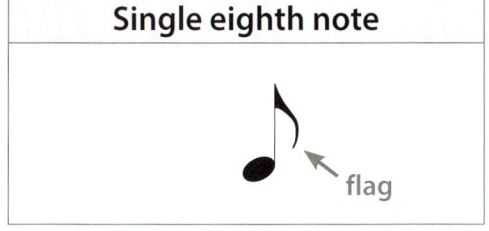

Single eighth note

flag

Eighth notes that occur *singly* are notated with a **flag** instead of a bar.

Here are some examples with *single eighth notes*. Combine quarter and eighth notes. Keep the 60bpm for the quarter notes on the metronome and count the eighth notes evenly:

Count aloud: *1 + 2 + 3 + 4 +.*

Speak aloud: *Ta ki Ta ki Ta ki Ta ki.*

Distribute the beats to your hands. This means:

Your 'strong' hand (*the right hand for right-handers, the left hand for left-handers*) plays the bass tone, your other, 'weaker' hand plays the edge tone. Grooves emerge that immediately make you think of a drum kit. They will still be required as building blocks resp. modules in the *Groove & Fill Concept* starting from *page 18*.

Single eighth	Eighth rest
♪	♩

Online video 05

Grooves with quarter and eighth notes

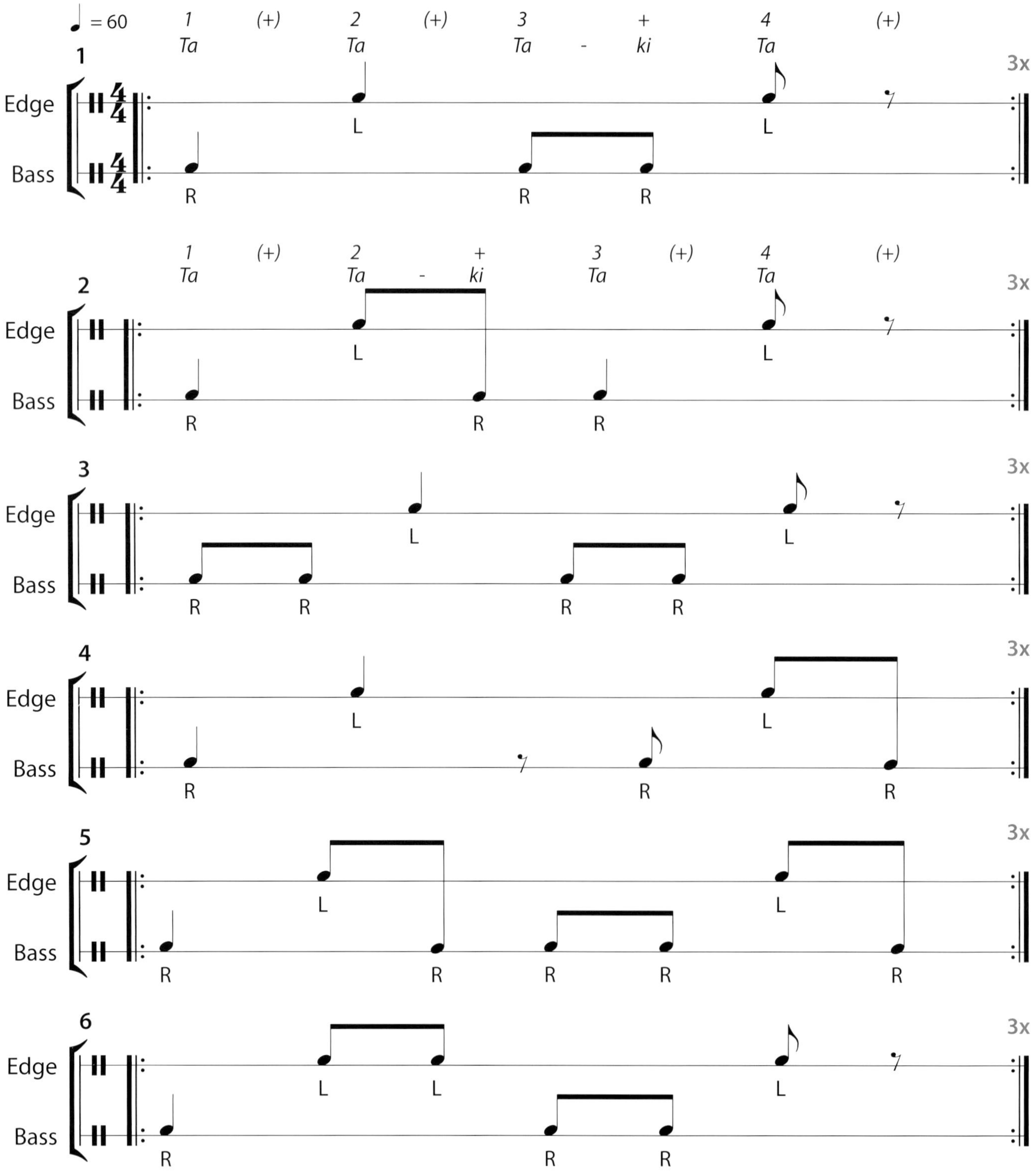

The next few exercises show *sixteenth notes*. Two sixteenth notes are exactly as long as one eighth note and four are as long as one quarter note. So *sixteen* sixteenth notes fit into one $\frac{4}{4}$ bar. The same applies, of course, to the *sixteenth rests*.

Sixteenth notes	Sixteenth rest

Sequential sixteenth notes are connected with **two bars**.

Count aloud: *1 e + a 2 e + a 3 e + a 4 e + a.*
Speak aloud: *Ta ki di mi Ta ki di mi Ta ki di mi Ta ki di mi.*

Online video 06

Exercises with sixteenth notes (bass & edge)

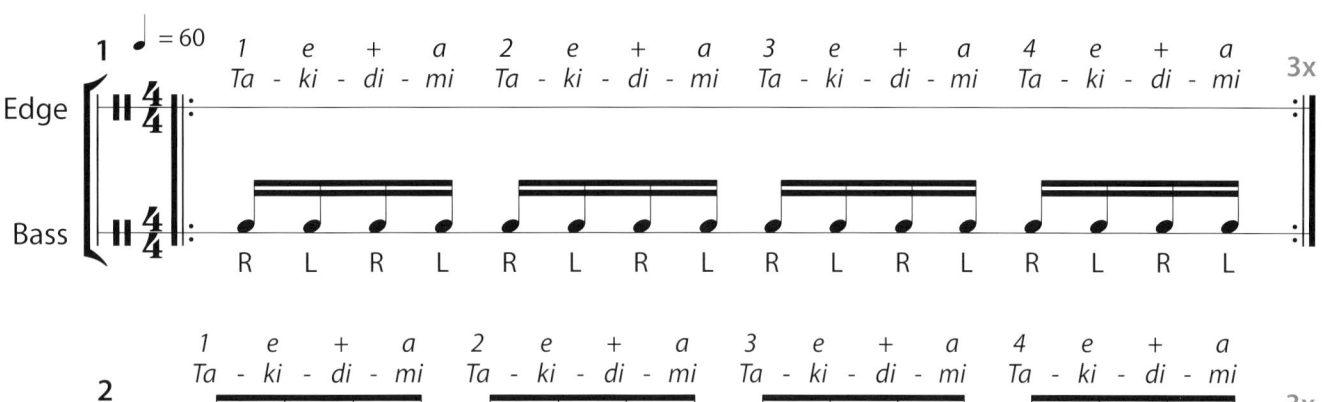

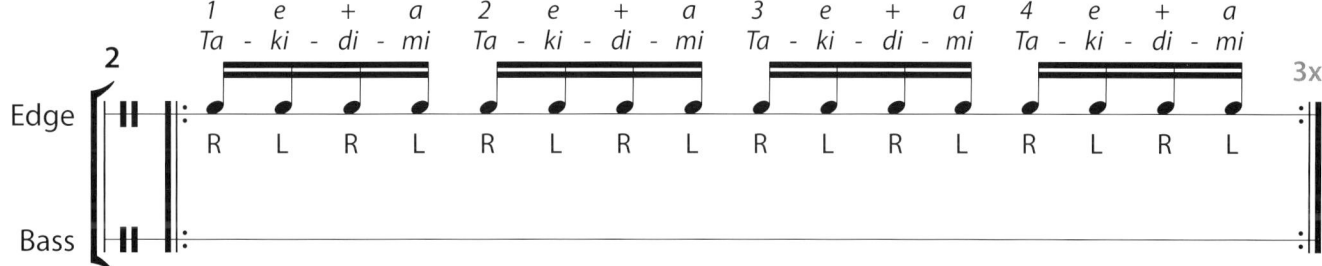

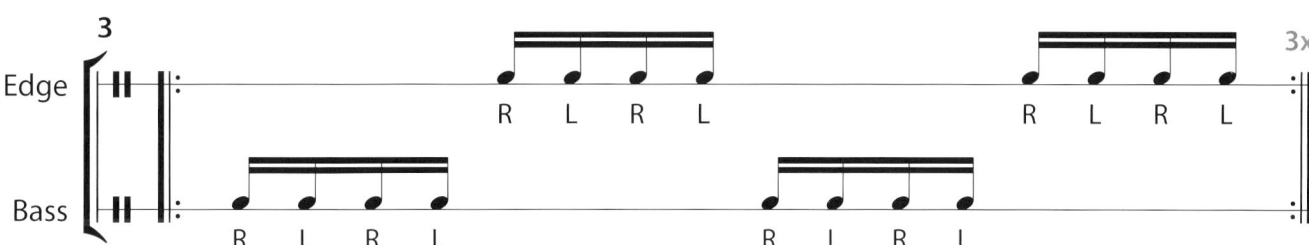

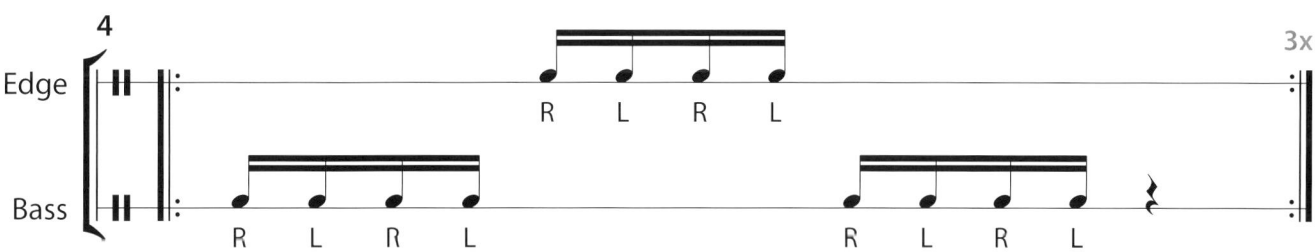

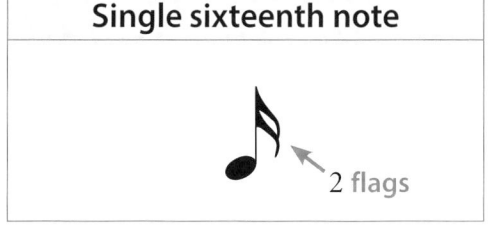

Sixteenth notes that occur *singly* are notated with **two flags** instead of two bars.

15

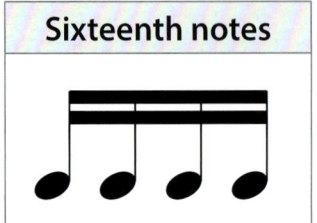

Sixteenth notes

Now you distribute the sixteenth notes also within the groups of four on bass and edge ...

Online video 07

Exercises with sixteenth notes (distributed)

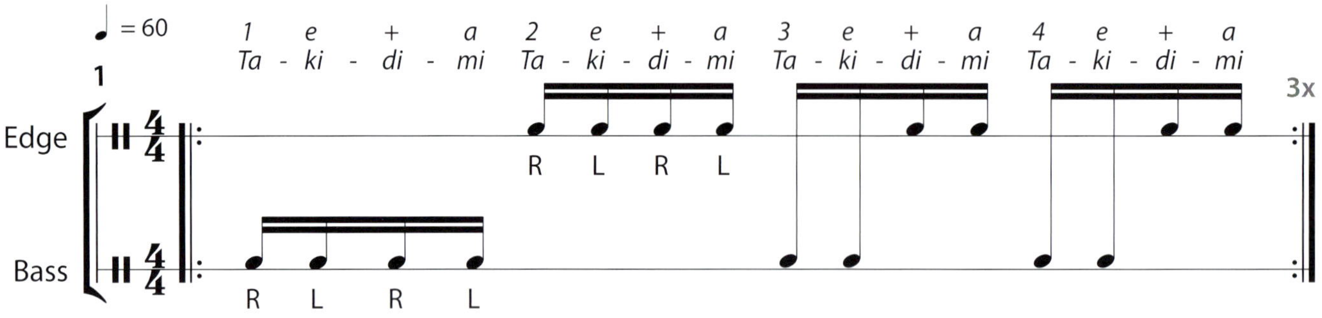

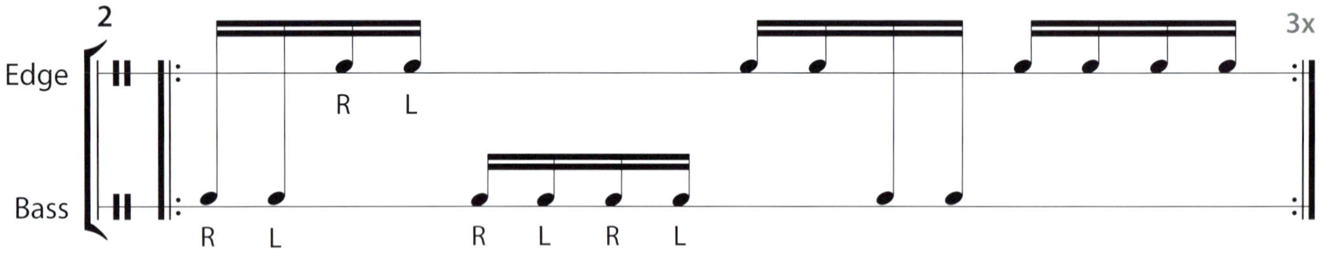

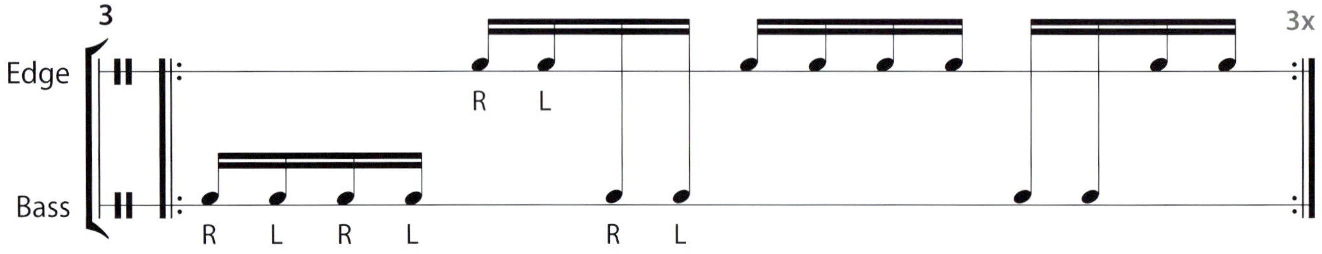

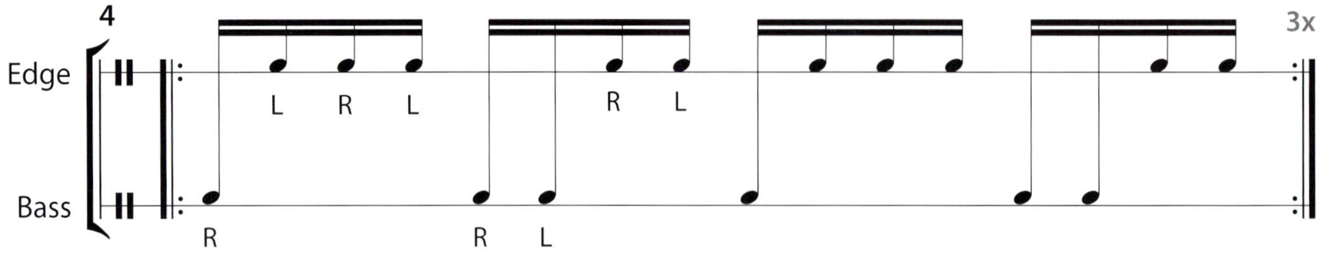

This and the following page can be used very well as fill-in variations in the *Groove & Fill Concept*. How this works, more on *page 18* ...

16

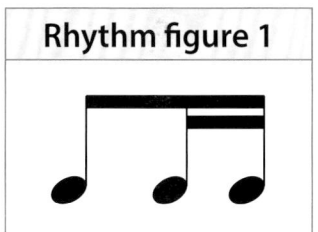

Rhythm figure 1

... and now combine eighth notes with sixteenth notes.

Count aloud: *1 + a 2 + a 3 + a 4 + a.*

Speak aloud: *Ta di mi Ta di mi Ta di mi Ta di mi.*

Pay attention to the hand stickings.

Online video 08

Combinations of eighth notes and sixteenth notes

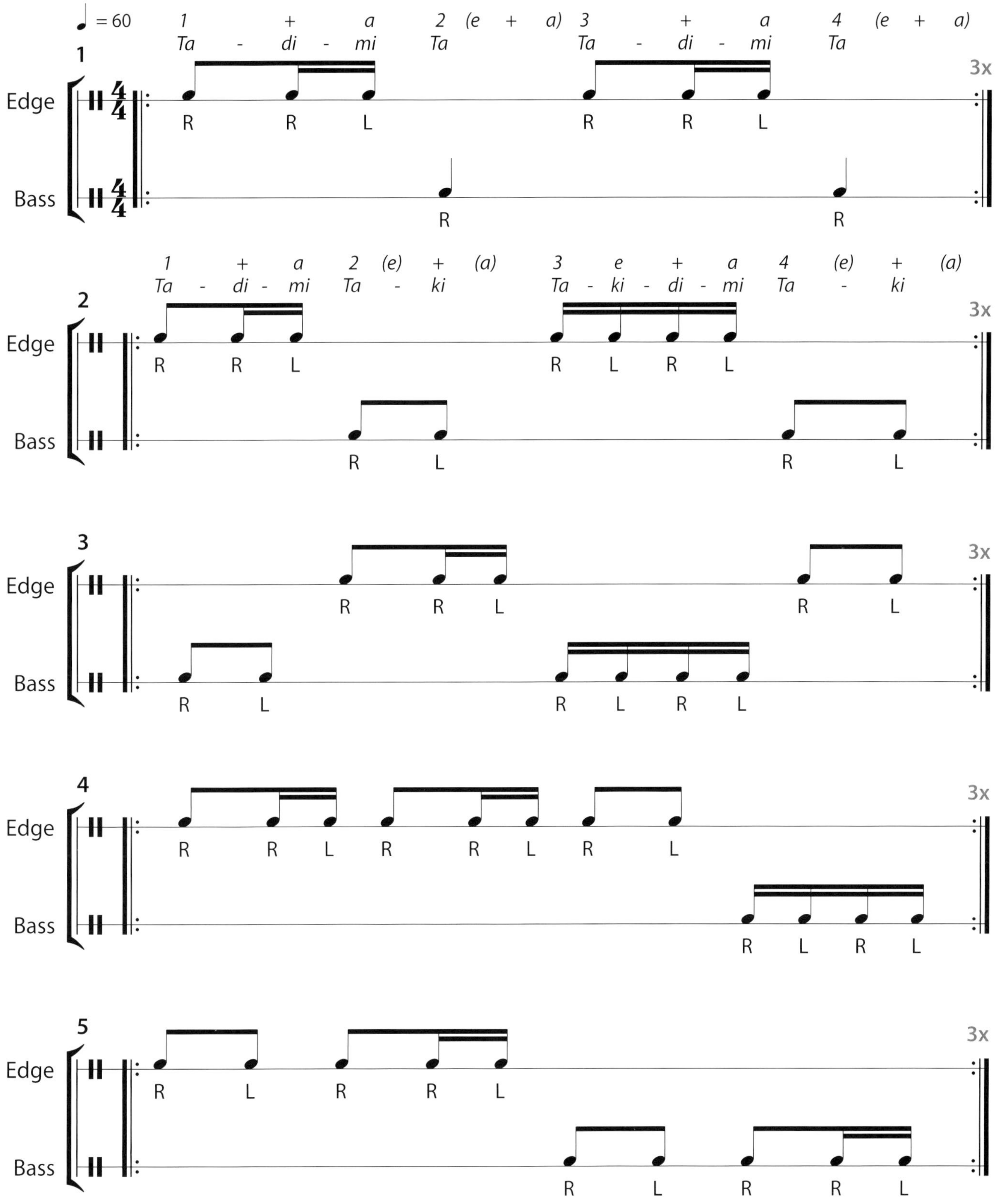

17

The Groove & Fill Concept

The *Groove & Fill Concept* will help you to create your own grooves to accompany pop songs in a modular system:

Select a rhythm line from the six grooves on *page 14* as a basic groove and play it three times. For the fourth time, choose a line from the sixteenth note exercises on the *previous two pages* as a fill-in. So your kit consists of:

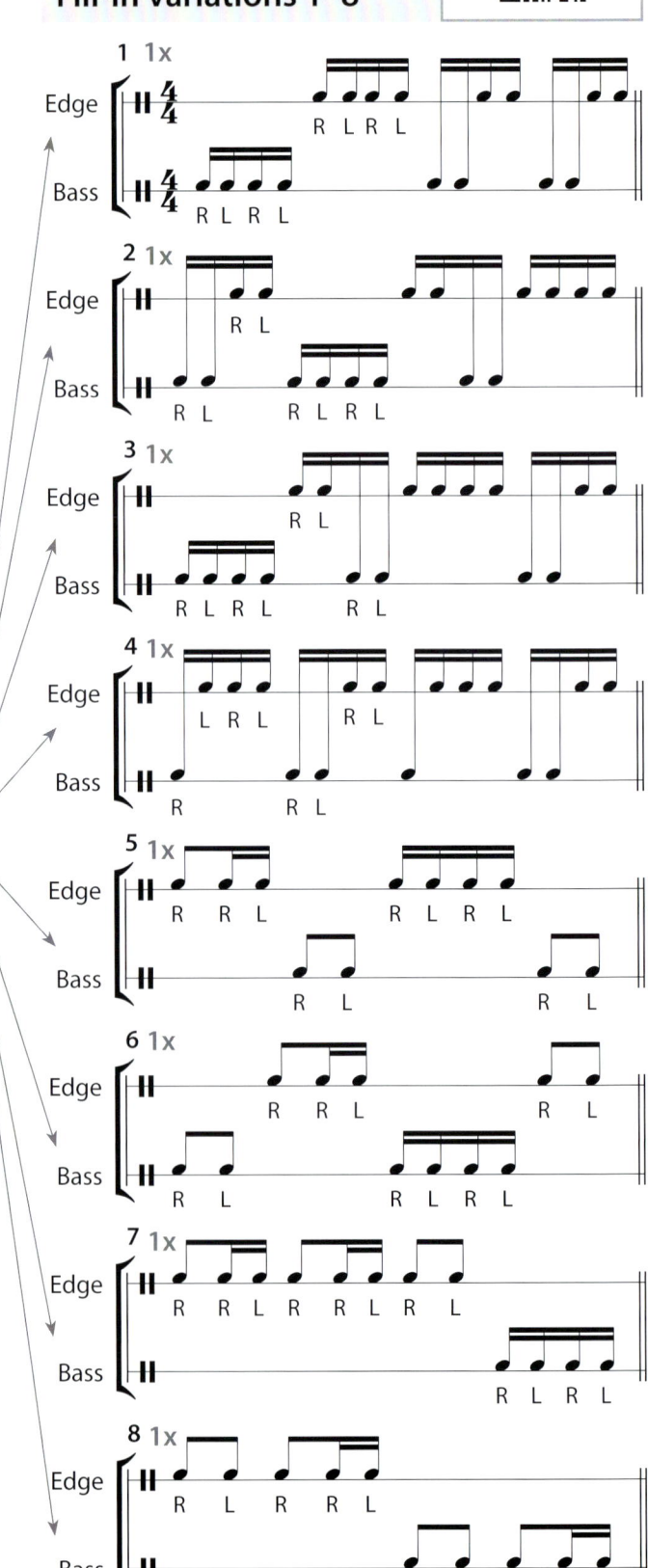

Fill-in variations 1–8

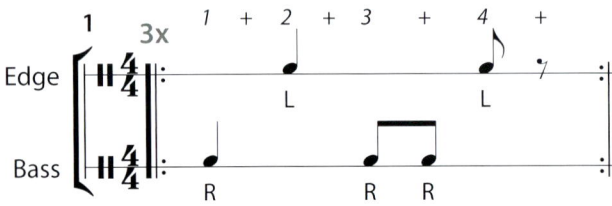

Basic groove 1

Now combine the other *grooves 2 to 6* from *page 14* in the same way with the *fill-in variations*. Basic groove three times, fill-in once. This way you get a four-bar form that is very common in pop music, which you can also use to develop your own grooves to accompany pop and rock music.

Basic grooves 2–6 **Fill-in variations 1–8**

IMPORTANT: *Try out your own rhythm patterns according to this Groove & Fill Concept. You will find versatile possibilities.*

Now simply reverse the *rhythm figure 1* from *page 17*. The eighth note now follows two sixteenth notes.

Count aloud: *1 e +   2 e +   3 e +   4 e +*
Speak aloud: *Ta ki di   Ta ki di   Ta ki di   Ta ki di*

Combinations of sixteenth notes and eighth notes

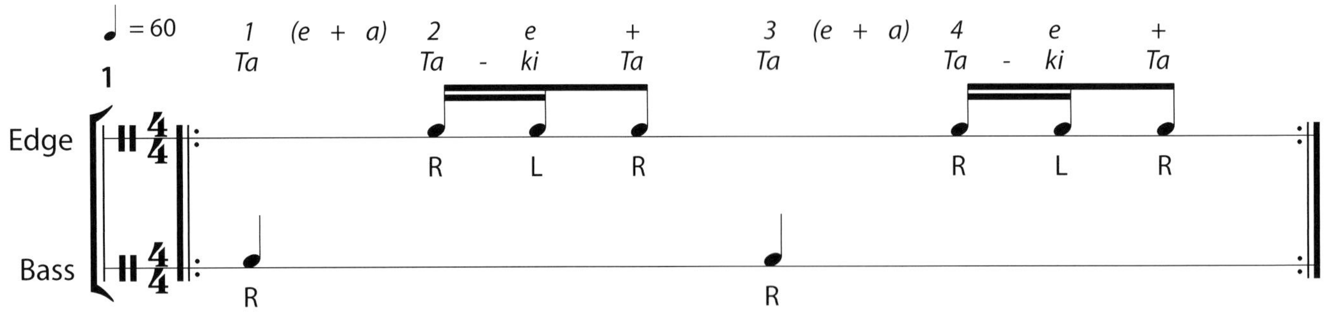

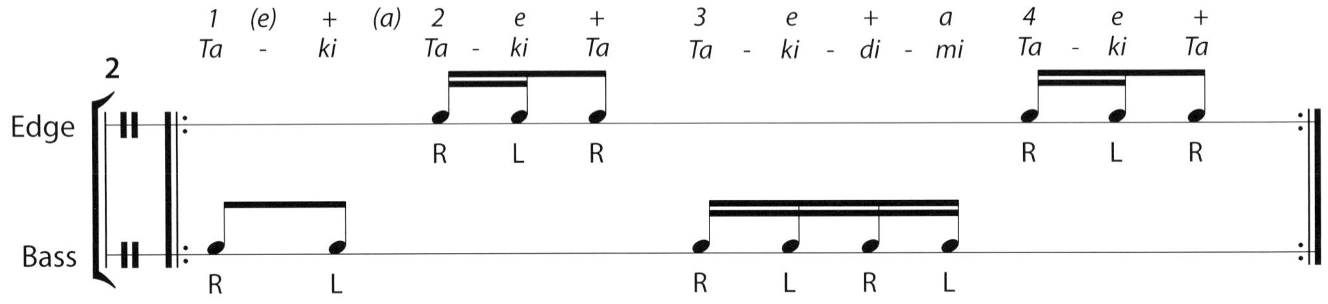

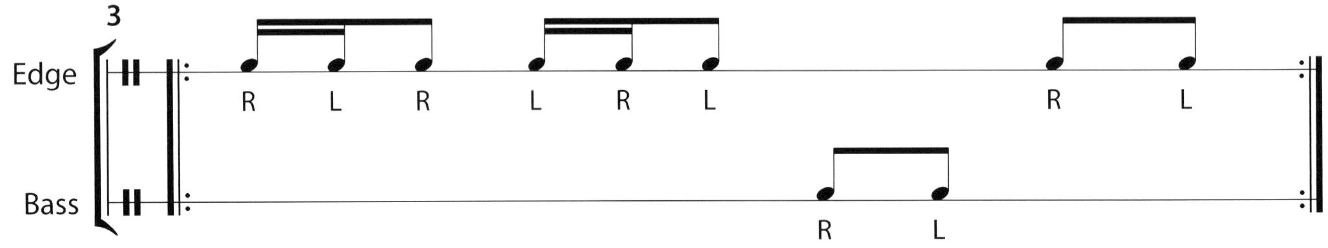

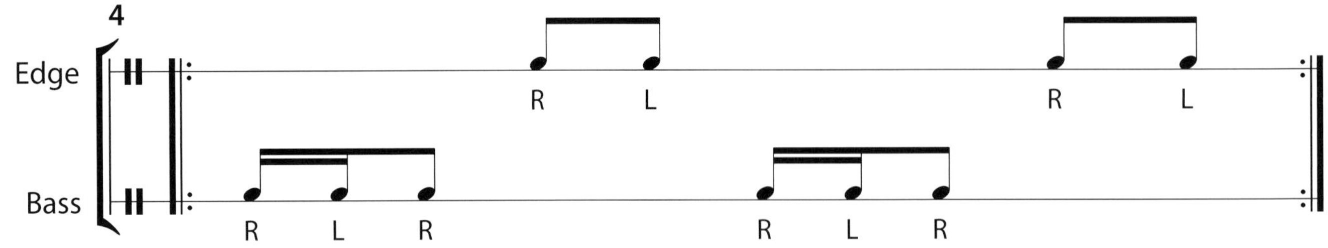

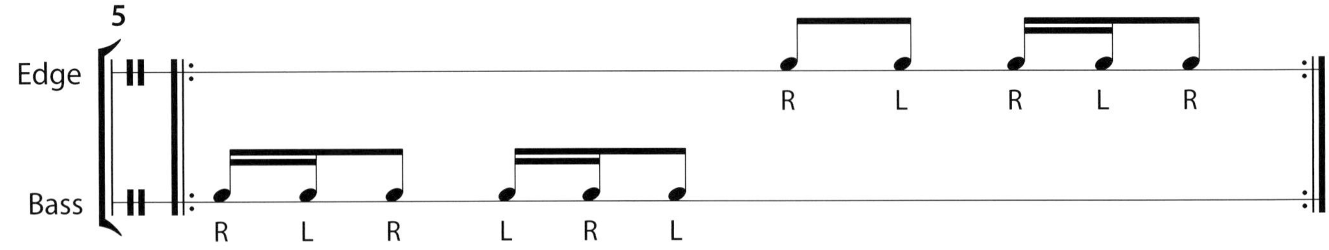

Rhythm figure 1	Rhythm figure 2

Consequently, it makes sense to combine both rhythm figures *with each other.*

Count aloud: *1* + *a* resp. *2 e + a* ...
Speak aloud: *Ta di mi* resp. *Ta ki Ta* ...

Combinations of Rhythm figure 1 and 2

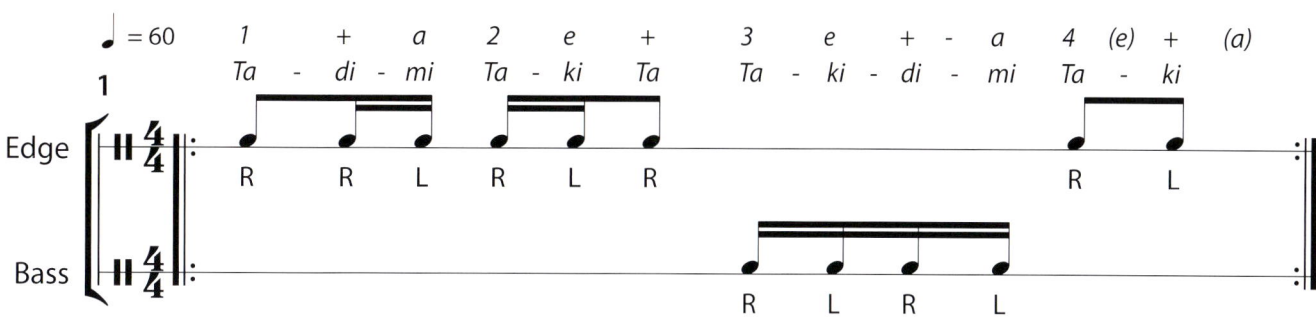

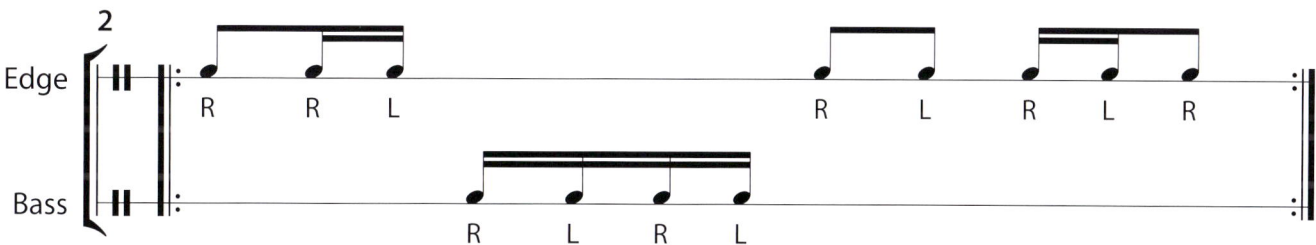

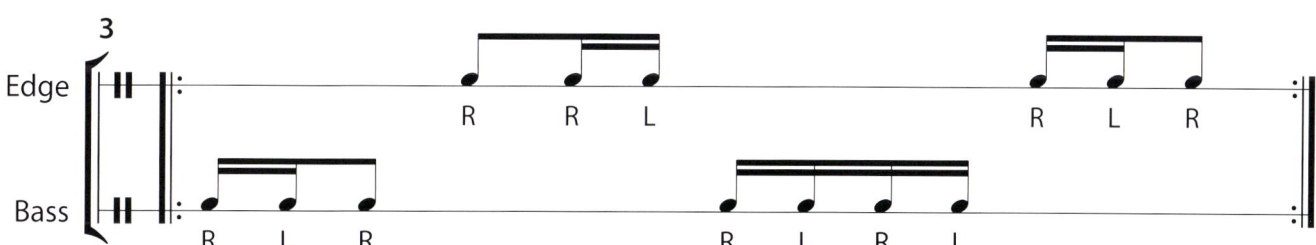

Similar to the *Groove & Fill Concept* from *page 18*, you can also compose the patterns with the rhythm figures 1 and 2 independently in the modular system:

Again, select a rhythm line from the six grooves on *page 14* as the basic groove and play it three times. For the fourth round, choose a line from the combination examples on the previous two pages as a fill-in. So your kit consists of:

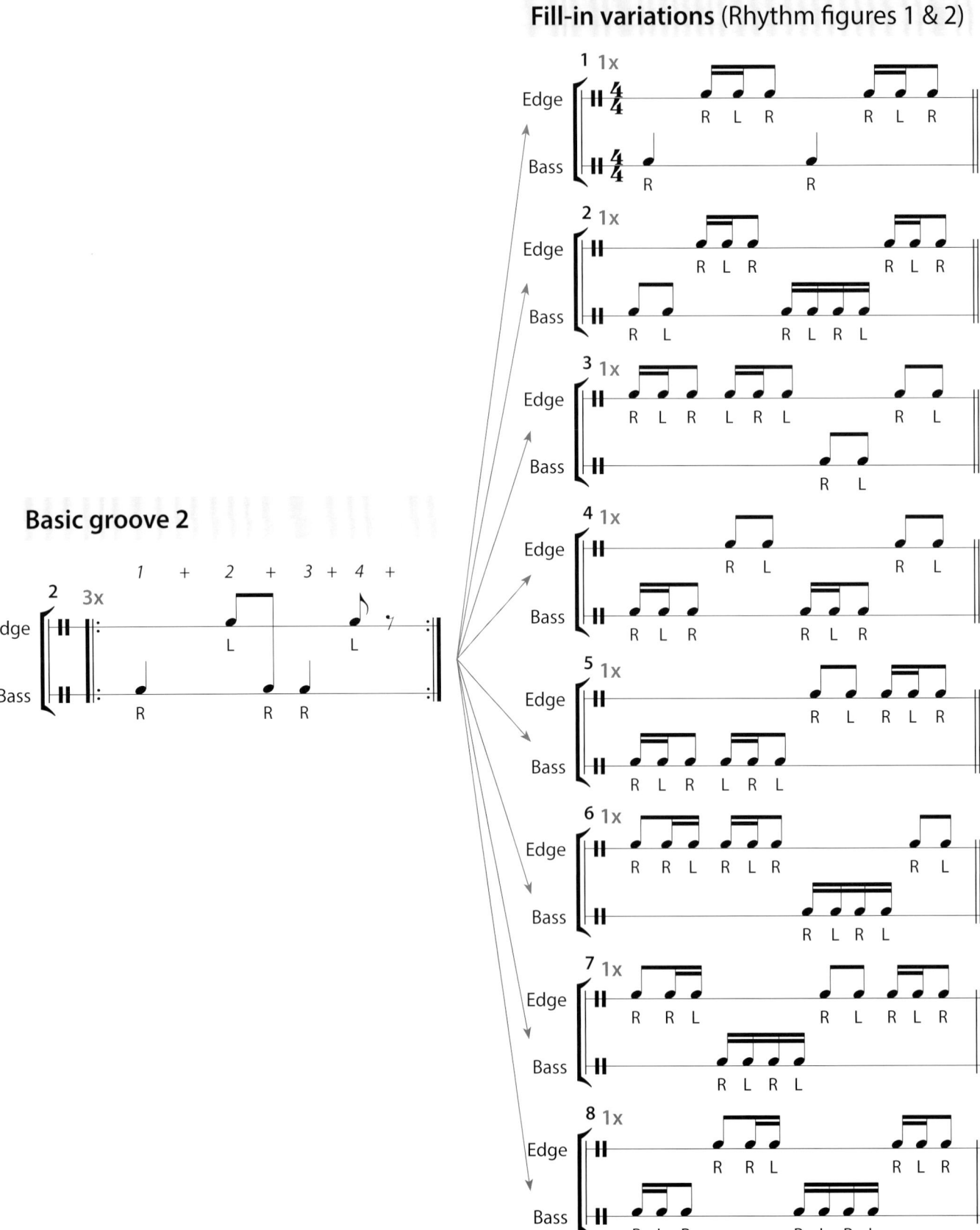

Basic groove 2

Fill-in variations (Rhythm figures 1 & 2)

Now combine the other *grooves 1 and 3 to 6* from *page 14* in the same way with the fill-in variations. Basic groove three times, fill once. This way you get more four-bar grooves common in pop music to accompany pop and rock pieces.

Don't forget: Try out your own grooves by using these fill-in variations from the modular system.

Basic grooves 1 and 3–6

Fill-in variations 1–8

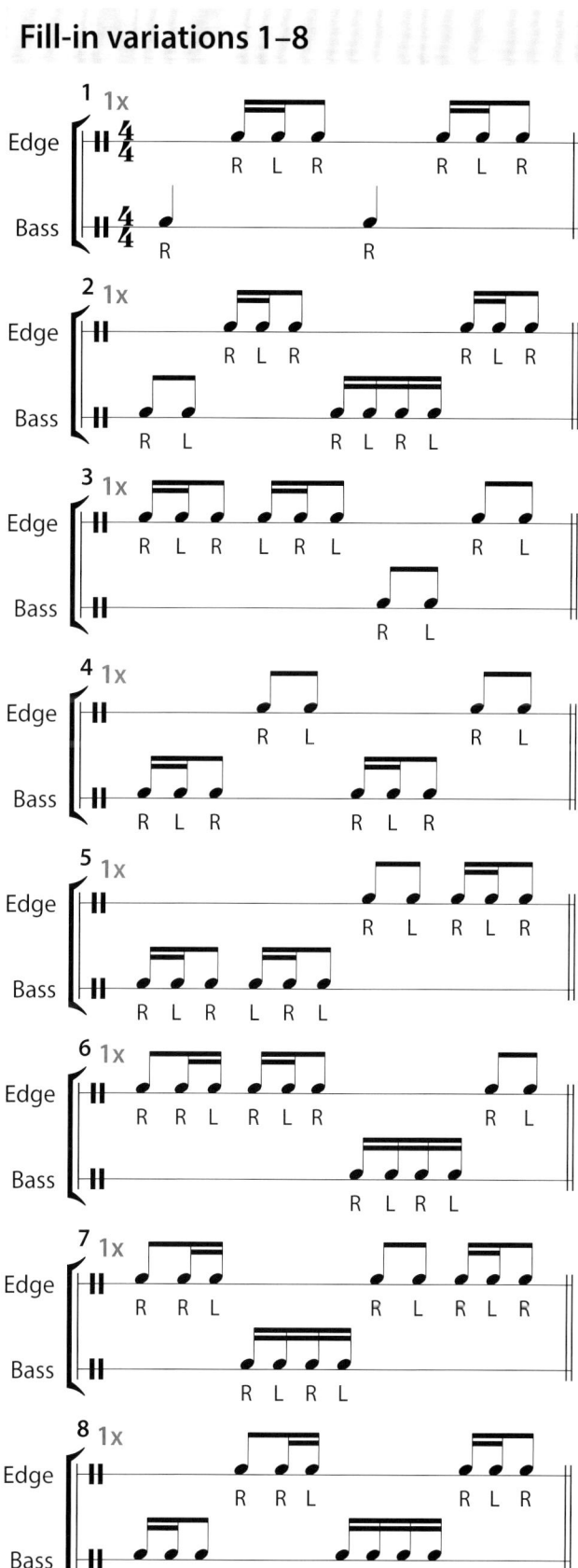

The Peruvian Way of Playing

The Peruvian way of playing differs from *the Cuban way* mainly in its volume. It could be described as a *soft style of playing*. However, this doesn't just mean hitting less forcefully, but also in a fundamentally different way. In the Peruvian style, the *edge tone* (commonly know as the **tip**) is used instead of the *open tone* and the *bass stroke* is also played differently.

BASS STROKE (Peruvian)		EDGE STROKE (Peruvian)	
With the **bass stroke**, cup your hands and hit the playboard just with the *very first part of your fingers*. Your *fingertips* 'stick' to the cajón surface. This gives you better control over the bass sound. Even in a reverberant church or basement vault, you won't predominate other acoustic instruments with your cajón.	Online video 11 	At the **edge**, you play as far up as possible so that the fingers just hit. The tonal distance from the bass to the edge tone is much larger in the Peruvian style than in the Cuban. To achieve colourful and dynamic cajón playing, it is essential to master both techniques.	Online video 12

BASS STROKE — Peruvian way of playing

 Small note head in brackets **on the bottom line** of the staff

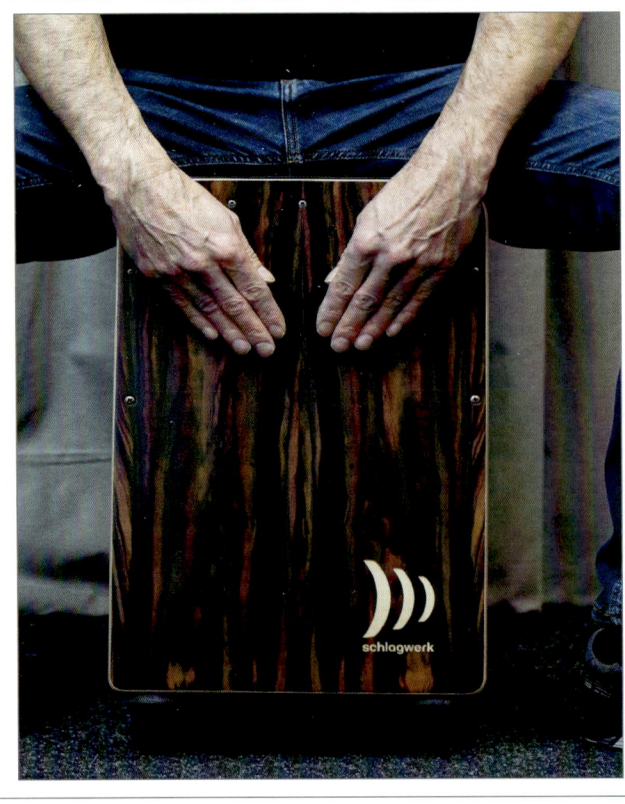

Position: Centered, just above the middle of the surface.

Execution: Hit with the hollow hand from the whole arm and control the volume with the fingertips 'sticking' on the cajón surface.

Sound: deep, warm, muffled, bassy

Function: bass drum (soft)

EDGE STROKE (TIP) — Peruvian way of playing

 Small note head in brackets **on the top line** of the staff

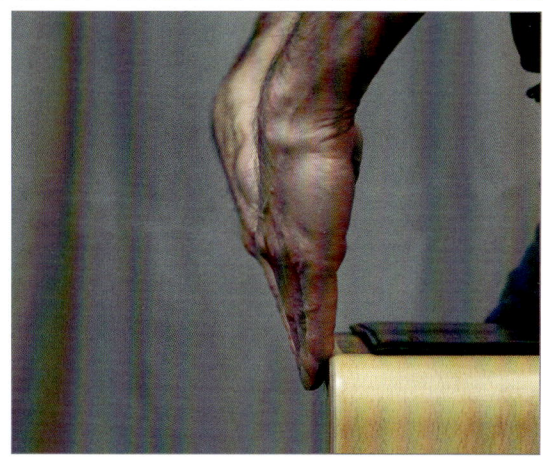

Position: Hit just below the top edge of the surface.
Execution: Hit with the fingertips only.
Sound: Softer than the *open tone*.
Function: *Fill strokes* mainly that keep the flow going like the *ghost notes* on the drum set.

Online video 13

Peruvian Bass strokes and Tips (bass & edge)

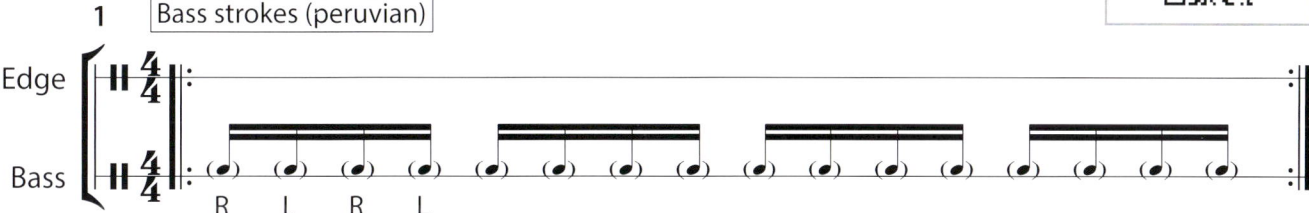

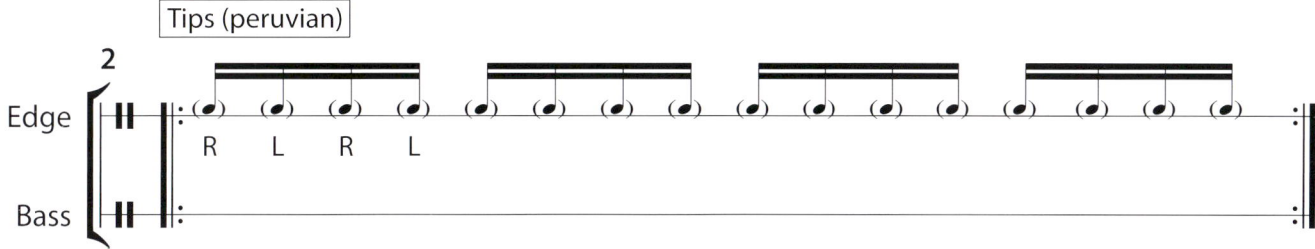

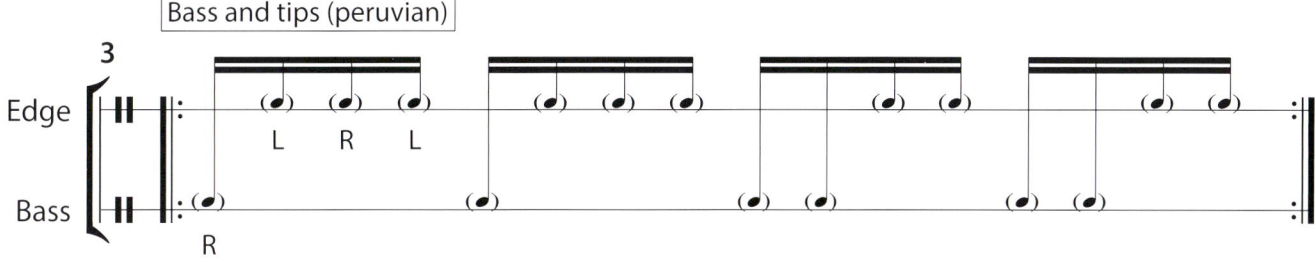

25

Rudiments

It is a good idea to practice these two Peruvian playing techniques with a few rudiments. These so-called *drum rudiments* were compiled by **Sanford A. Moeller** in his *The Moeller Book* for the snare drum as early as 1918. They are still used today as technique exercises on the snare drum in drum lessons. In the 1950s the *National Association of Rudimental Drummers* (*N.A.R.D.*) defined 26 exercises as 'American Standard Rudiments.' **Alfred author Claus Hessler** has highlighted their importance for modern drumming in his book *Camp Duty Update*. Thus, rudiment figures such as the *long roll*, the *mill*, and the *paradiddle* have become established in rock, pop, and fusion music.

Paradiddle

We will practice the Peruvian bass and tip strokes by using the *paradiddle*, *a combination of single and double strokes*, as an example. The name paradiddle is the onomatopoeic transcription of the succession of *two single strokes* (*para*) and a *double stroke* (*diddle*).

Starting with a regularly *alternating sticking* (R L R L) over *two double strokes* (R R L L) you arrive at the *paradiddle*, from which there are several derivations (*see e.g. inverted paradiddle*).

For the cajón, the paradiddle results in new, interesting patterns between bass and tip—not only in the Peruvian way of playing.

Make sure that the bass strokes and the tips are played precisely.

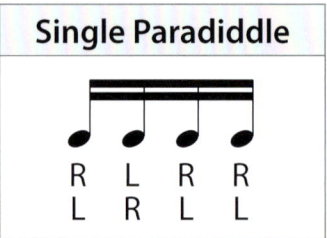

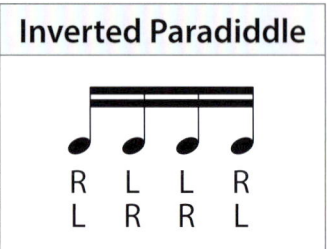

Online video 14

Bass (Peruvian)	Tip (Peruvian)
(♪)	(♪)

Single Paradiddles (derivation)

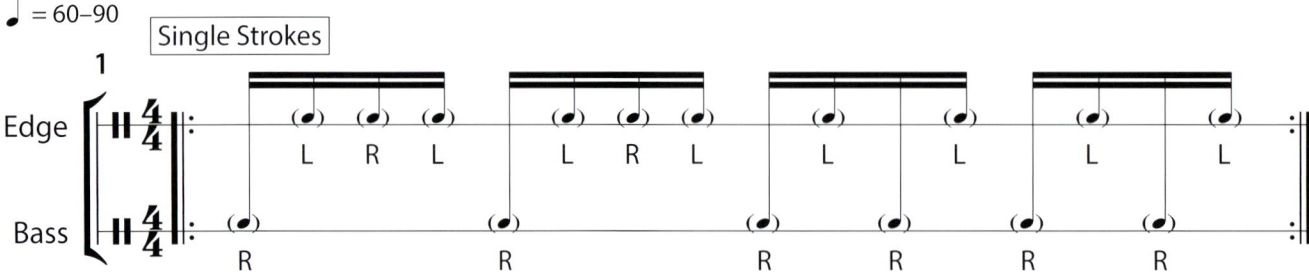

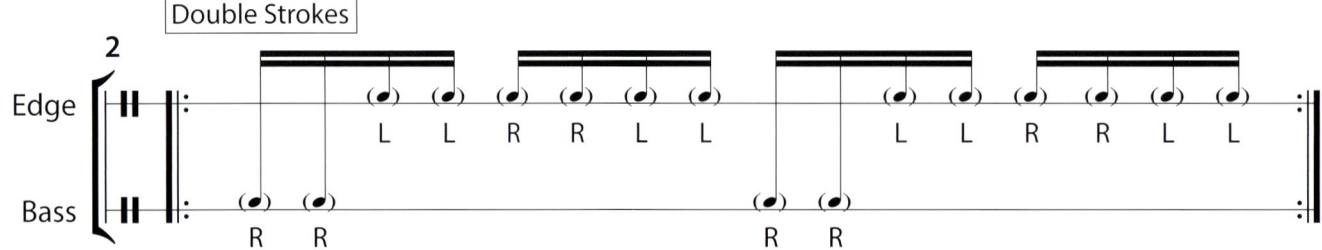

26

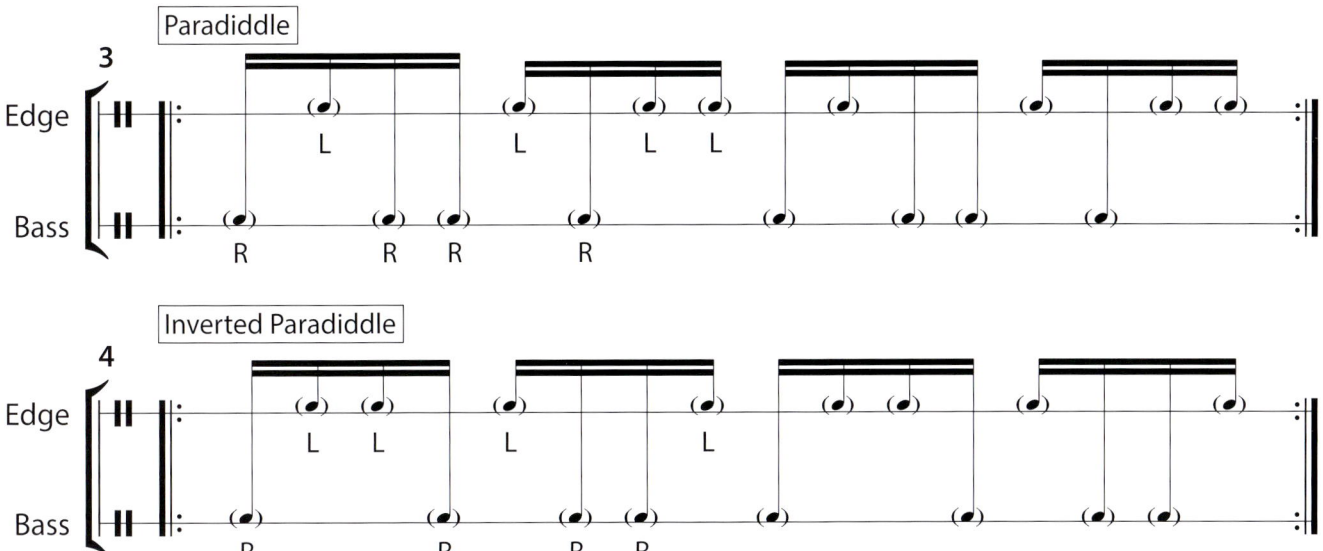

Other derivatives are the *paradiddle-diddle* and the *double paradiddle*.

Paradiddle-diddle

In paradiddle-diddle, *the double strokes are doubled.* This results in the sticking: **R L R R L L** or **L R L L R R**.

For this reason it is easier to think of the sticking of the paradiddle-diddle as a *group of 6*.

Double Paradiddle

In double paradiddle, the *single strokes are doubled.* This results in the sticking: **R L R L R R** or **L R L R L L**.

Here, too, it is easier to think of the Double Paradiddle sticking as a *group of 6*.

Since *Paradiddle-diddle* and *Double Paradiddle* result in a total of only *12 strokes*, we *fill up* the following two exercises with four strokes.

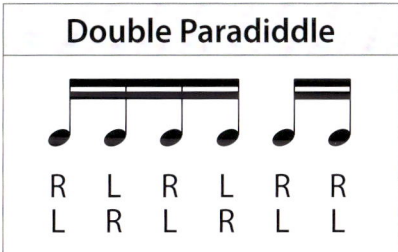

Paradiddle-diddle and Double Paradiddle plus 4 strokes

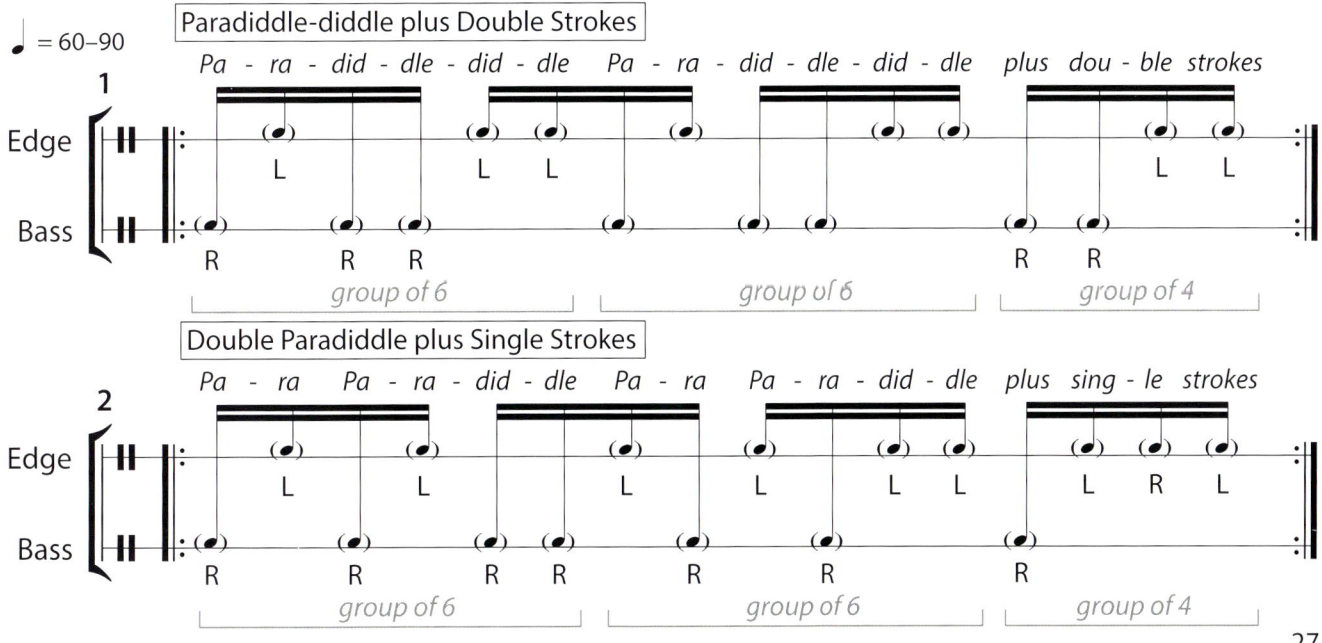

27

Practice the next lines separately first. Then play them one after the other in one go. The stickings change in each line. From the second line on, interpret them in groups of 6 and and 4 which will make it easier.

More Paradiddle variations

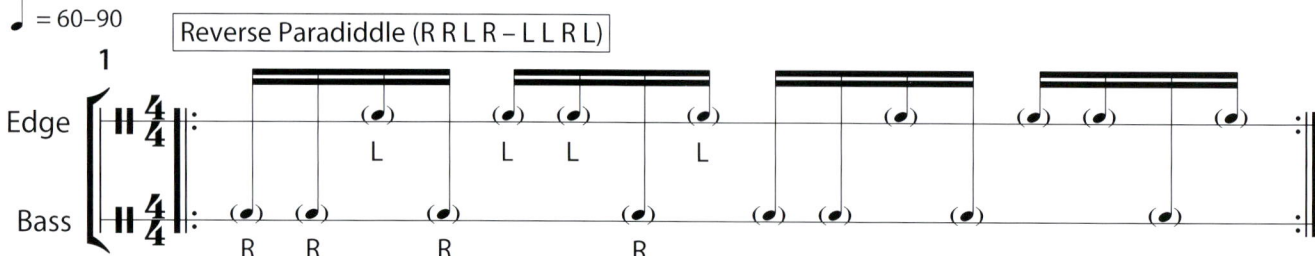

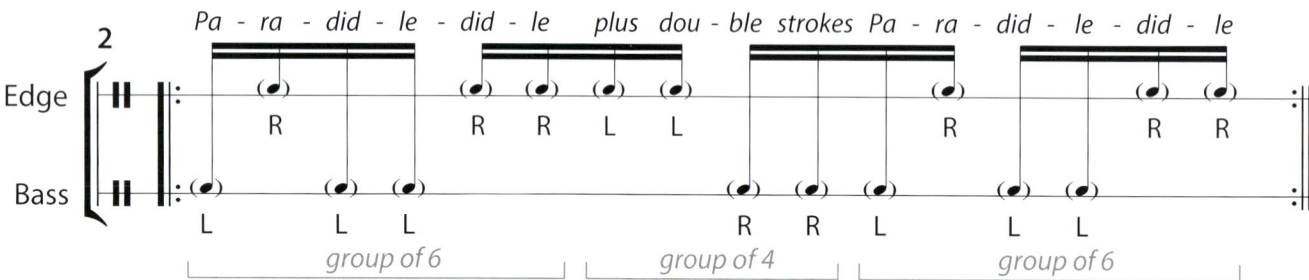

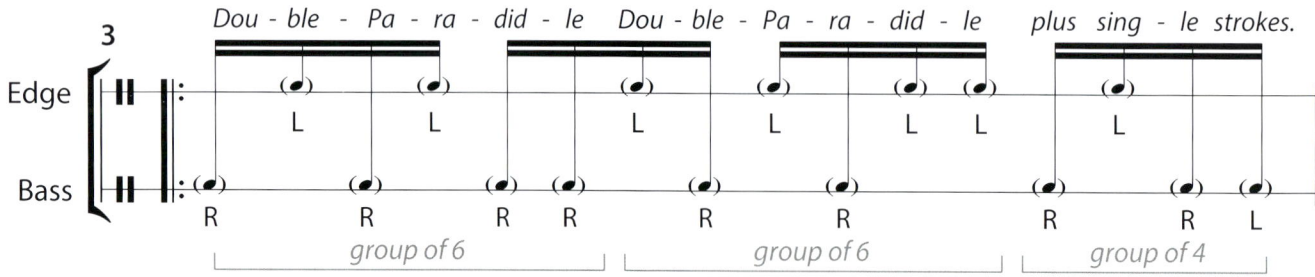

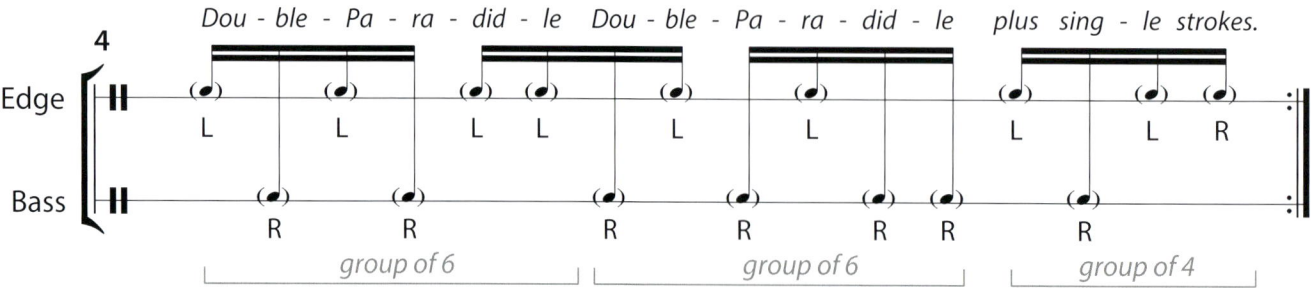

IMPORTANT DYNAMICS EXERCISE:

Once you have automated the rudiment patterns, vary in dynamics. This means you alternate between the Cuban and Peruvian styles of playing.

Also combine the rudiment patterns with one of the basic grooves from the pages 22 to 23!

In the following two-bar exercise, you'll find more groups of 6 and 4.

More groups of 6 and 4

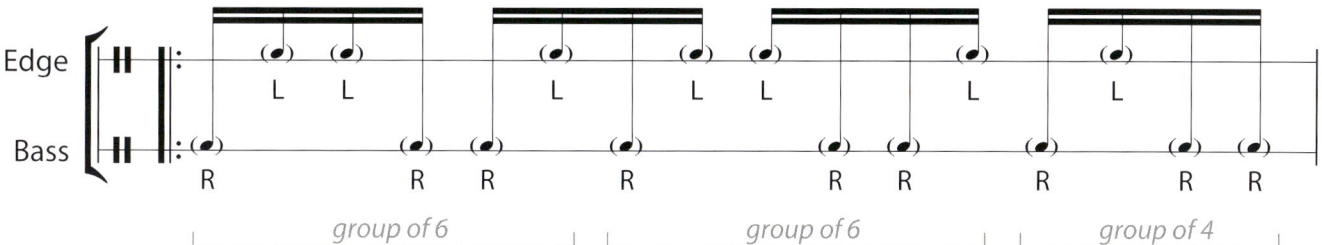

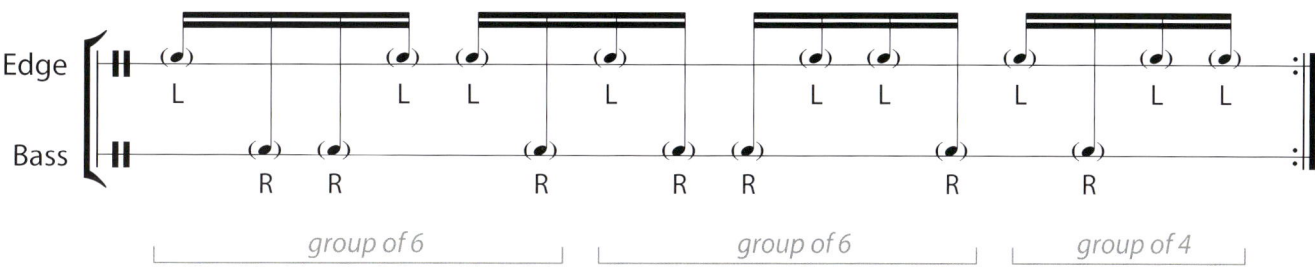

Matt at the Saulkrasti Jazzfestival Latvia in 2009

The Slap Strokes

Slaps are *loud, accented beats* that give your playing a 'melody' and a special character. Depending on the *position on the edge* of the cajón, the slap has *different tone colors*. I distinguish between the *light slap* and the *dark slap*.

Online video 15
Dark Slap

SLAP

✕ **The dark slap: cross on the top line** of the staff

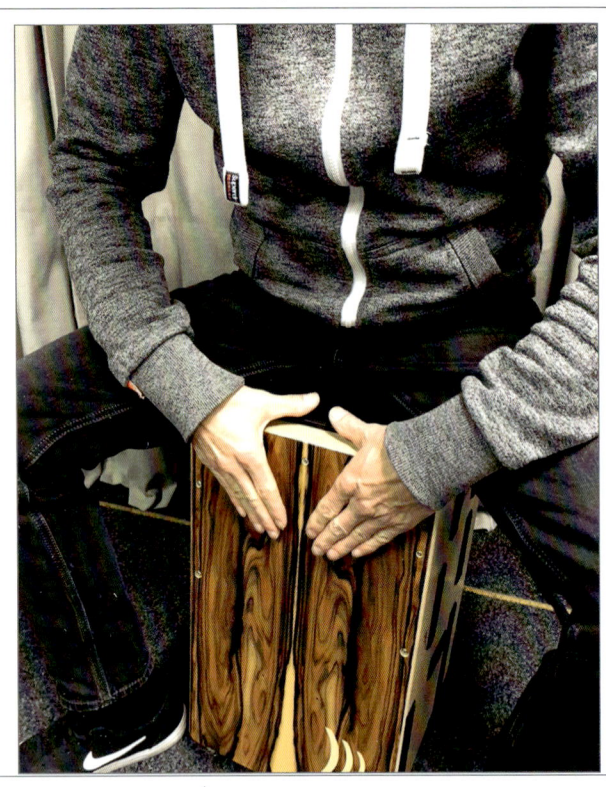

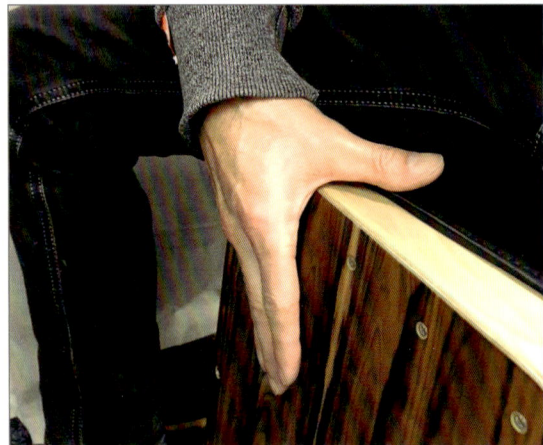

Position: As with the *open tone* at the top edge. From the player's point of view, the hand hits *below* the base of the finger. The thumb is stretched out to the side.
Execution: Shoulder slightly forward. Hit from the whole arm with a slightly arched, somewhat tense hand parallel to the cajón surface. The wrist is stiff.
Sound: brighter than *the open tone*, gaudy, loudest tone.
Function: accented beat, melodic rhythm.

(✕) **The light slap: cross** in brackets **on the top line** of the staff

Online video 16
Light Slap

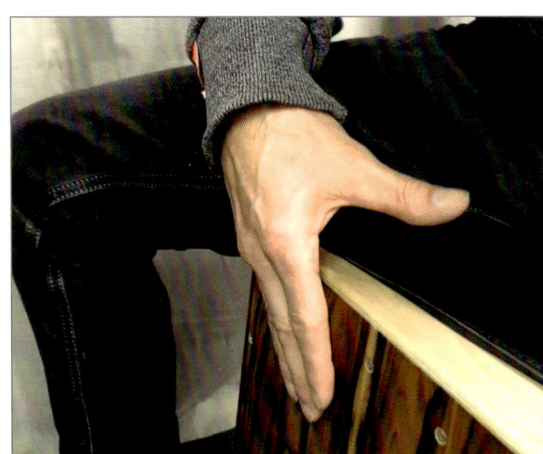

Position: At the upper edge exactly between tip and open tone. From the player's point of view, the hand hits *above* the base of the finger.
Execution: Like the *dark slap*. The hand hits evenly with great movement from the whole arm.
Sound: brighter than the *dark slap*.
Function: Accented stroke for softer playing.

Practice both the dark and the light slap in combination with soft tips played at the very edge of the cajón (*see page 25*).

Online video 17

Slap and Tip

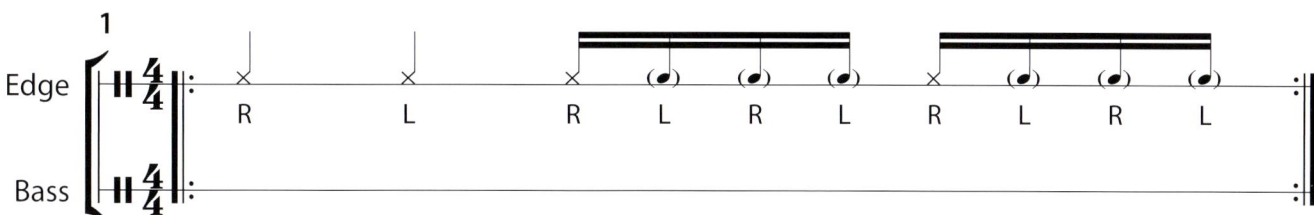

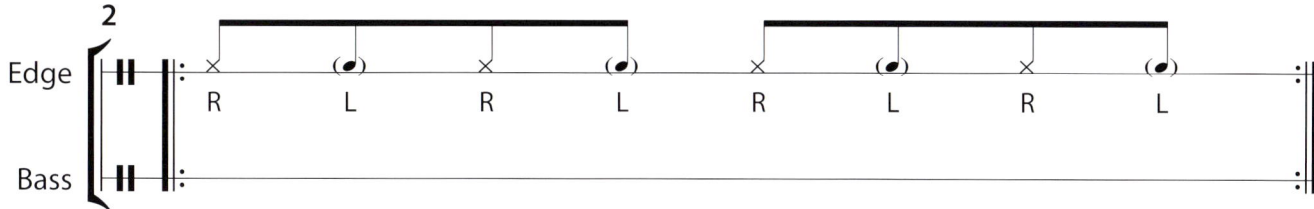

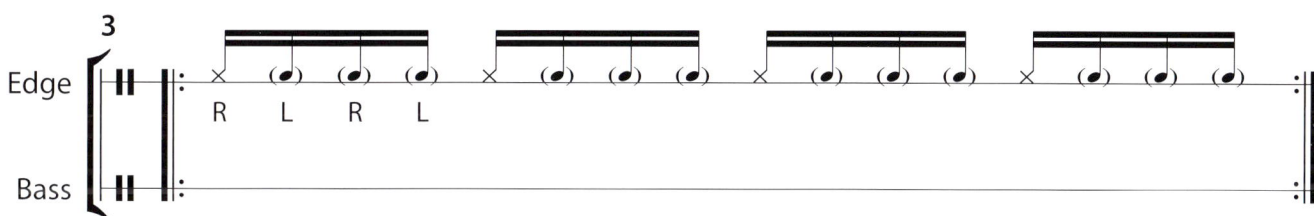

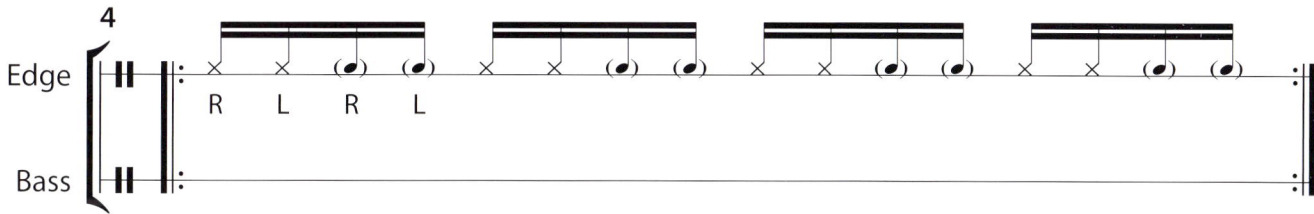

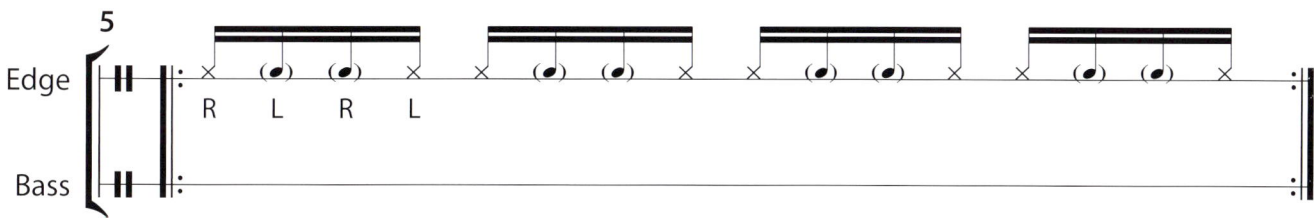

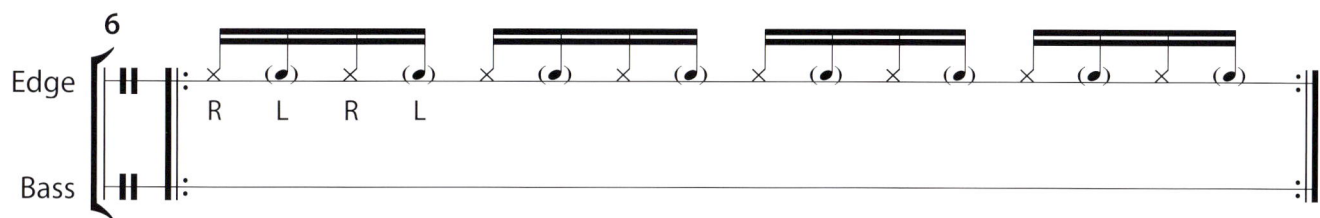

The Melody Concept

Now start with your own ideas and create your own 'melodies.' Your *loud slaps* are played alternately with soft filling strokes (*tips*, see page 25), the so-called *ghost notes*. This opens up a versatility of variations. Start with the following *initial pattern* with slaps in the right hand:

Online video 18

Initial pattern 1 (slap accents)

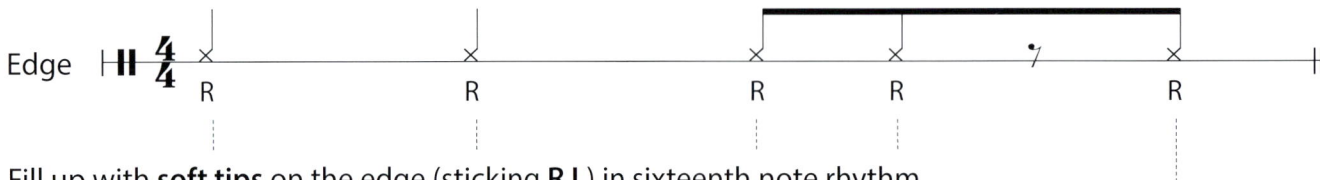

Fill up with **soft tips** on the edge (sticking **R L**) in sixteenth note rhythm.

Step 1: Fill up with tips in sixteenth notes

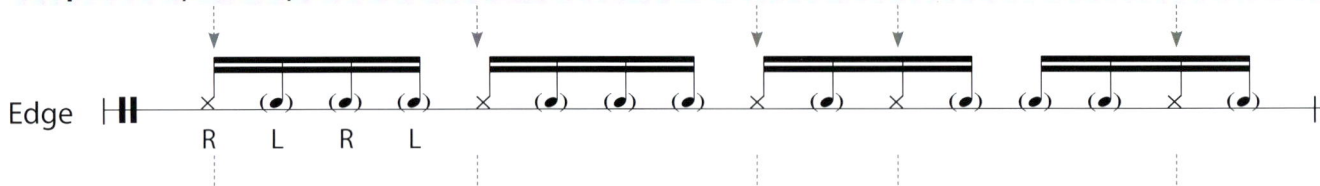

In the second step, you *orchestrate* the slap accents, meaning, you divide them between **bass** and **edge**.

Step 2: Divide the slap accents between bass and edge

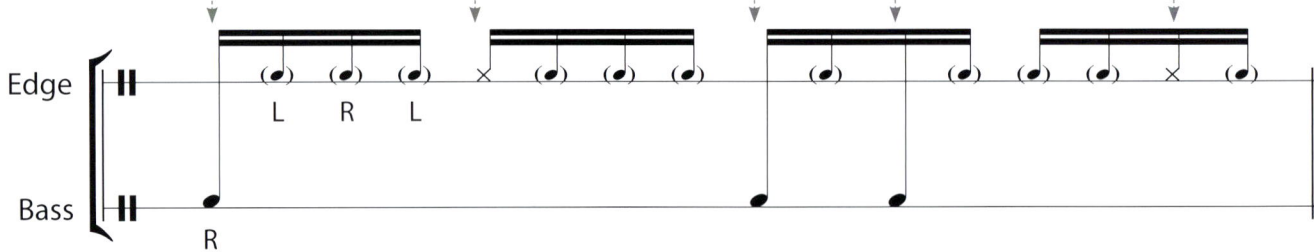

Initial pattern 2 (slap accents)

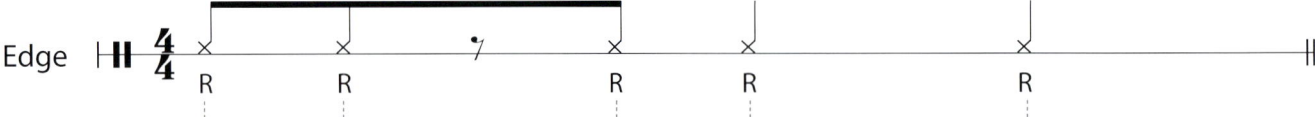

Step 1: Fill up with tips in sixteenth notes

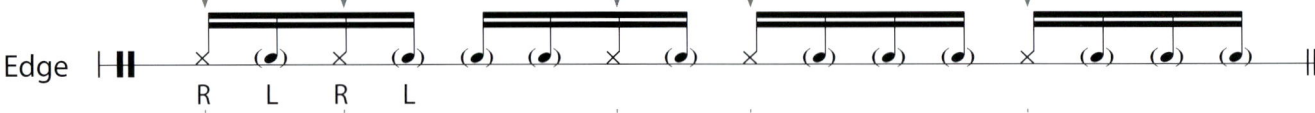

Step 2: Divide the slap accents between bass and edge

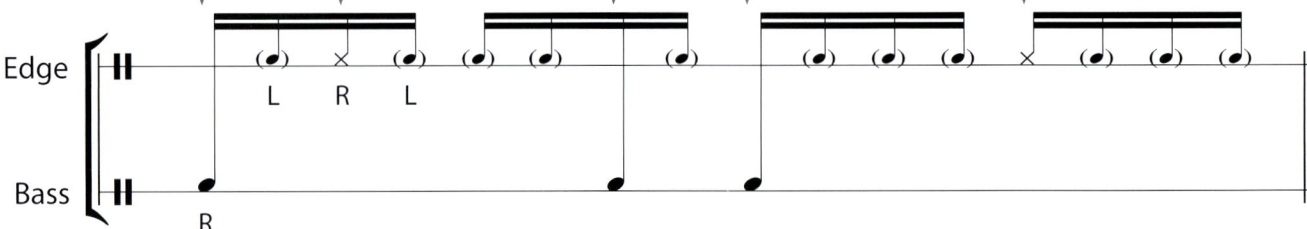

IMPORTANT: *You can play all of the following exercises that contain slap accents both Cuban — that is, with the dark slap — and Peruvian — that is, with the light slap.*

The next accent melodies should inspire you to find your own interpretations and rhythms. Proceed with the initial patterns according to the *melody concept (Step 1 and 2)*, fill up with tips and orchestrate bass and slaps. Try to memorize the 'slap melody' and a lot of it will happen naturally.

Initial pattern 3 (Extend the slap accents with Step 1 and 2)

Step 1: Fill up with tips in sixteenth notes

Step 2: Divide the slap accents between bass and edge

Initial pattern 4 (Extend the slap accents with Step 1 and 2)

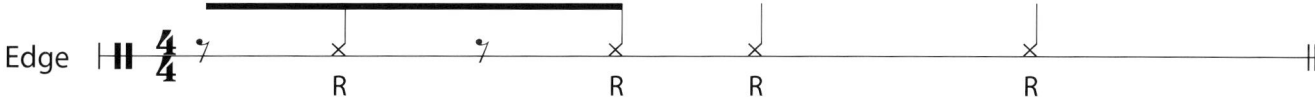

Step 1: Fill up with tips in sixteenth notes

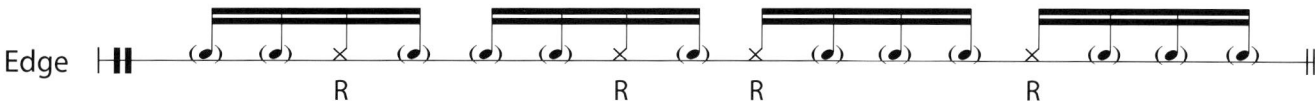

Step 2: Divide the slap accents between bass and edge

Initial pattern 5 (Extend the slap accents with Step 1 and 2)

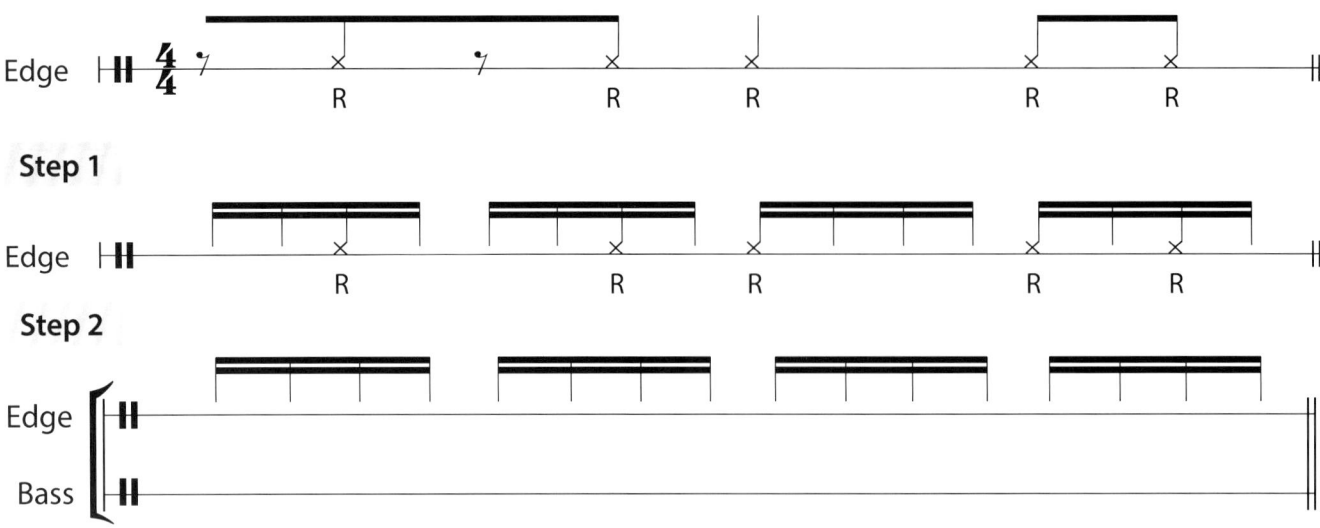

Initial pattern 6 (Extend the slap accents with Step 1 and 2)

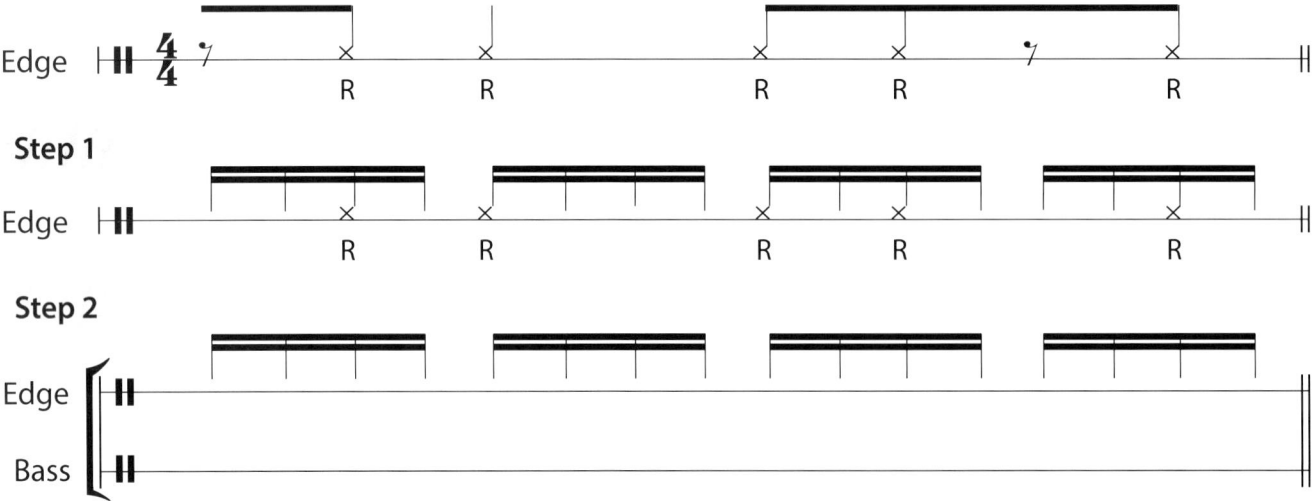

Initial pattern 7 (Extend the slap accents with Step 1 and 2)

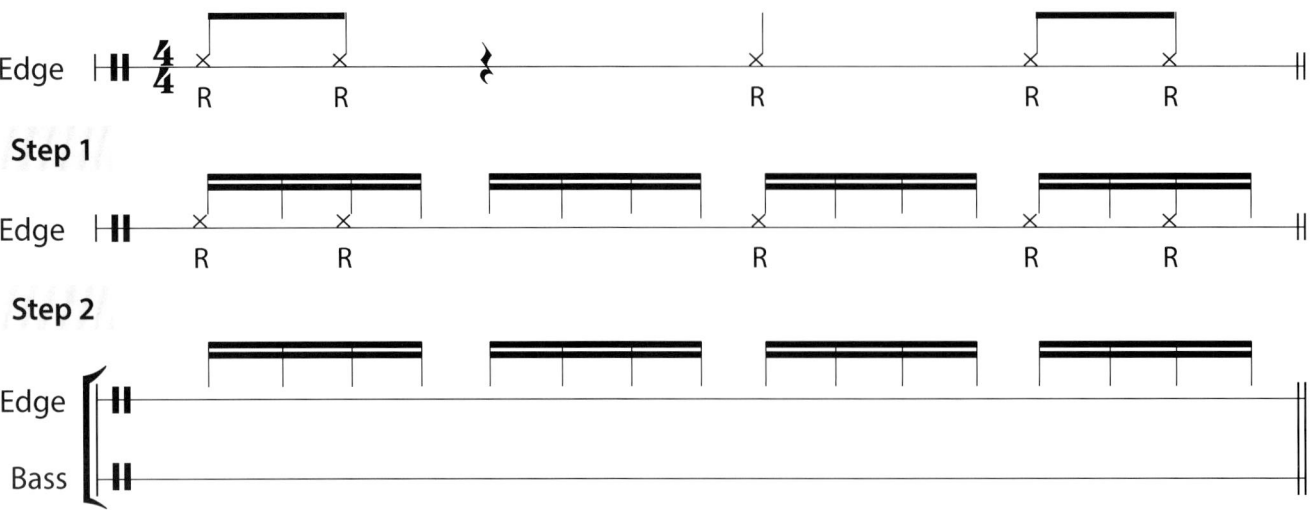

Find your own 'melodies' as starting patterns and implement them in the individual steps of the melody concept.

Your initial pattern 1 (Fill-in your slap accents and extend with Step 1 and 2)

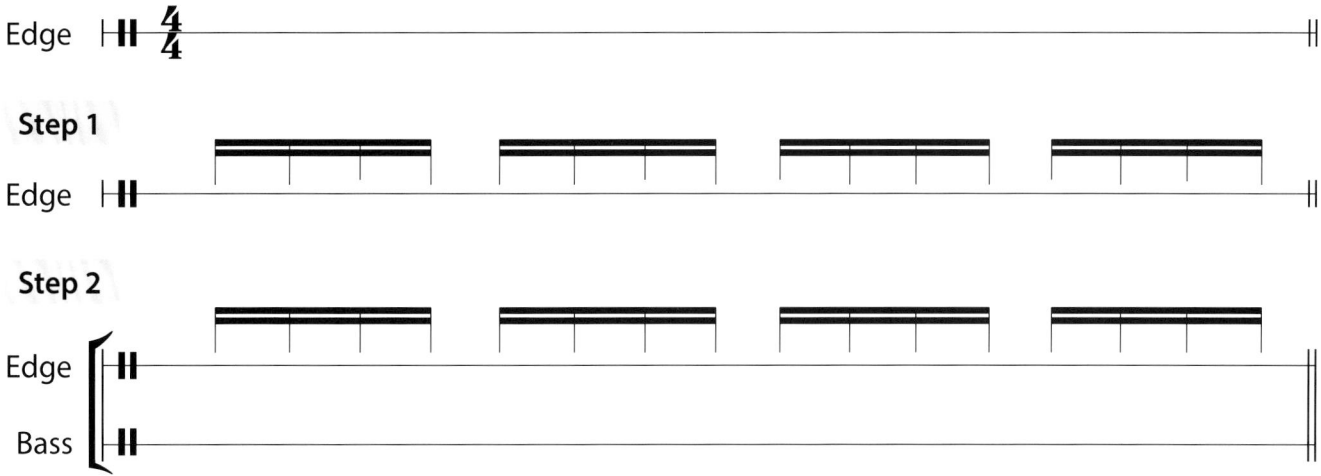

Your initial pattern 2 (Fill-in your slap accents and extend with Step 1 and 2)

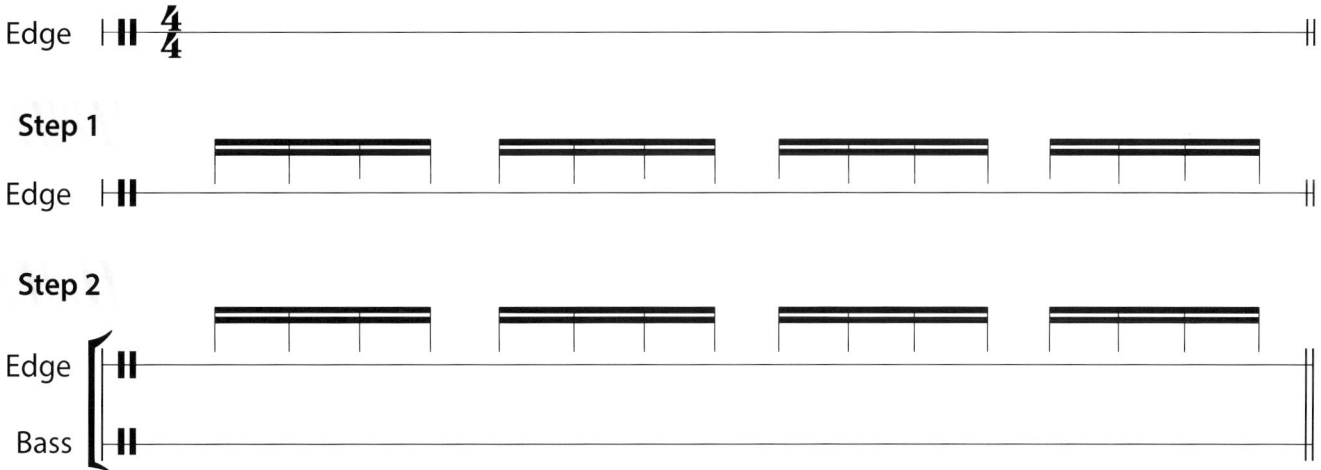

Your initial pattern 3 (Fill-in your slap accents and extend with Step 1 and 2)

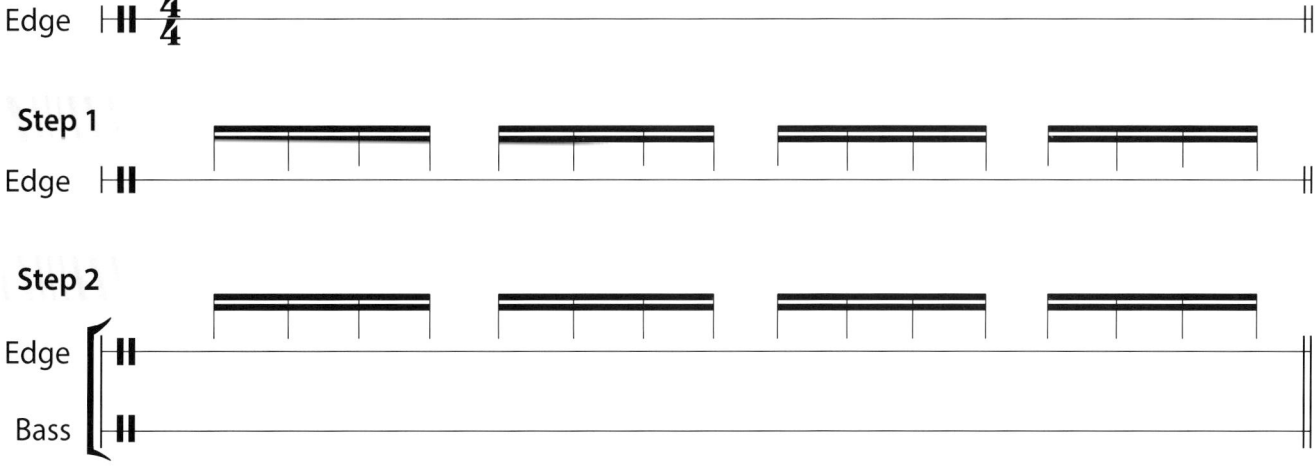

The Melody Concept using authentic and traditional patterns

The Clave

Rhythms from Brazil and Cuba are often based on the *rhythm figure* of the **clave**. It is a pattern from the African-influenced *Latin American music*, which — played with *two claves* — builds the rhythmic, recurring basis of a piece.

The Son Clave

The **Son Clave** is a two-bar pattern from Cuba. It is a characteristic of many Afro-Cuban rhythms and consists of a total of *five beats*, which are distributed in different ways over the two bars. The *dotted quarter note* plays a central role here.

The dotted quarter note	Note	Rest
The dot after a note extends its value by half. For the dotted quarter note, this means it sounds as long as *three eighth notes* or *a quarter plus an eighth note:*		

In even time signatures — such as $\frac{2}{4}$ or $\frac{4}{4}$ — this 'odd' division into three eighths makes up its special charm. This is because you always have to add an 'even' note value to one or two dotted notes to fill the bar. This is especially evident in the *son clave.*

The Son Clave 3/2

As its name suggests, the five beats in the **Son Clave 3/2** are distributed over the two bars in a **3:2 ratio**. Because it rolls better, we use the *sixteenth note syllables* here for the quarter and eighth notes:

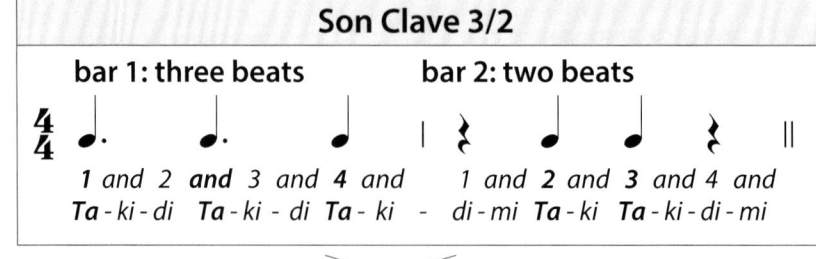

The Son Clave 2/3

Its inversion is the **Son Clave 2/3** with *two beats in the first bar* and *three beats in the second bar* (*see page 70*).

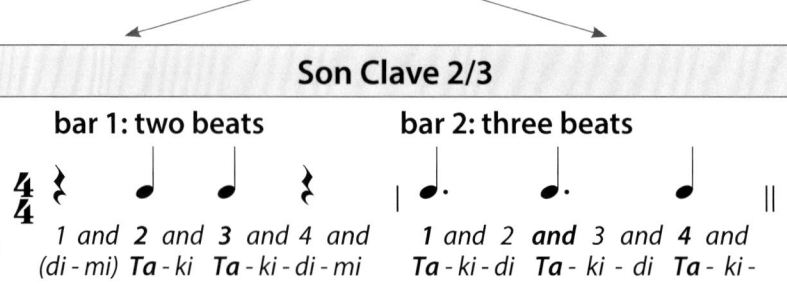

In addition, there are many other clave 'melodies,' such as the *rumba clave* (*see page 38*) and the *bossa clave* (*see page 39*). Basically, any concise rhythm pattern can be called a clave [*Spanish: key or code*].

Let's start arranging the **Son Clave 3/2** according to the individual steps of our *melody concept*. This time, however, you fill in with *eighth notes*.

Tip: Always clap the first syllable (see Step 1) of each group (see Step 2) to get the Son Clave 3/2. Increase by speaking the first syllable of each group louder and clapping the $\frac{4}{4}$ beats.

Son Clave 3/2 (initial pattern)

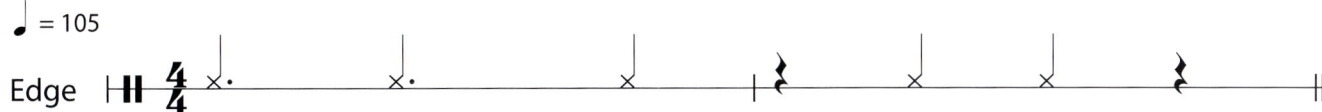

Step 1: Fill up with eighth notes as soft tips in R L stickings

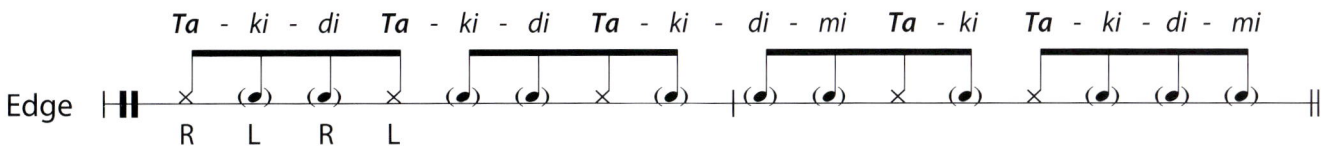

Step 2: Orchestrate by distributing the slap accents between bass and edge

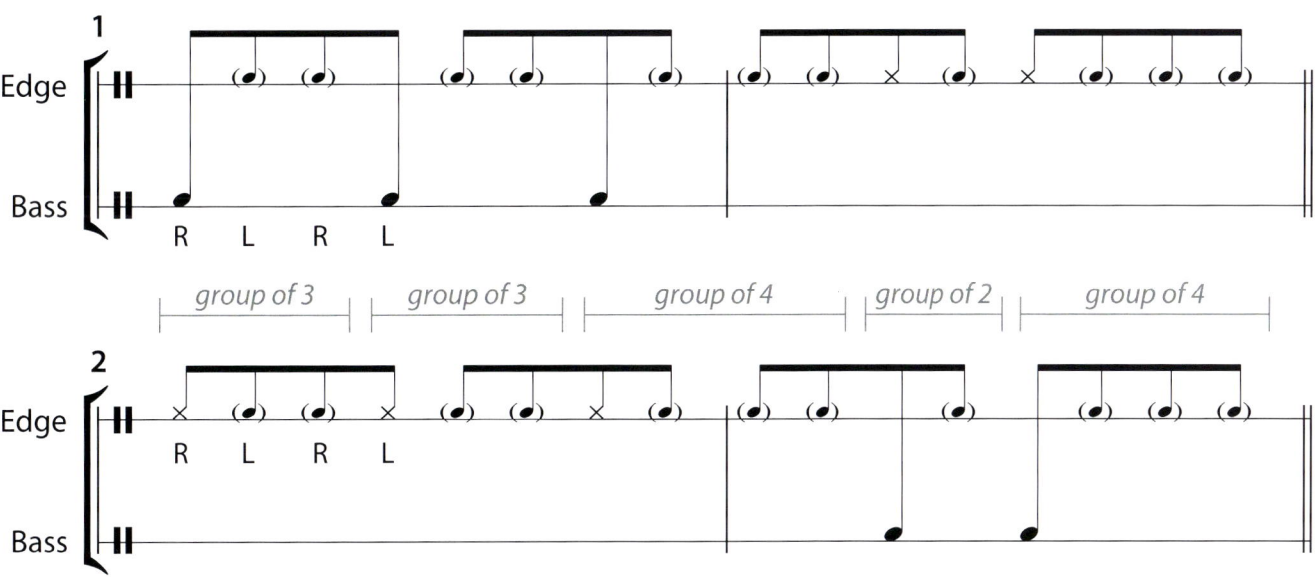

For the **Son Clave 2/3**, perform the individual steps according to the same principle.

Son Clave 2/3 (Extend the slap accents with Step 1 and 2)

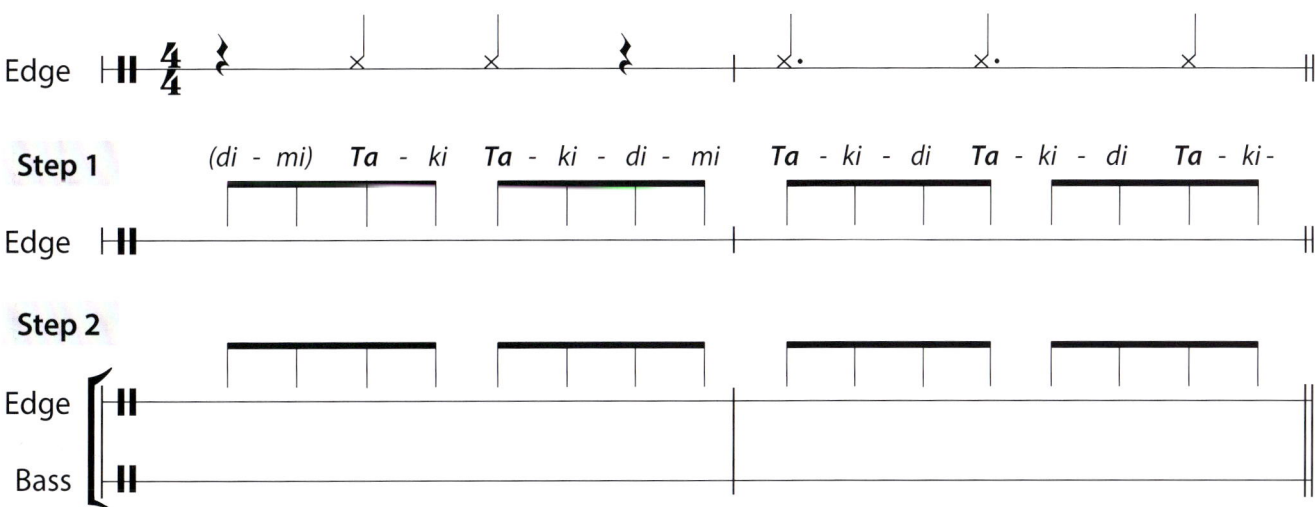

The Rumba Clave

The **Rumba Clave** differs from the *Son Clave 3/2*. The beat is shifted from the **4** to **4and** in the *first bar*. The Rumba Clave can also be reversed to a **2/3** version. Follow the same melody concept as with the *Son Clave* ...

Rumba Clave

bar 1 (*3rd beat on 4and*)   bar 2 (*similar to Son Clave 3/2*)

1 and 2 and 3 and 4 and   1 and 2 and 3 and 4 and
Ta - ki - di Ta - ki - di - mi Ta - ki - di Ta - ki Ta - ki - di - mi

Rumba Clave (initial pattern)

$\bullet = 100-144$

Edge

R   R   R   R   R

Step 1: Fill up the left hand with soft played tips in eighths. **WATCH** for loud, even-sounding slap accents and soft fill beats played at the very edge.

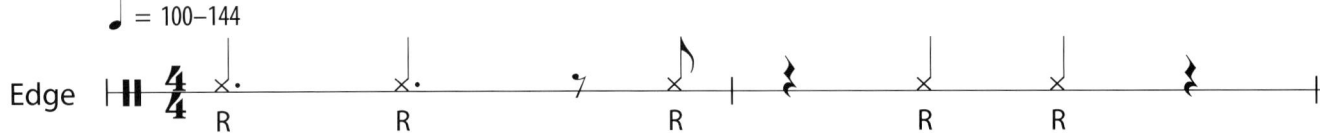

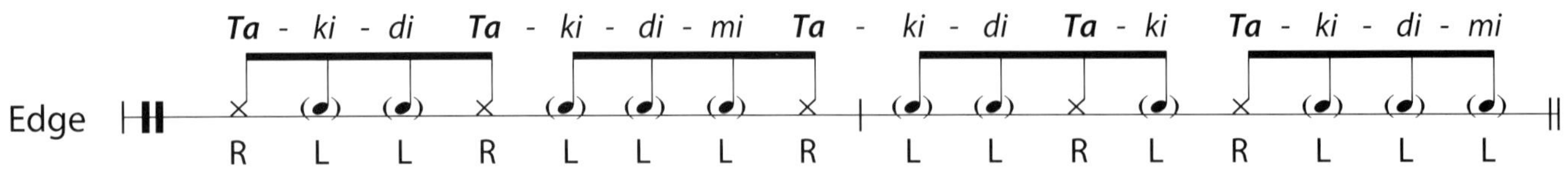

Ta - ki - di   Ta - ki - di - mi   Ta - ki - di   Ta - ki   Ta - ki - di - mi

Edge

R   L   L   R   L   L   L   R   L   L   R   L   R   L   L   L

Step 2: Some suggestions for orchestration. Be sure to practice both hand stickings!

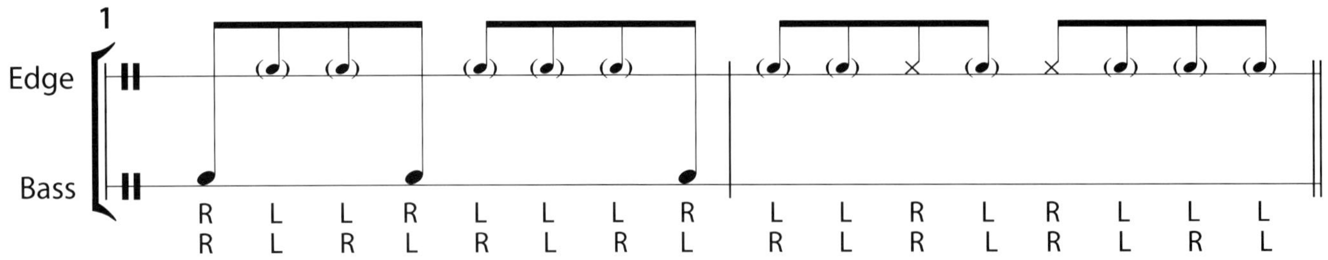

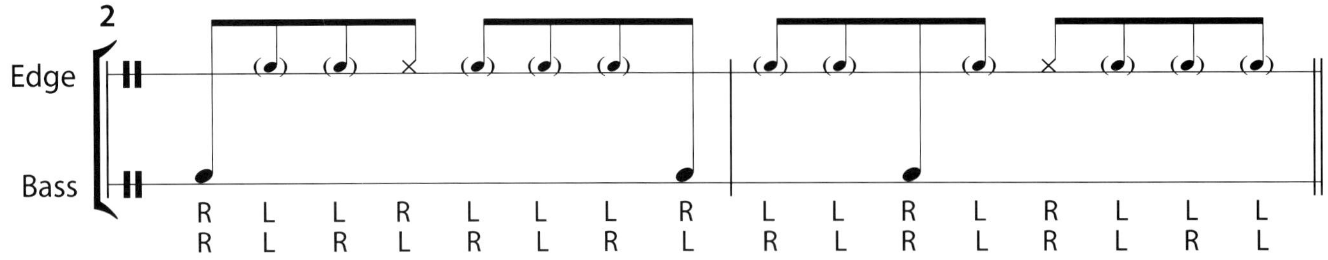

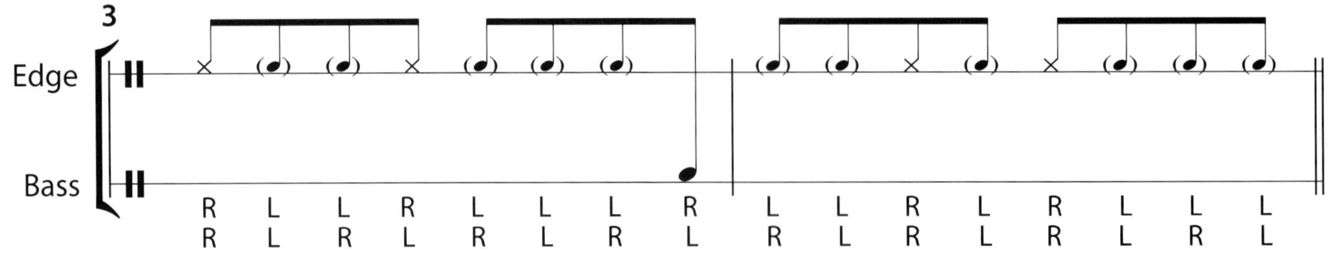

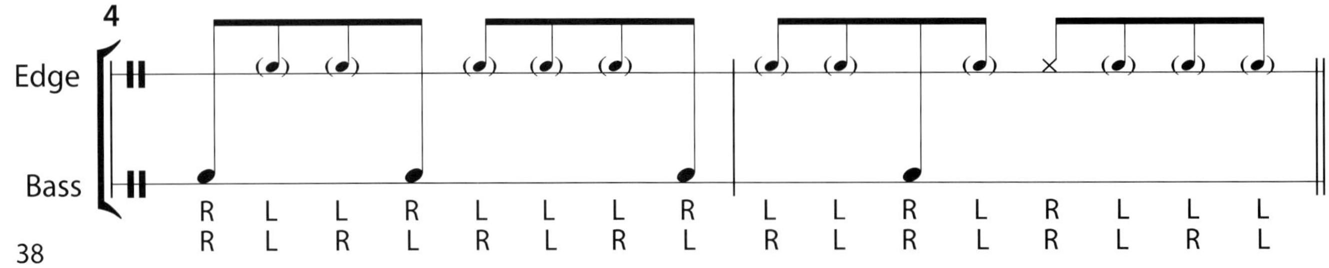

1

Edge

Bass

R   L   L   R   L   L   L   R   L   L   R   L   R   L   L   L
R   L   R   L   R   L   R   L   R   L   R   L   R   L   R   L

2

Edge

Bass

R   L   L   R   L   L   L   R   L   L   R   L   R   L   L   L
R   L   R   L   R   L   R   L   R   L   R   L   R   L   R   L

3

Edge

Bass

R   L   L   R   L   L   L   R   L   L   R   L   R   L   L   L
R   L   R   L   R   L   R   L   R   L   R   L   R   L   R   L

4

Edge

Bass

R   L   L   R   L   L   L   R   L   L   R   L   R   L   L   L
R   L   R   L   R   L   R   L   R   L   R   L   R   L   R   L

The Bossa Clave

In Brazil, the clave is used in the music of *bossa nova* and *samba*, among others. Let's start with the **Bossa Clave**. It is very similar to the *Son Clave 3/2* from Cuba, but differs in the *second bar* by the last beat on the count of **3and** instead of **3**. It is usually played by the *Agogôs* (*metal bells* connected by a hoop) or by the *Caixas* (Brazilian snare drum).

Bossa Clave

bar 1 (*sim. to Son Clave 3/2*) bar 2 (*2nd beat on 3and*)

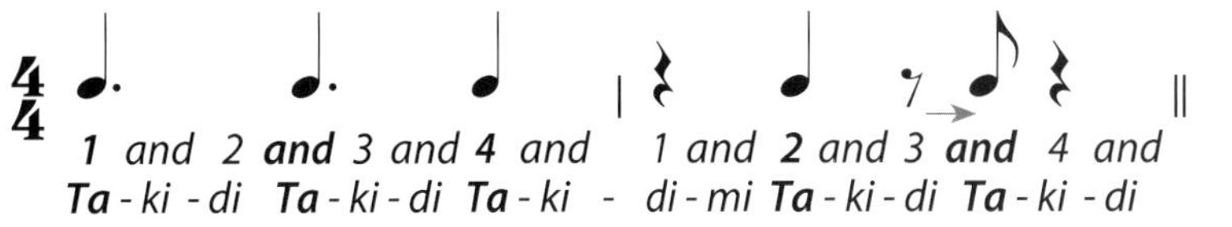

Online video 20

Bossa Clave (initial pattern)

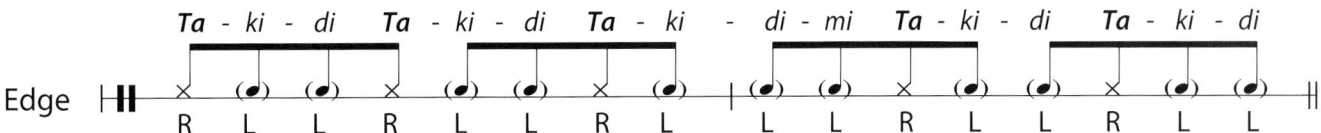

Step 1: Fill up the left hand with soft played tips in eighths. **WATCH** for loud, even-sounding slap accents and soft fill beats played at the very edge.

Step 2: Again some suggestions for orchestration. Be sure to practice both hand stickings!

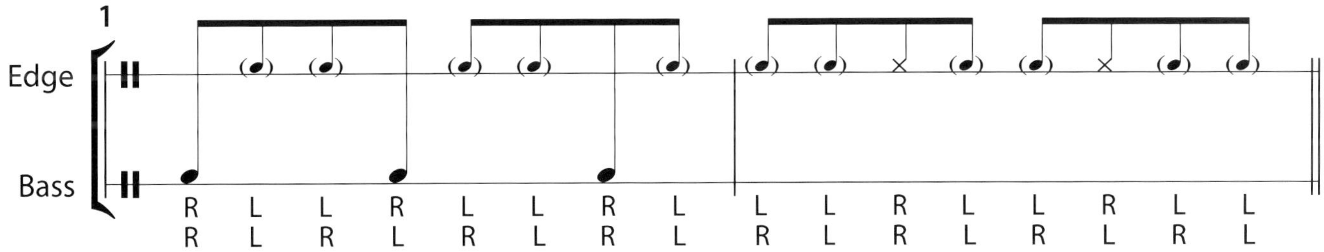

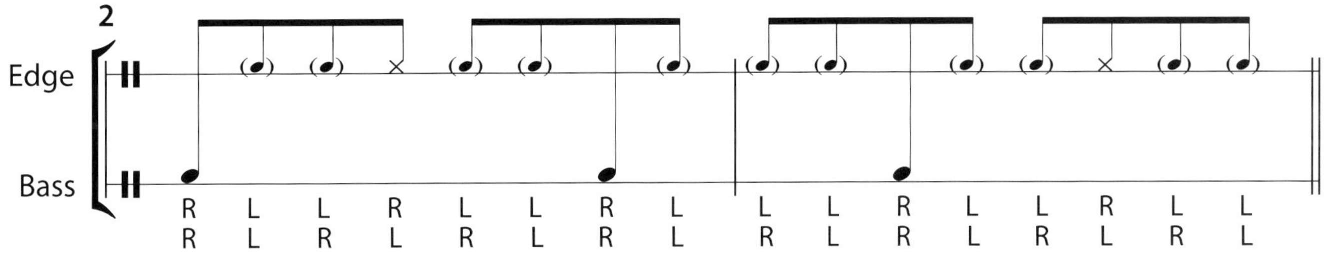

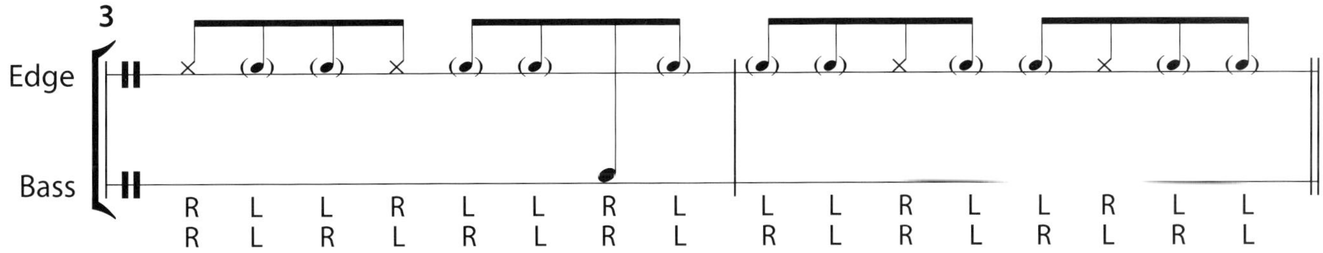

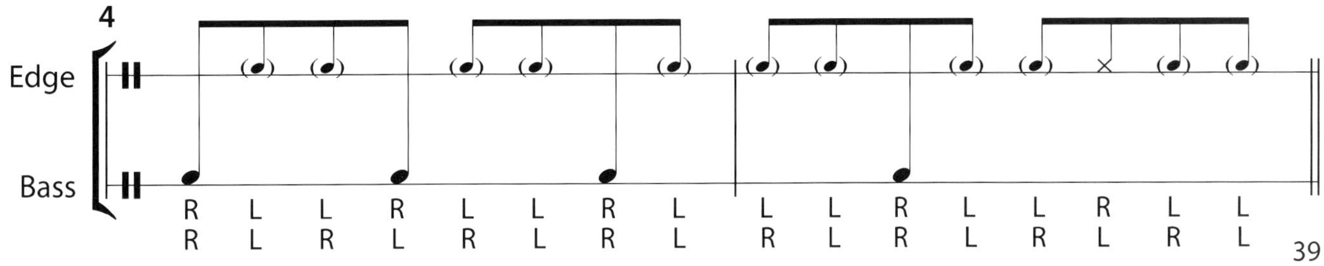

39

The Samba Clave

Proceed in the same way with the **Samba Clave**. The tempo of the samba is much faster in the original with up to 116 bpm than the bossa nova with 60 bpm.

Online video 21

Samba Clave (initial pattern)

♩ = 100–116

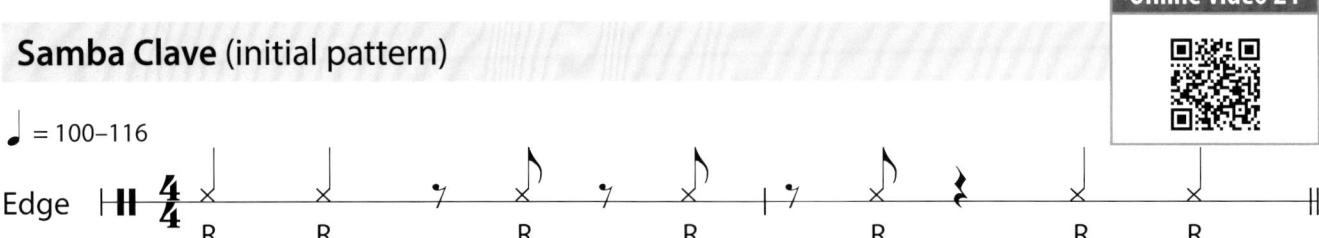

Step 1: Fill up the left hand with soft played tips in eighths. **WATCH** for loud, even-sounding slap accents and soft fill beats played at the very edge.

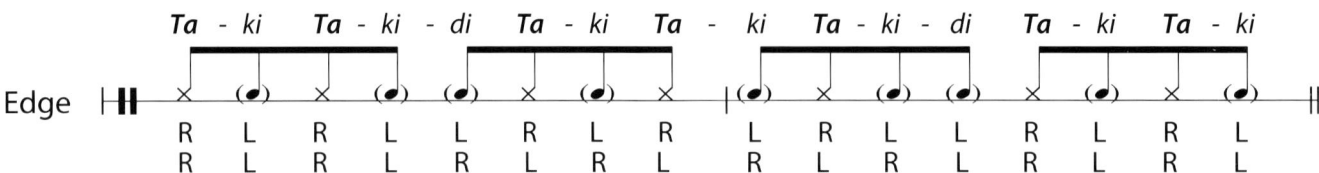

Step 2: Some suggestions for orchestration. Be sure to practice both hand stickings!

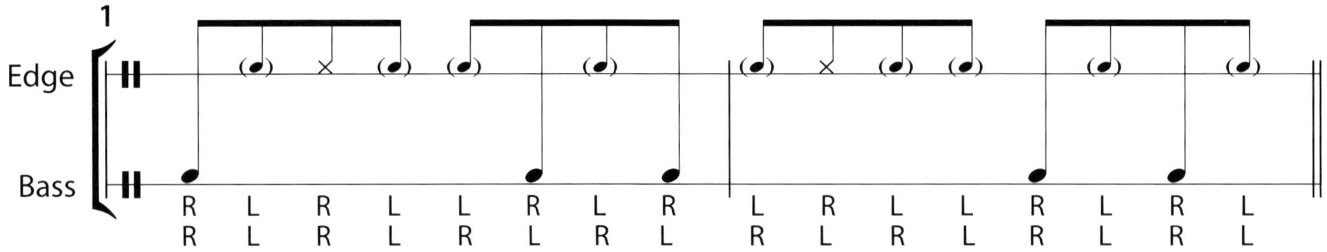

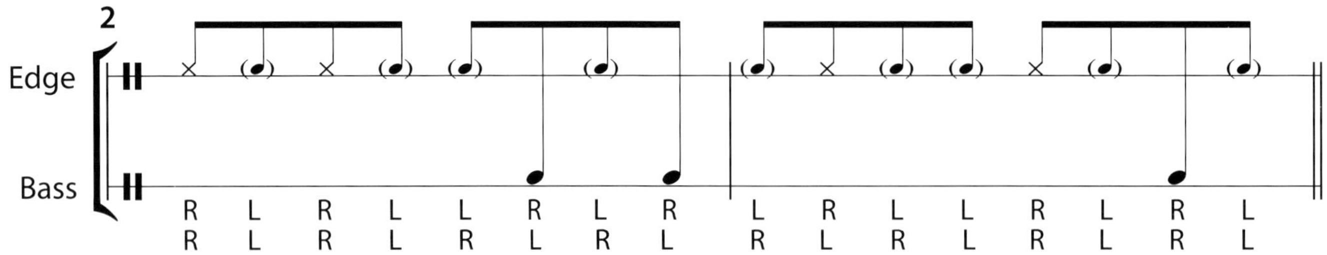

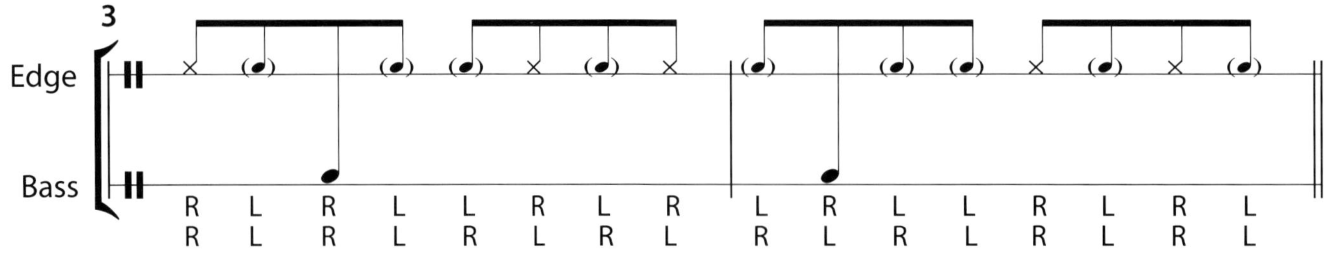

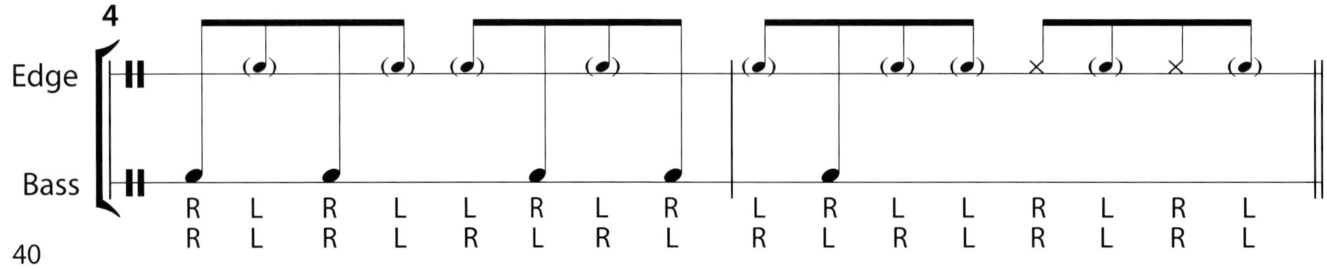

40

Groupings

A completely different form of movement and instrumentation on the cajón is playing *groupings within a sixteenth note grid*.

> **IMPORTANT:**
>
> *Always think in this 16th note grid, the 'illusion'[1] of a new meter is created exclusively by the groups.*

3 over 4

Again, we start with a *basic pattern* at a tempo of **60 bpm**, e.g.:

Basic pattern in a 16th note grid (60 bpm)

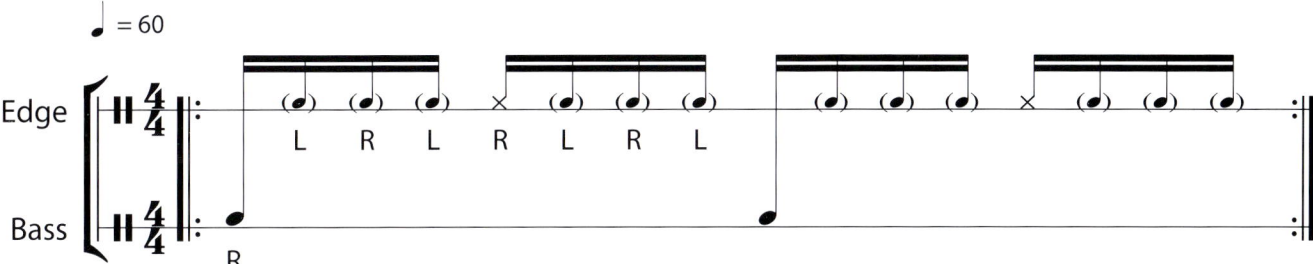

The idea: groups of *three* beats with a *slap accent* on the *first beat* ('odd' division of three beats in an 'even' $\frac{4}{4}$ = **3 over 4**).

Important: If you still find **R L** sticking difficult, play all slap accents with the strong hand first and fill in with the weak hand: **R L L** or **L R R**.

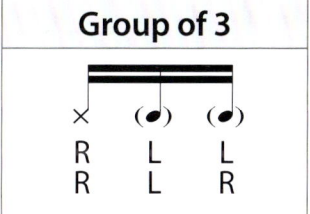

Groups of 3 (with slap accent on the first beat) **plus 1 beat**

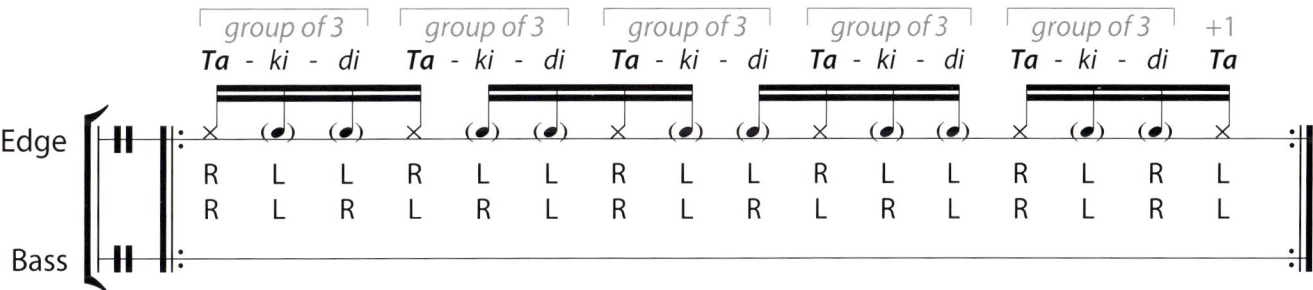

PRACTICE SYSTEM:

STEP 1: Play the basic pattern slowly: **60 bpm**

STEP 2: Practice the **3 over 4** 'illusion.'

STEP 3: Use the 'illusion' as a fill-in or variation, ie:
   3 bars of basic pattern plus 1 bar of 'illusion.'

STEP 4: Orchestrate the 'illusion' as a fill-in or variation by distributing the accents to the bass and edge.

---

[1] *The term 'illusion' is used by Gavin Harrison in his book* **Rhythmic Illusions** *(1998) to describe this phenomenon of the supposed, temporary change of meter or tempo.*

Practice the following groups according to the same system.

This form of *rhythm within rhythm* again offers infinite variations and always gives the listener the feeling that you are setting a different meter, a different pulse with this 'illusion.'

5 over 4 (plus 1 beat)

Group of 5

STEP 1: Play the basic pattern slowly: **60 bpm**:

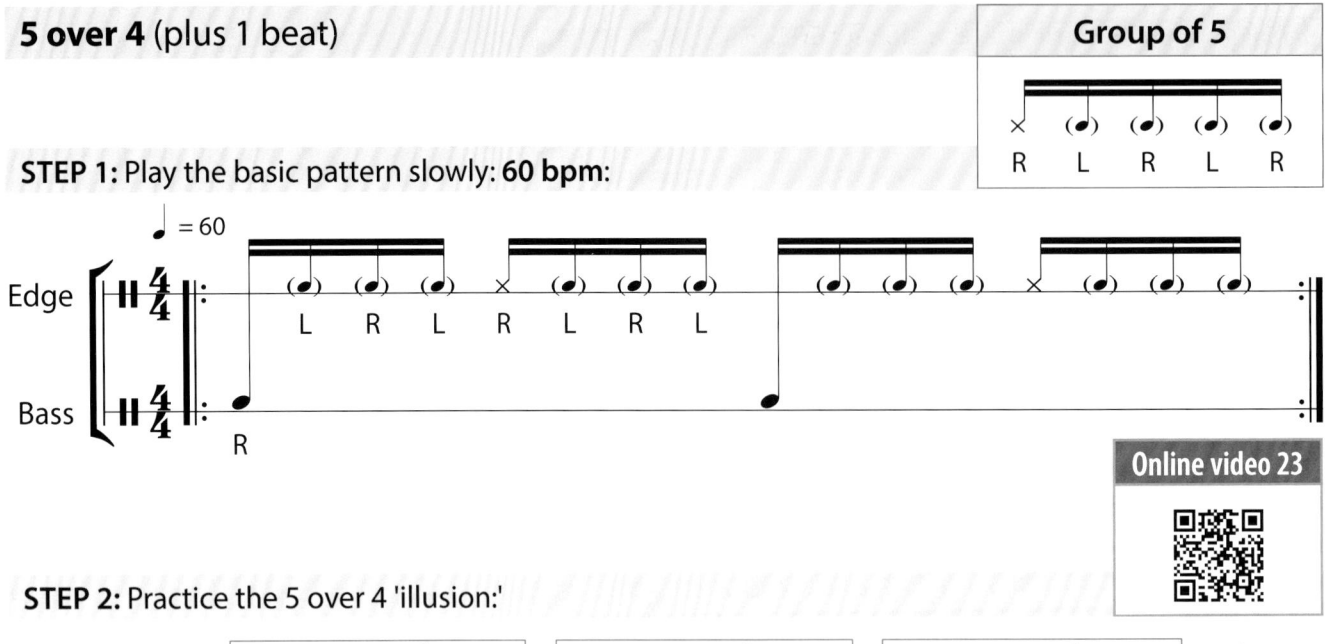

Online video 23

STEP 2: Practice the 5 over 4 'illusion:'

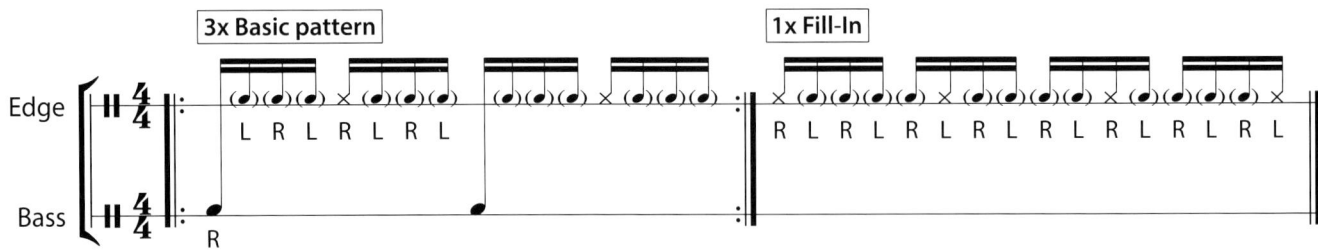

STEP 3: Use the 'illusion' as a fill-in or variation (*see Groove & Fill Concept on page 18*):

STEP 4: Independently orchestrate the slap accents distributed on bass and edge:

1

Edge

Bass

2

Edge

Bass

42

7 over 4 (plus 2 beats)

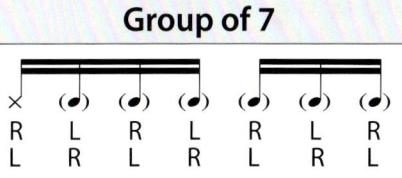

Group of 7

Groups of 7 we put together from two groups, here: **4 + 3**!

STEP 1: Play the basic pattern slowly: **60 bpm:**

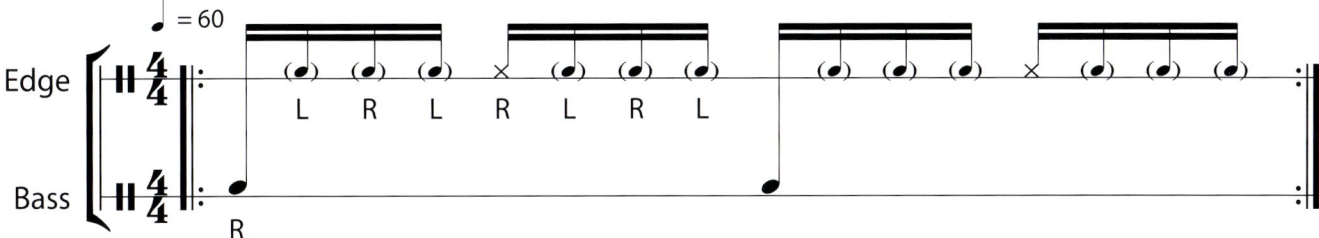

STEP 2: Practice the 7 over 4 'illusion:'

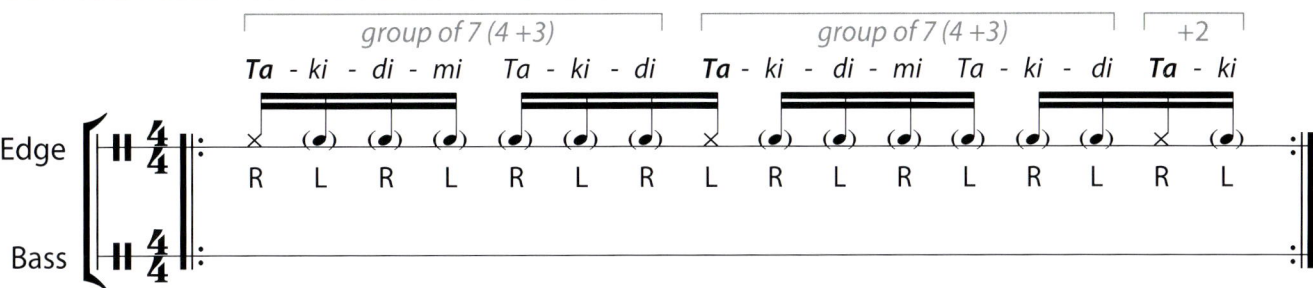

STEP 3: Use the 'illusion' as a fill-in or variation (*see Groove & Fill Concept on page 18*):

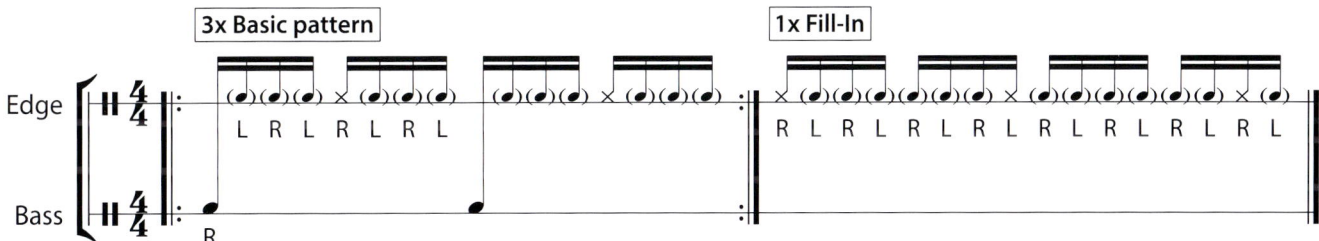

STEP 4: Independently orchestrate the slap accents distributed on bass and edge:

Grouping combinations

It is also very interesting to *combine* the groups with each other. When speaking the syllables in the following combination exercises, emphasize the slap accents highlighted in bold.

3 + 2 combination over 4 (plus 3 beats)

Combination 3 + 2

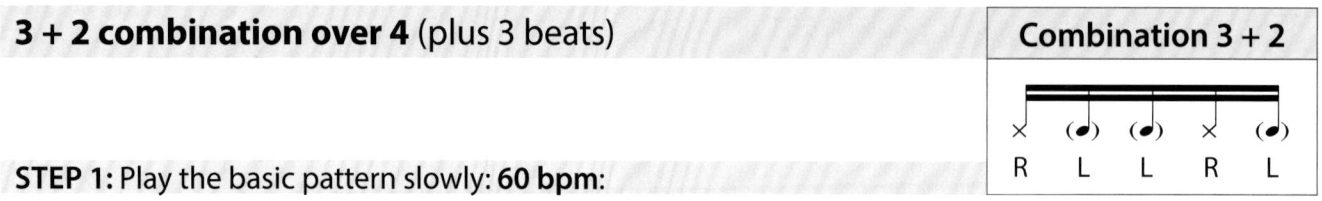

STEP 1: Play the basic pattern slowly: **60 bpm:**

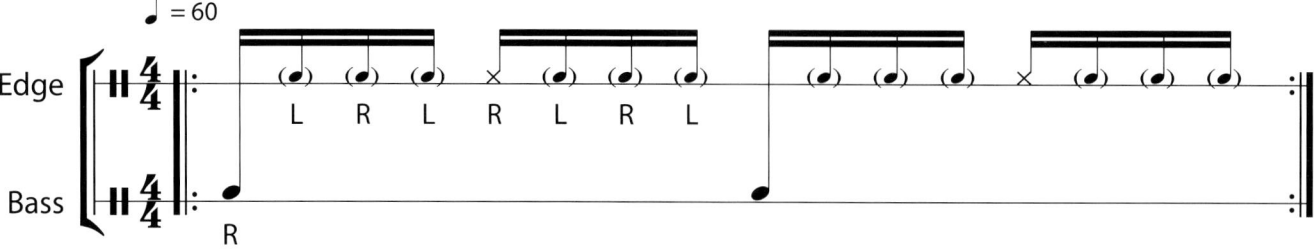

STEP 2: Practice the 3+2 combination over 4:

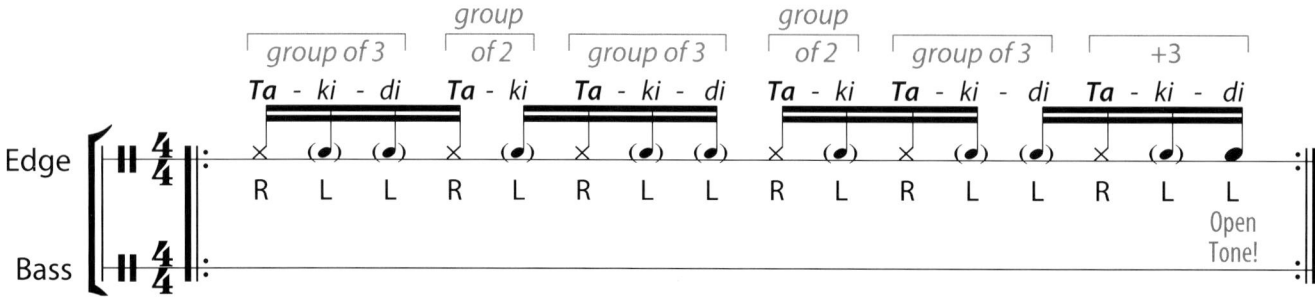

STEP 3: Use the 3+2 combination as a fill-in or variation:

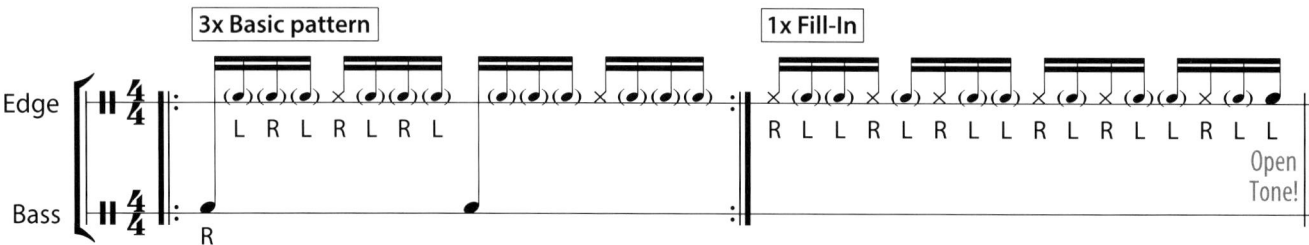

STEP 4: Orchestrate the slap accents distributed on bass and edge:

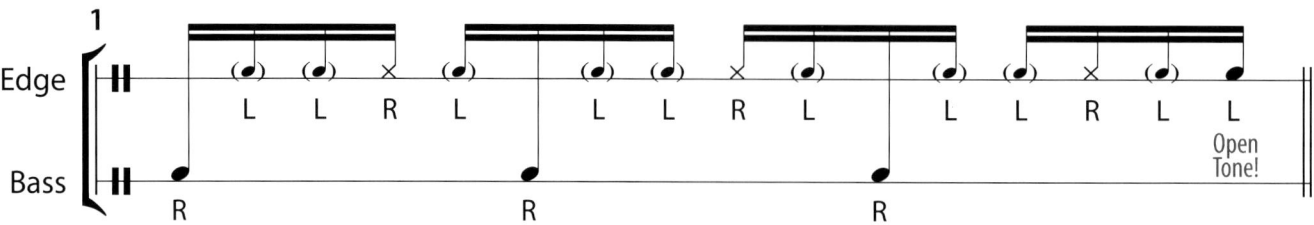

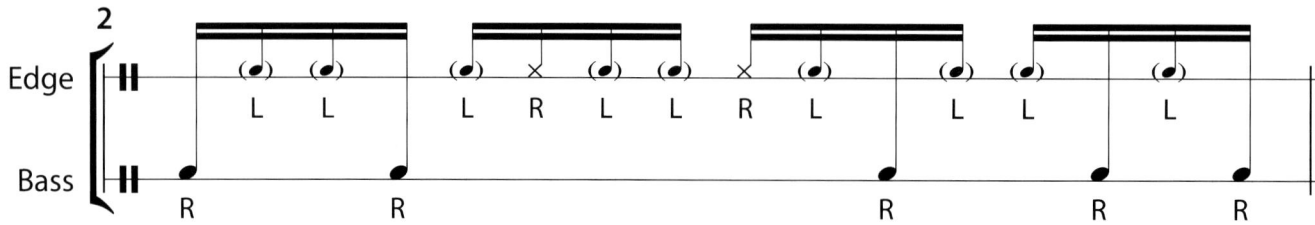

2 + 3 combination over 4 (plus 4 beats)

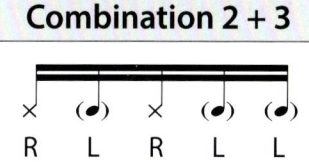

Combination 2 + 3

STEP 1: Play the basic pattern slowly: **60 bpm:**

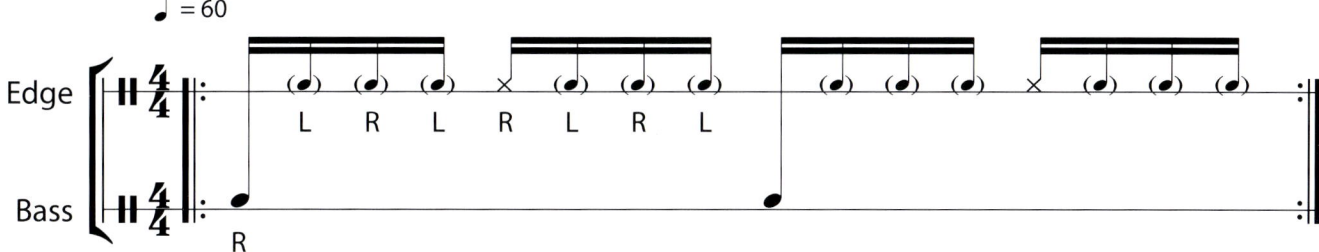

STEP 2: Practice the 2+3 combination over 4:

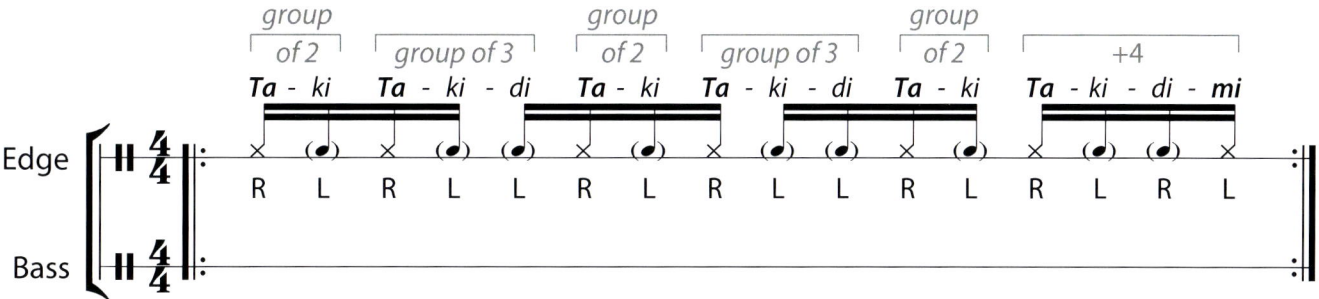

STEP 3: Use the 2+3 combination as a fill-in or variation:

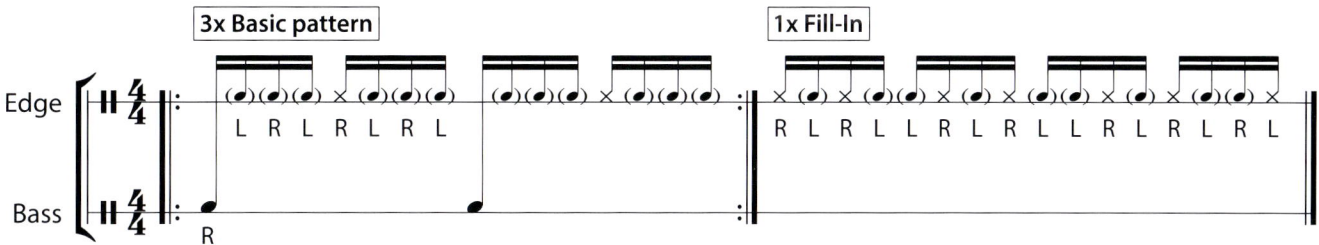

STEP 4: Orchestrate the slap accents distributed on bass and edge:

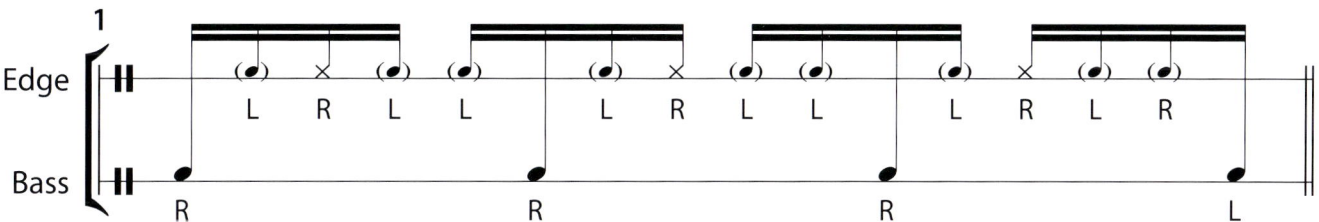

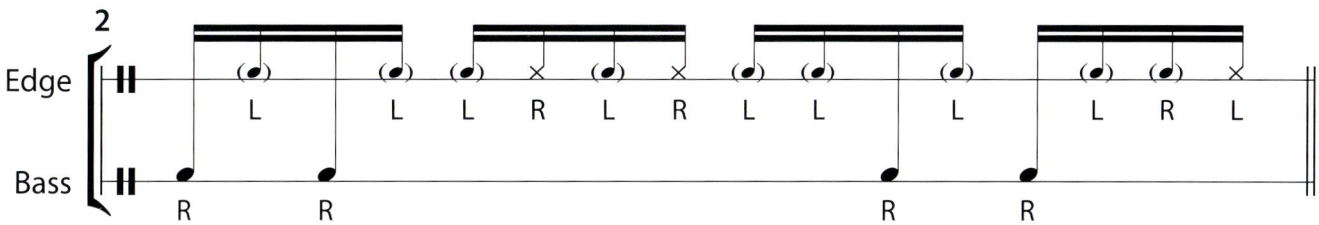

Now combine *three groups* together. Start with a *group of 7*, which you divide into **3+2+2**. Proceed in the usual way with steps 1 to 4.

3 + 2 + 2 combination over 4 (plus 2 beats)

STEP 4: Orchestrate the slap accents (bass and edge):

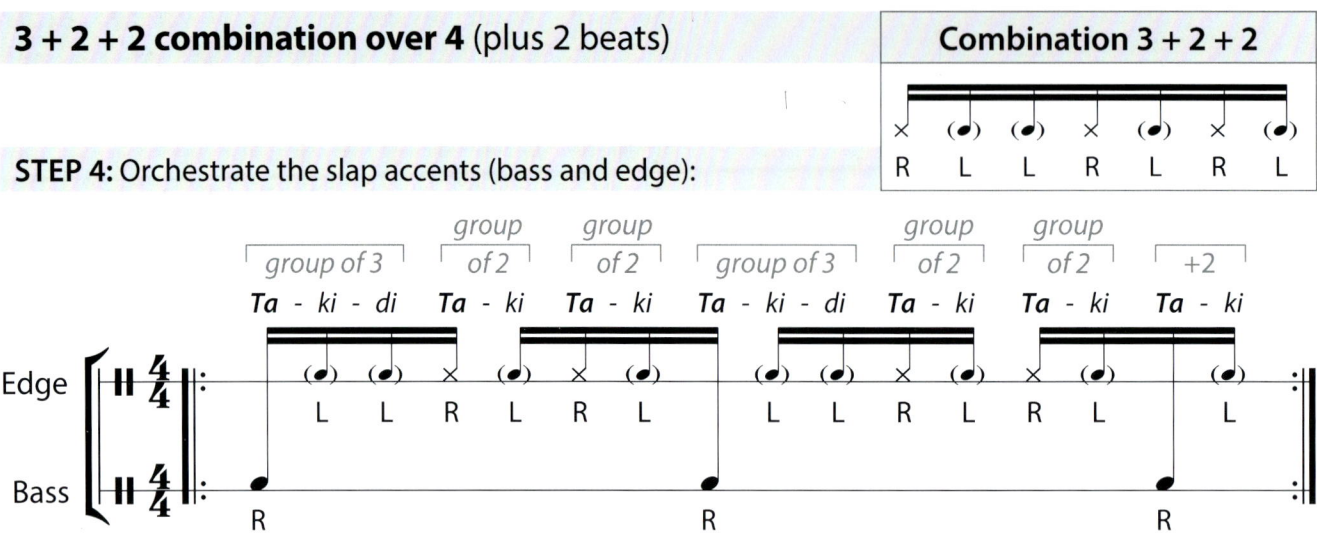

Reverse the 3+2+2 combo to **2+2+3** and proceed in the single steps Step 1 to 4.

2 + 2 + 3 combination over 4 (plus 2 beats)

STEP 4: One of the orchestrations might look like this:

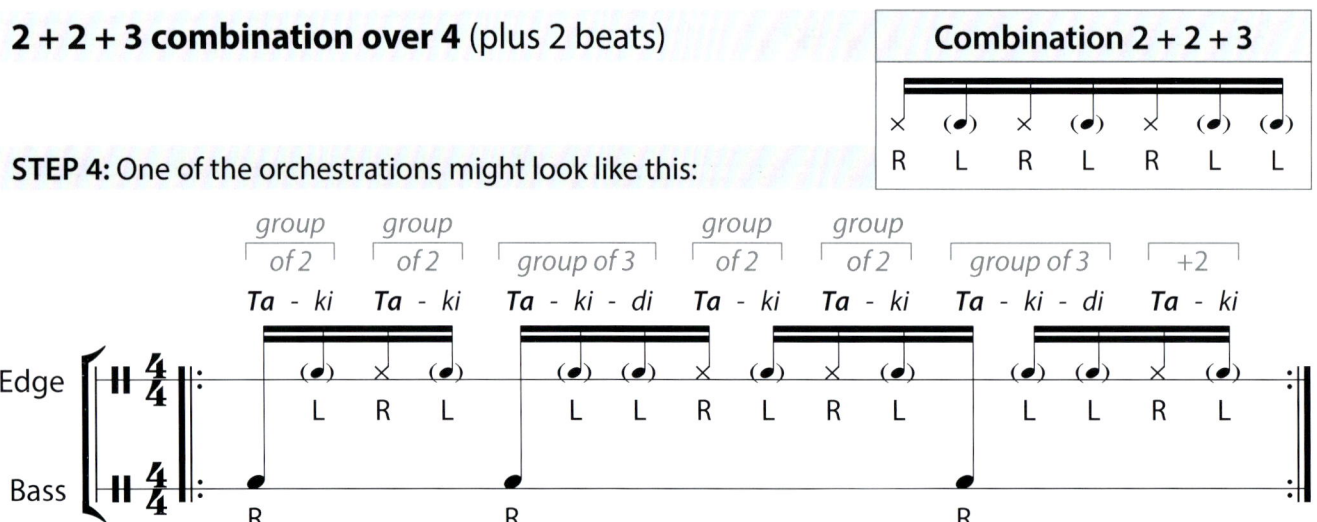

Or in the third and final option: **2+3+2**:

2 + 3 + 2 combination over 4 (plus 2 beats)

STEP 4: A proposal for instrumentation:

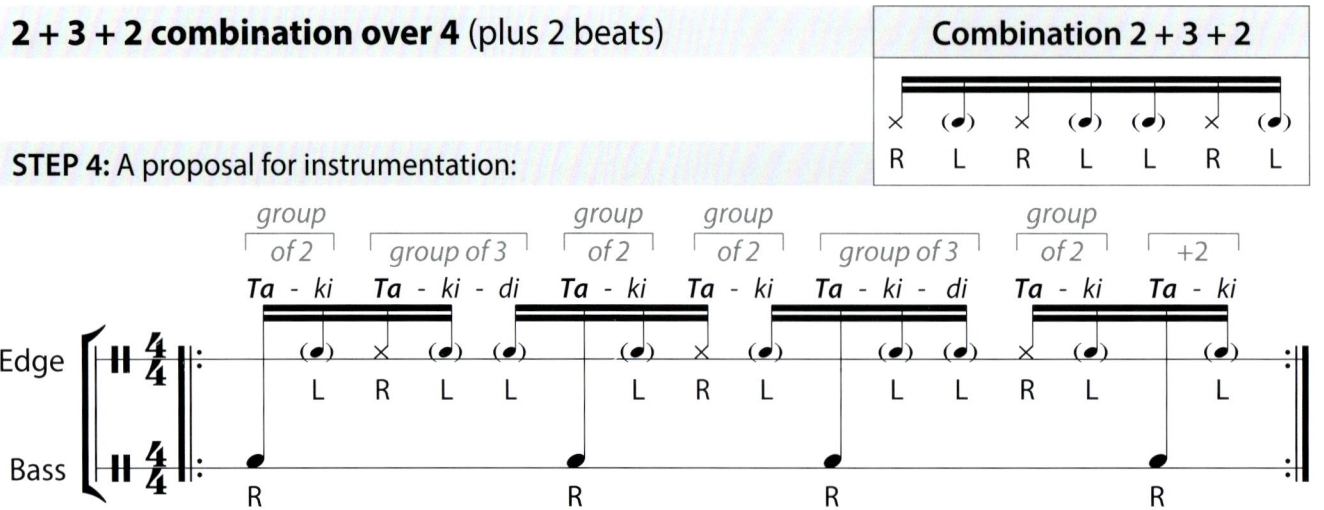

Now start with a group of 8 in the division **3+3+2** and proceed as usual in the single steps 1 to 4:

3 + 3 + 2 Combination over 4

STEP 4: A proposal for instrumentation:

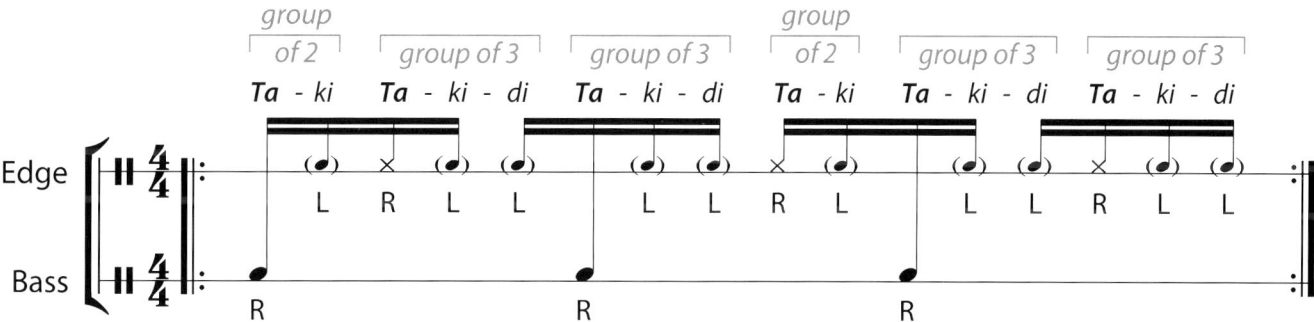

Now: **2+3+3**:

2 + 3 + 3 combination over 4

STEP 4: One of the orchestrations might look like this:

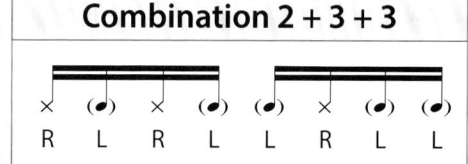

> **IMPORTANT:**
>
> *Practice the groups slowly and always as a fill-in alternating with the basic pattern.*

Many rhythms from Eastern Europe and the Middle East work with groups of 2 and 3. This often results in so-called *odd meters* like $\frac{5}{8}$, $\frac{7}{8}$, $\frac{9}{8}$ etc. In the next example, I have written down a *Kalamatianos*, a Greek folk dance in $\frac{7}{8}$ time.

Kalamatianos (3 + 2 + 2 combination: 8ths = 100 bpm)

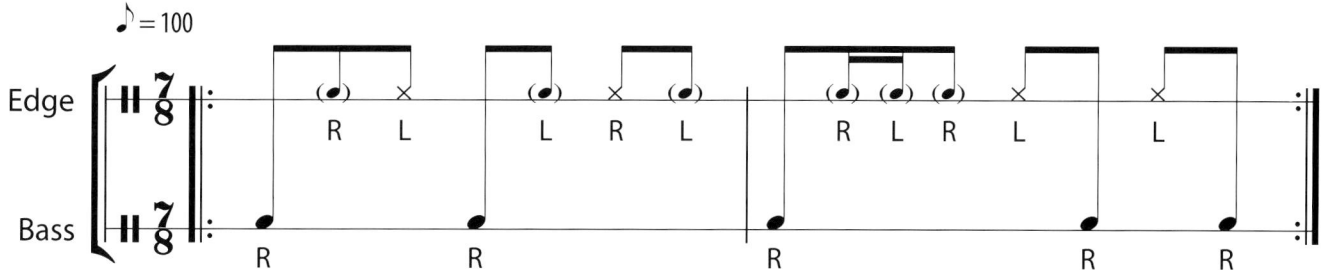

Triplets and Groupings in the Flow of R L

So far, we have mainly used a sixteenth note grid to create the groups and their 'illusions.' Now the triplet becomes the new basis.

The eighth-note triplet

Until now, we have divided the note values — such as quarter notes, eighth notes, and sixteenth notes — into two equal parts only. Thus, one quarter note becomes two eighth notes and one eighth note becomes two sixteenth notes. This is called *binary rhythm* [*Latin: double or pairs*].

The **triplet**, on the other hand, is the basis of the *ternary rhythm* [*lat.: ter = three times*]. It arises when you divide a note value into *three equal parts*. Instead of the usual two eighth notes, a quarter note becomes *three eighth notes of equal length*, the so-called *eighth-note triplet*. In musical notation, it is marked with an *italicized '3'* above or below the eighth bar.

Start with the basic triplet pattern, which you should play by heart to have it ready as a reference for the next triplet exercises.

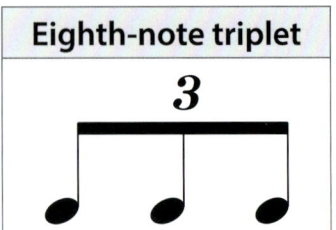

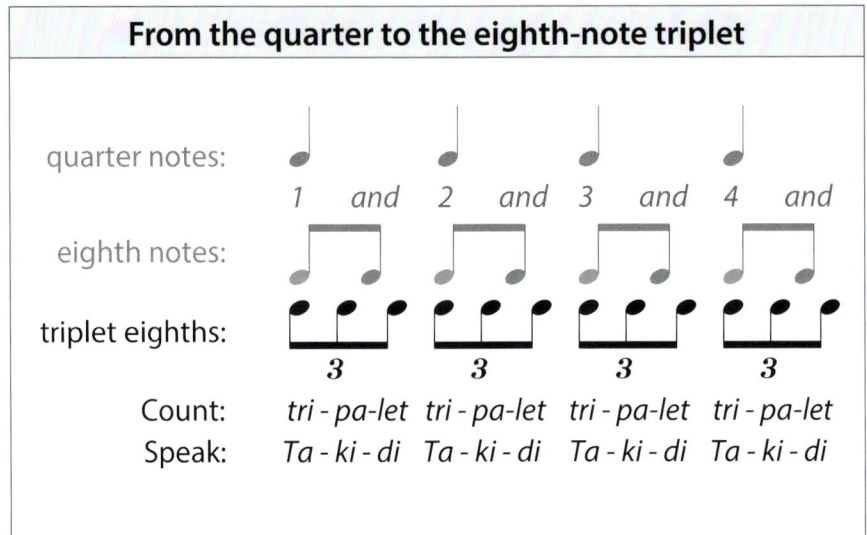

Basic pattern in a triplet grid (60 bpm)

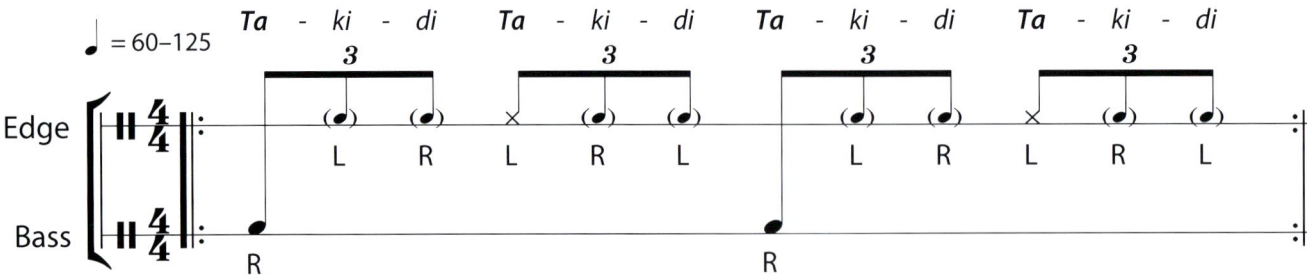

Groups of 2 in triplet sequences

Now start to play the slap with the strong hand on the edge and fill up with *tips* in the weaker hand:

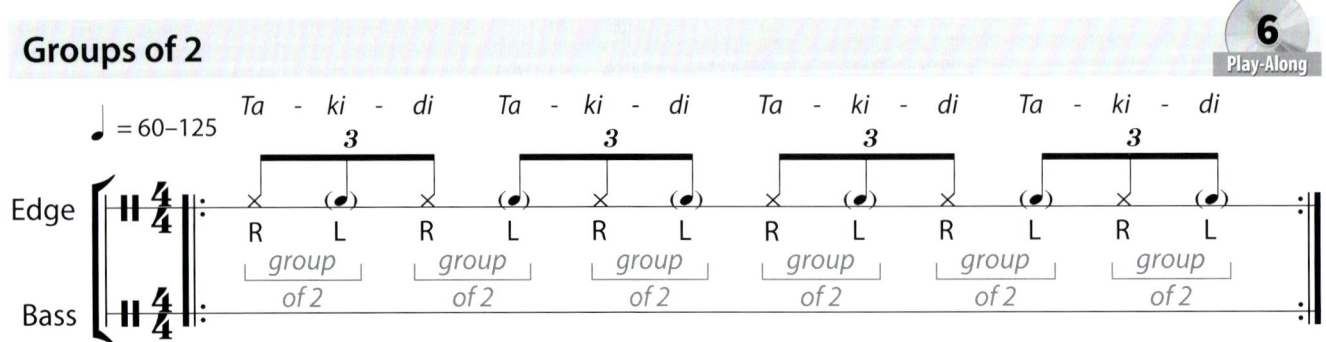

48

These groups of 2 in triplet sequences are the first step towards *polyrhythmic figures*. If you play edge and bass line alternately — as shown in the following example — you will understand what I mean. This is also called **3 against 2** (**3** = accents in the bass; **2** = main pulse: accents on the edge on the $\frac{4}{4}$ beats).

Practice this polyrhythm as follows (tempo: $\quad = 60$ bpm):

1. Start with the *left hand* in the bar you play *at the edge* of the cajón and then switch to the *bass bar* you play with the *right hand only*. Always switch back and forth between both hands.

2. Now play both parts *at the same time*, but very slowly. Pay attention to the exact balance in volume between accent and tip (ghost note).

3. Now leave out the tips (fill beats) and play *only the accents* with both hands *at the same time*. What you hear is **3 against 2** in its purest form!

Online video 26

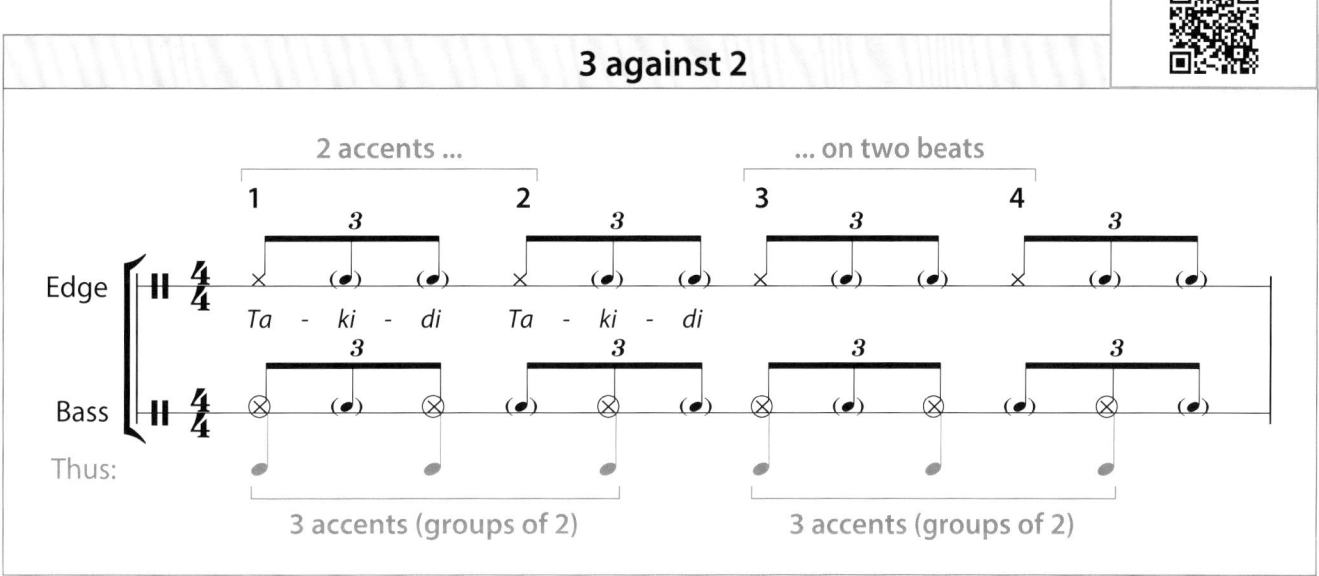

Orchestrate the accents in the right hand:

Slap accents (distributed on bass and edge)

6 Play-Along

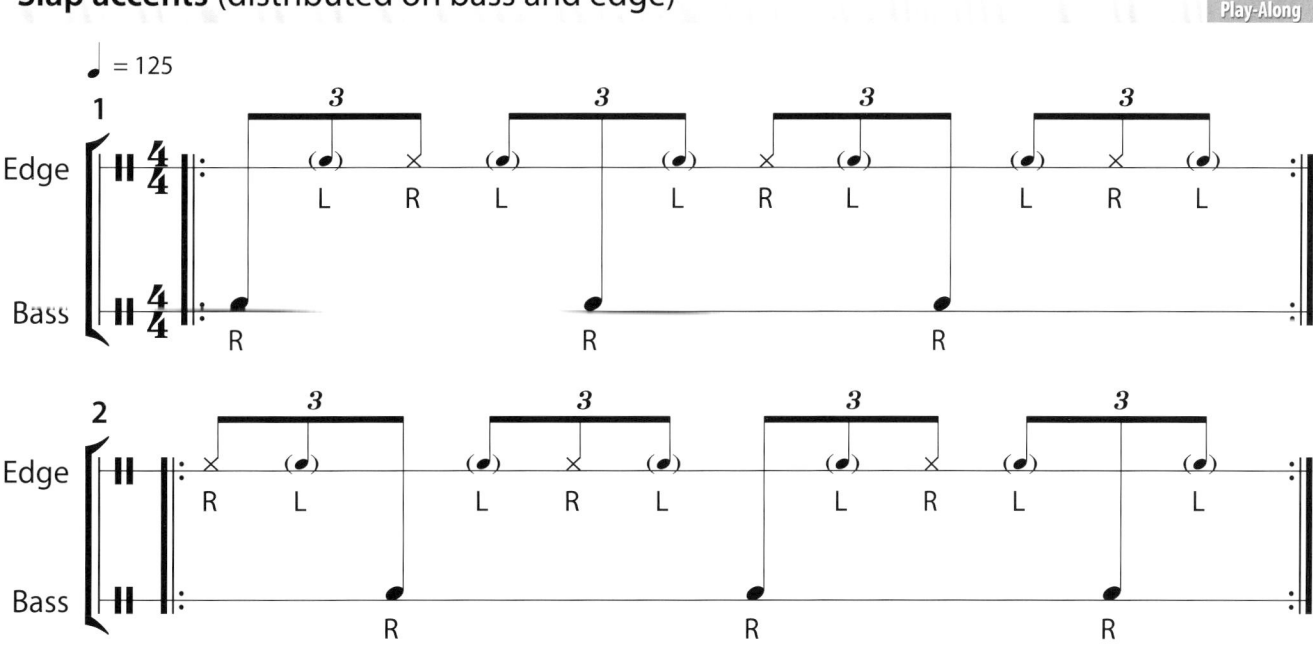

Groups of 4 in triplet sequences

You achieve a new 'illusion' with *groups of 4*:

Groups of 4 (orchestrated)

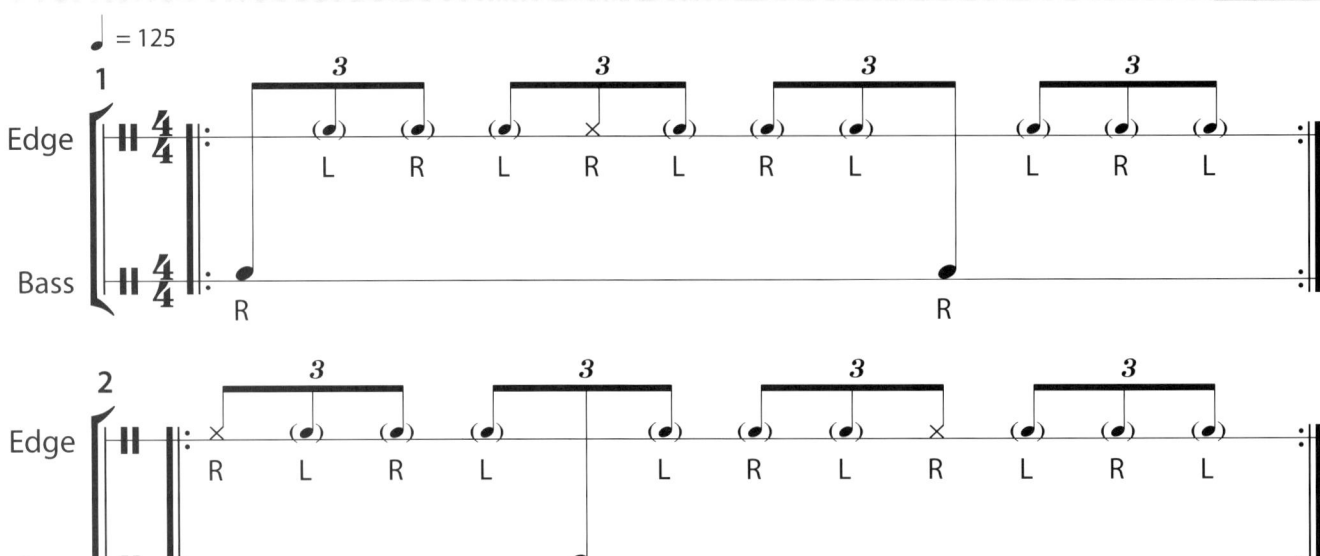

Now it gets more challenging, because you move the starting point of your groups of 2 and 4 to the *second eighth* of a triplet. This means that the first slap accent is on the second note of the first triplet group. The 'illusion' starts one triplet beat later.

The sticking continues to alternate consistently between **R** and **L**, so that this time the accents are performed with the supposedly weaker hand. Practice the five lines separately first.

Then combine each line again with your basic pattern. Once with the basic pattern plus once with the 'illusion' (one bar of the 2 or 4 group variations).

As a reminder, here is the **basic pattern** from *page 48* again:

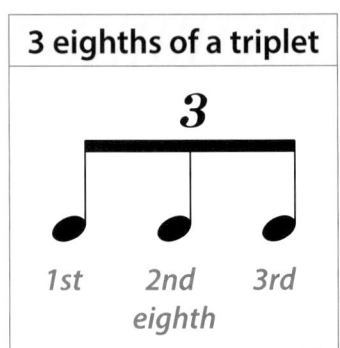

Basic pattern in a triplet grid (60 bpm)

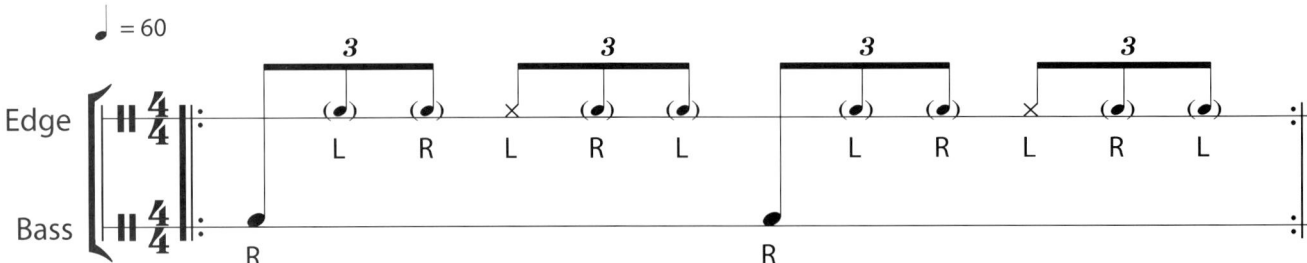

Here are the five exercises with groups beginning on the second triplet eighth:

Slap accents (groups of 2 and 4: start on the 2nd eighth)

6 Play-Along

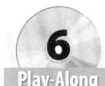

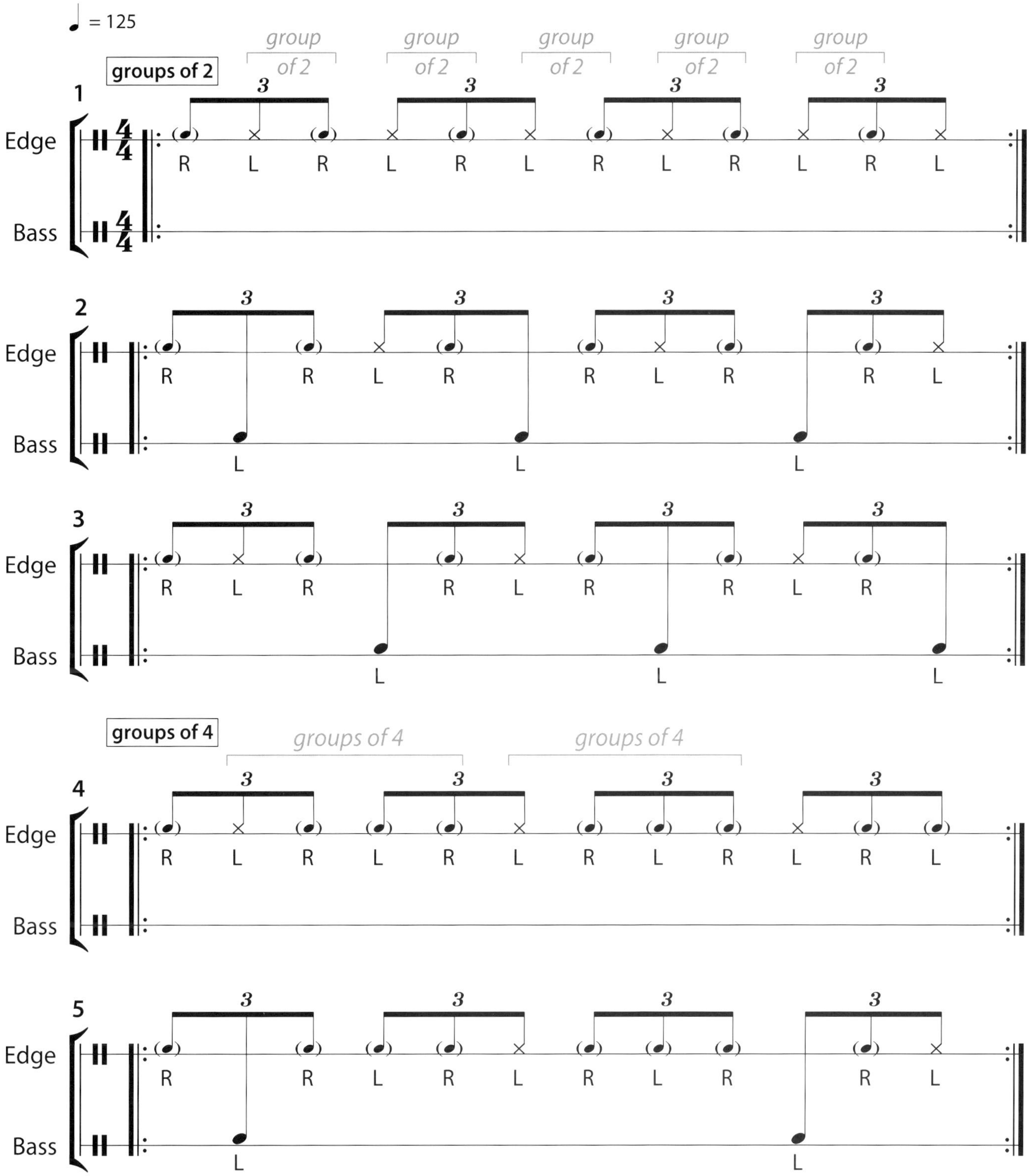

IMPORTANT:
Always practice according to the system: once basic pattern and once 'illusion.'

Multiple accents

Now play *double accents* in groups of 2 and *triple accents* in groups of 4:

Double accents and triple accents (in groups of 2 and groups of 4)

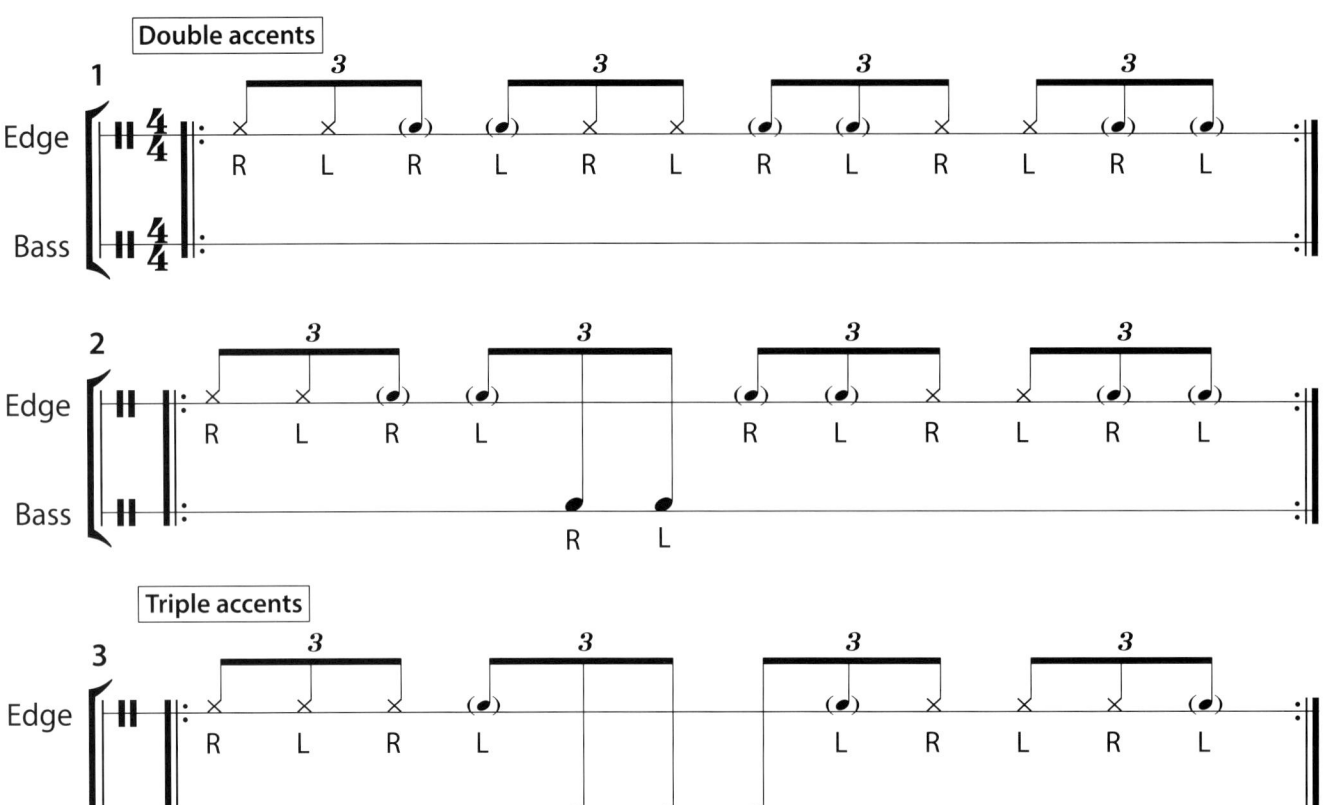

The Bembe rhythm

It's just as interesting to incorporate the melodic accents of traditional rhythms into your accent/non-accent scheme. The next example shows you the melody of the bembe, a traditional Afro-Cuban beat in $\frac{6}{8}$ metrum.

The $\frac{6}{8}$ time is one of the *compound, 'odd' time signatures* more common in Latin American music. It is composed of *six eighth notes* that are divided into *two groups of three* with different accents:

Time signature

$$\frac{6}{8}$$

	6/8 time					
accentuation	heavy	light	light	semi-heavy	light	light
beats	**1**	2	3	**4**	5	6

The *melody of the bembe* looks like this. Play the accents always with your strong hand (R for right-handers; L for left-handers):

Bembe (6/8 time)

Now we transfer the $\frac{6}{8}$ accents into the $\frac{4}{4}$ time. The triplets are a good choice for this, since they — like the $\frac{6}{8}$ time — are subject to a tripartite division. This results in wonderful $\frac{4}{4}$ grooves.

Online video 27

Bembe (Transcription in 4/4 time with eighth-note triplets)

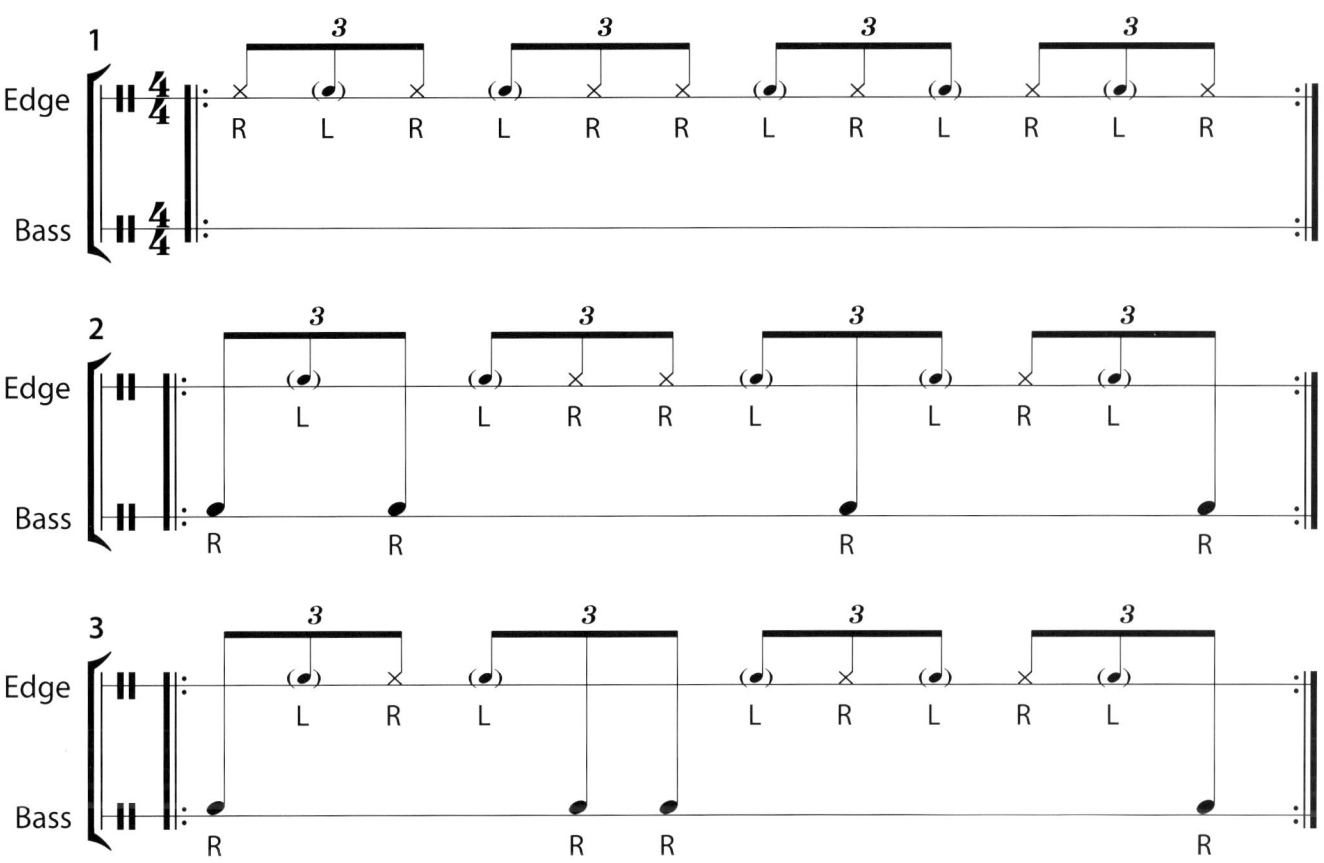

Below you will find variations of more African patterns and their application.
First are the patterns played on the edge only:

More African patterns (edge only)

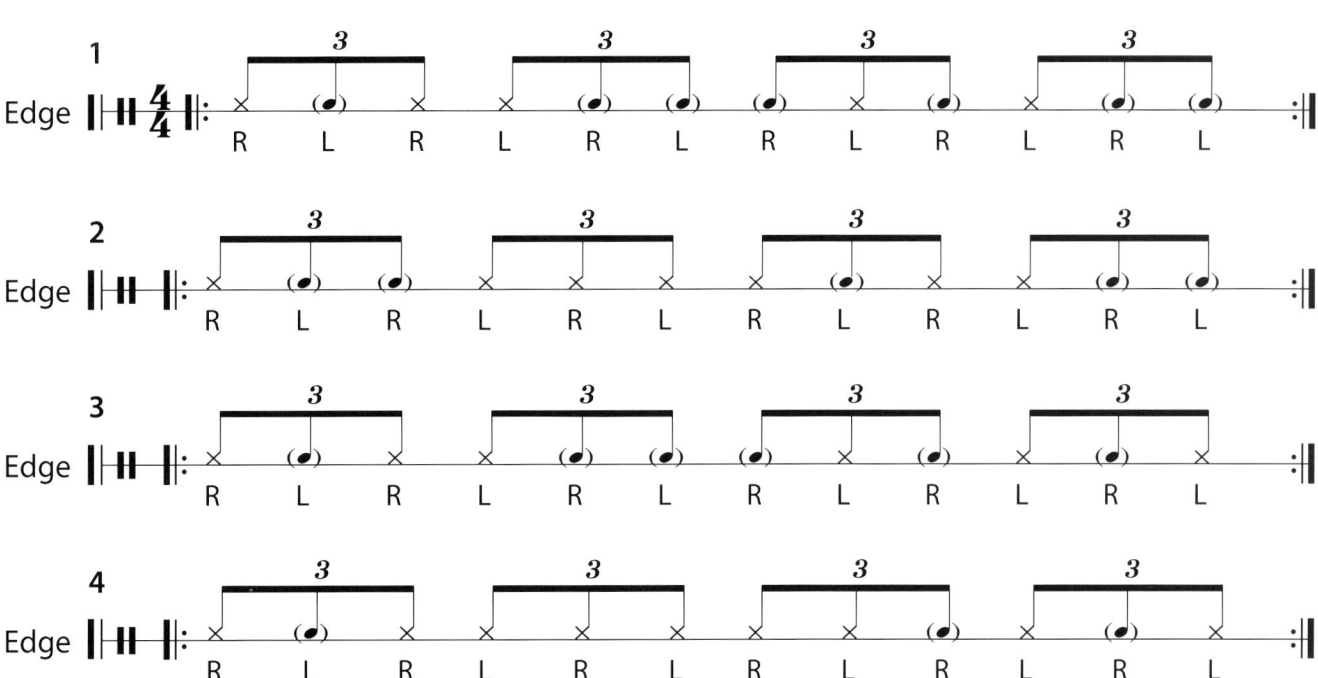

Then split between bass and edge as a complete groove:

More African patterns (bass and edge)

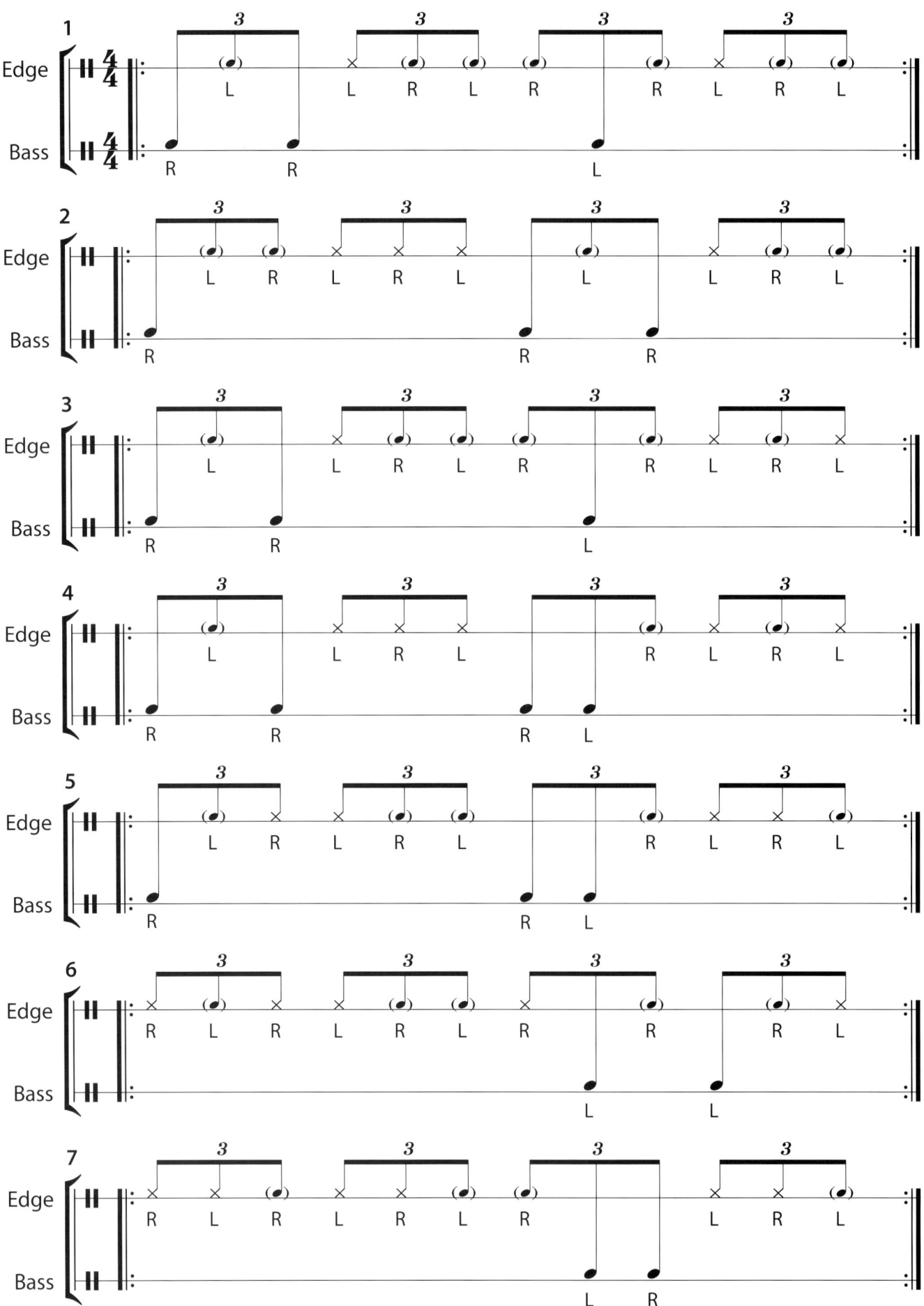

PART 2: GROOVES & STYLES

The Cajón as a Drum Set and for Song Accompaniment

In **PART 2** you learn to play the cajón like a *drum set*.

The strong hand in the bass replaces the *bass drum* and the supposedly weaker hand on the edge replaces the *snare drum* of a drum set.

The rhythms listed below vary only in the right hand (bass) and are mostly based on the rhythmic figure of the bass player in the band. Together you are the rhythm section of a formation.

Pop Grooves

When practicing, pay attention to *balance in dynamics*, i.e. less bass and more edge tones make the rhythms more balanced. Combine the basic pattern—according to the *Groove & Fill Concept* (*see page 18*)—with one of each of the four variations listed below.

Online video 28

7 Demo Track 8 Play-Along

Variations 1–4

Basic pattern (bass | snare)

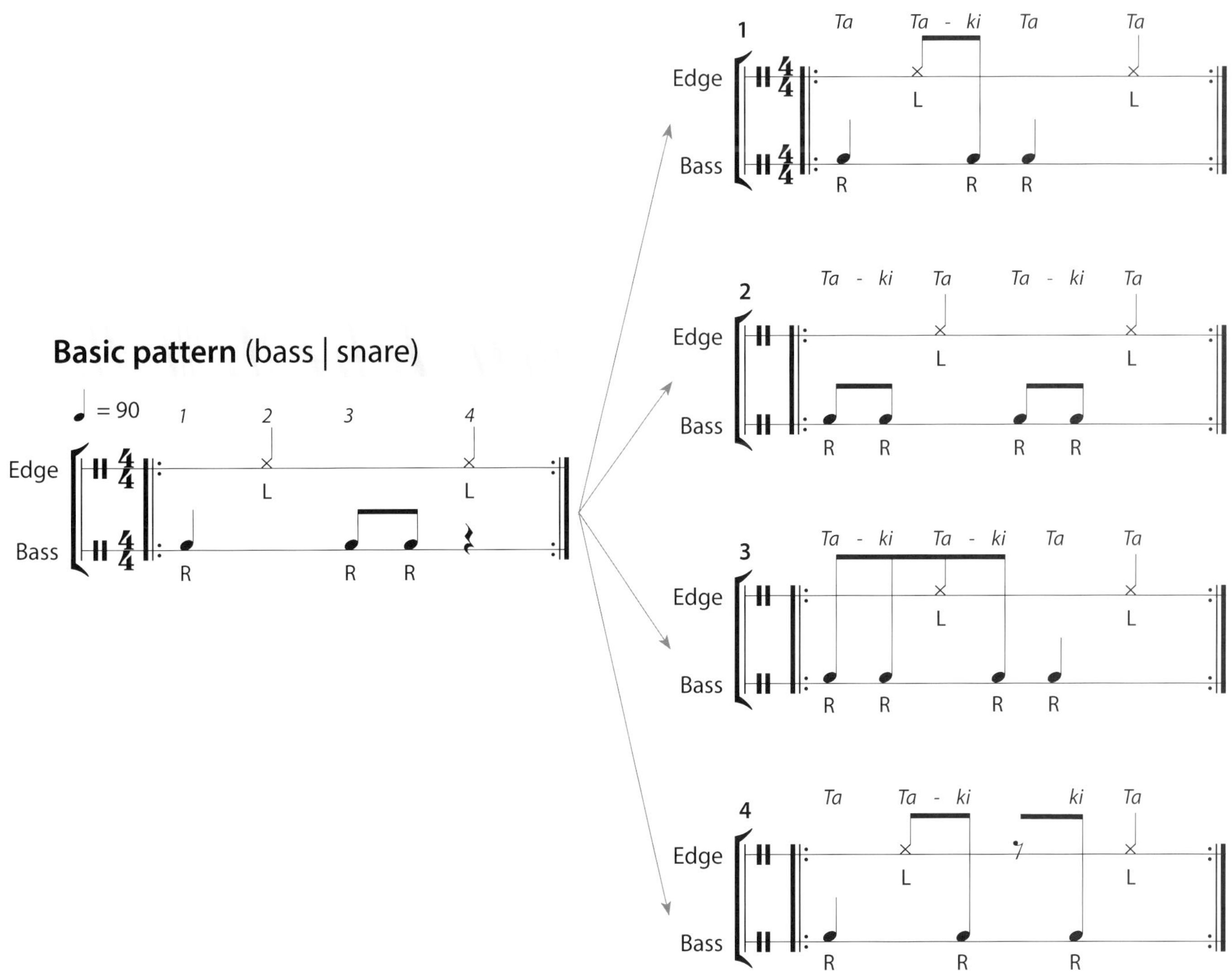

Such *two-bar patterns* are important and interesting.

Now compose further two-bar patterns on your own from the four variations on *page 55* according to the same principle. First with line 1 as the basic pattern (*see below*) …

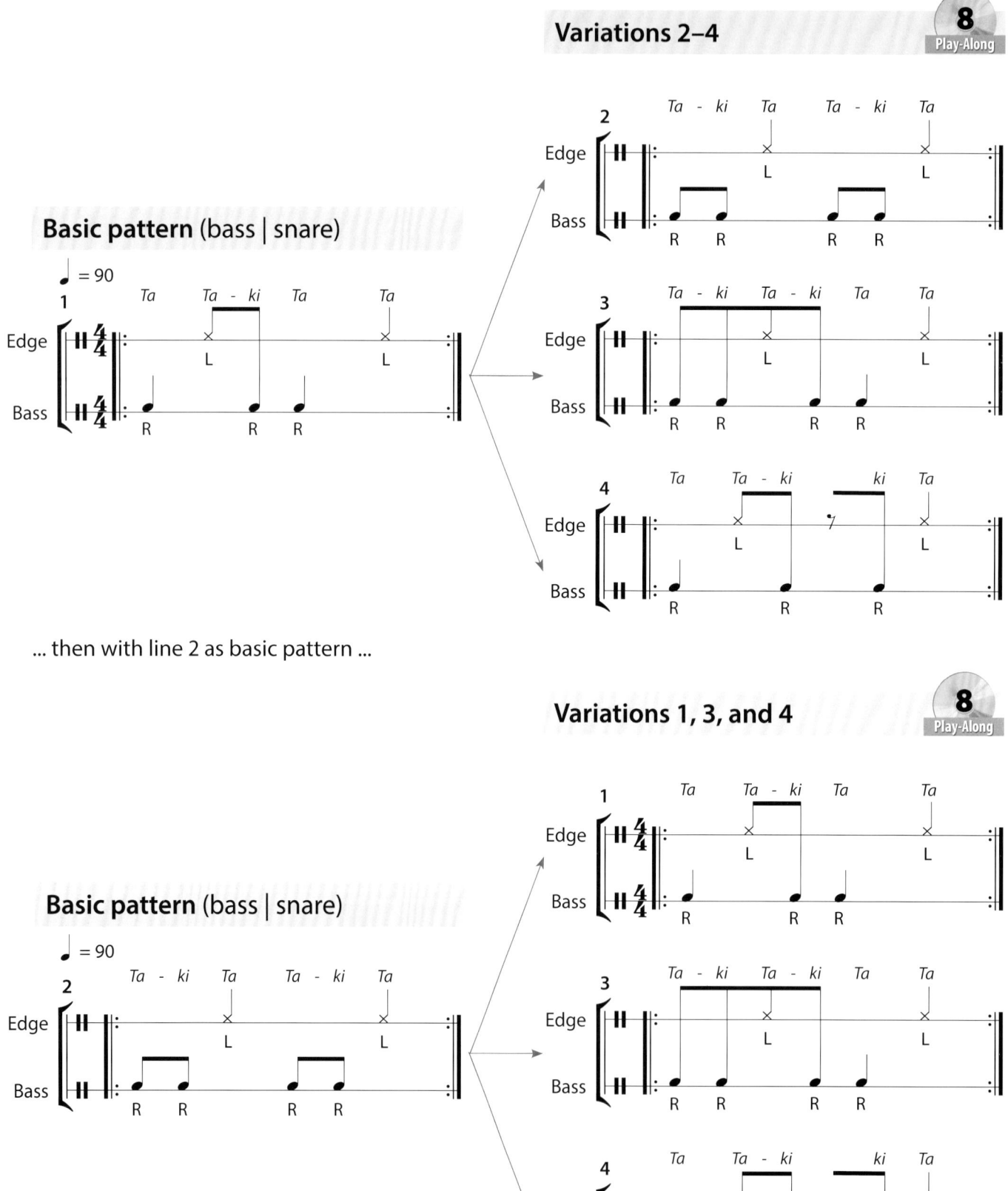

… then with line 2 as basic pattern …

… then with line 3 and finally with line 4 as the basic pattern.

These two-bar patterns can of course be combined into longer grooves.

You can listen to the following **pop groove** on the *audio CD* and play along (**Pop Basic**).

Pop Basic Groove (eight bars)

Hand-to-Hand

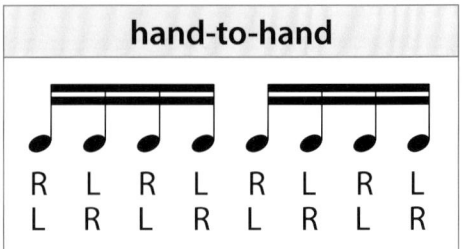

Rhythms sound very nice in **R L-** or **L R-sticking**, also called *hand-to-hand*, which means the hand changes with each beat.

Here are some examples of a pop groove. If you want to accompany in *fast tempos*, a **Country Pop Groove** in *Peruvian style* is recommended:

Country Pop Groove (Peruanian style)

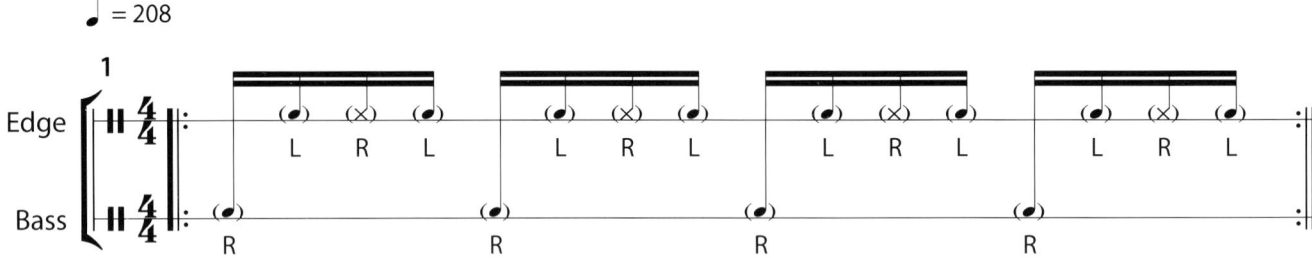

Or even a **Zydeco** as another style popular to this day.

Zydeco pattern (uptempo)

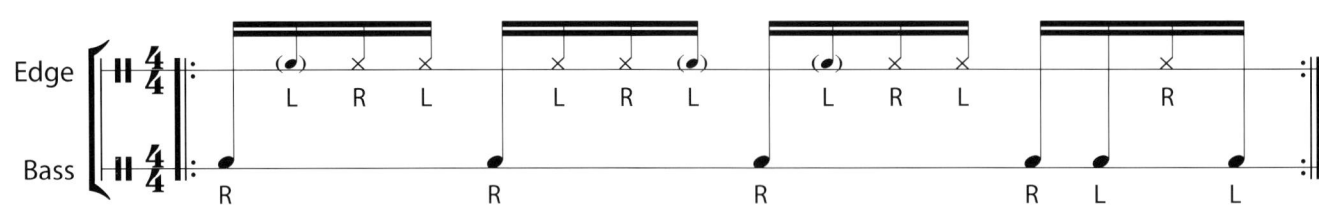

Online video 29

Hand-to-hand patterns (medium down to slow tempos)

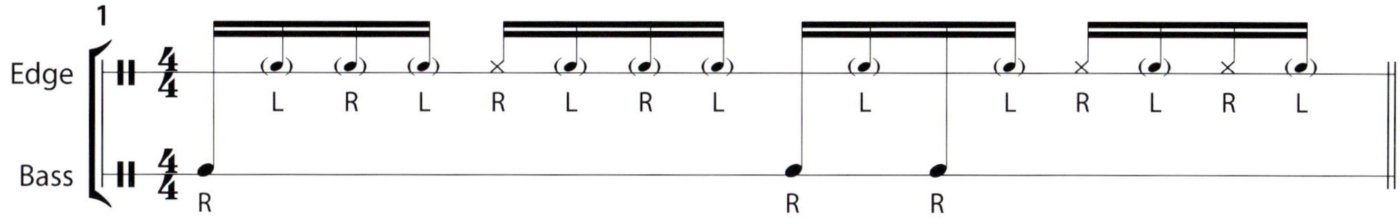

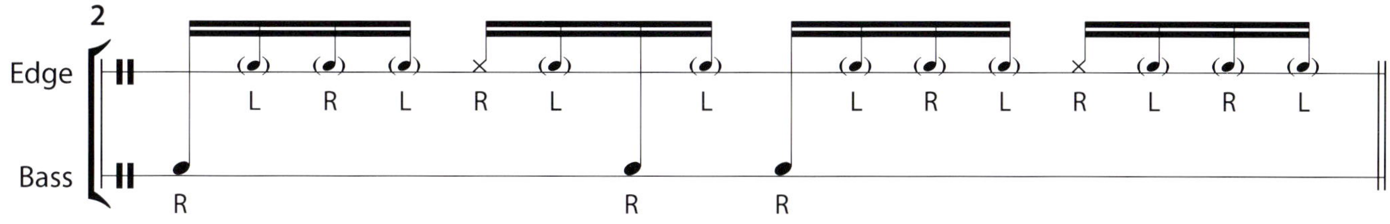

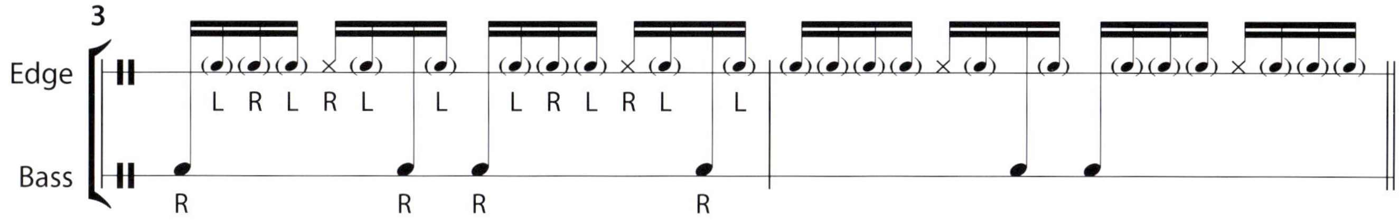

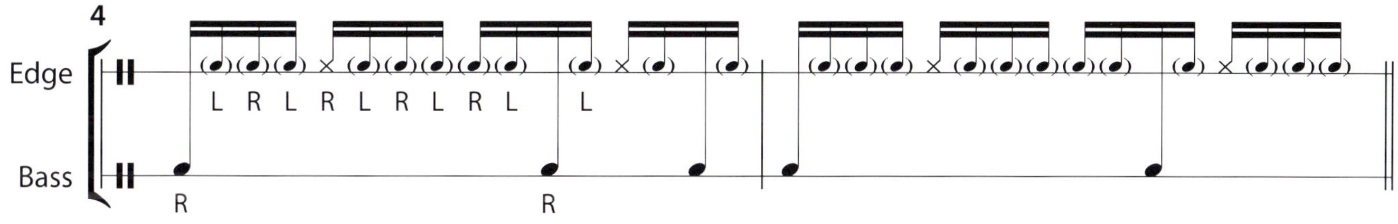

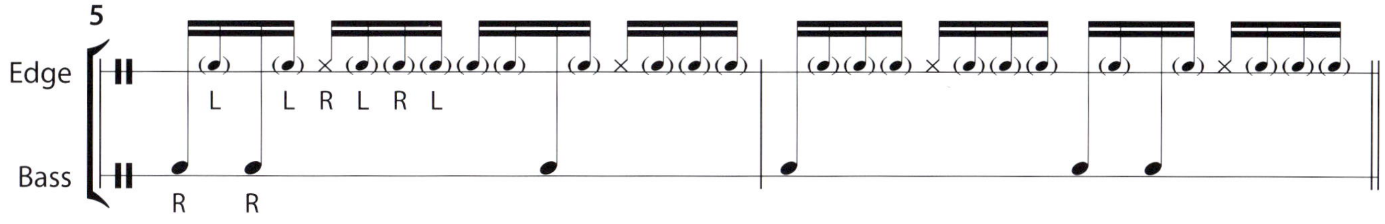

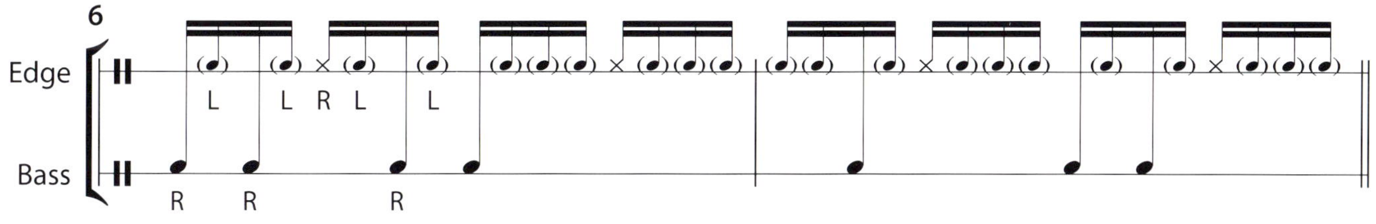

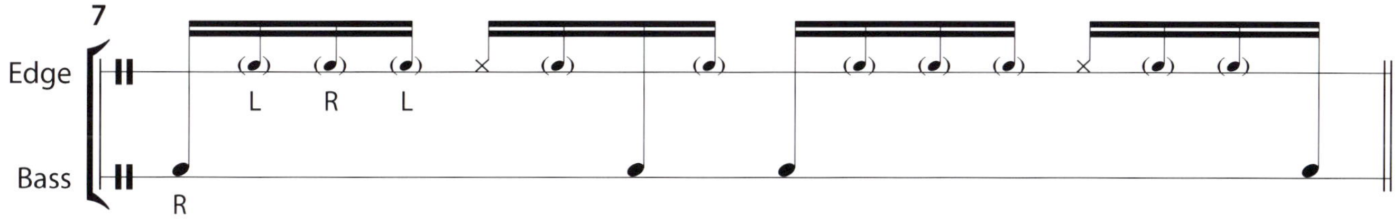

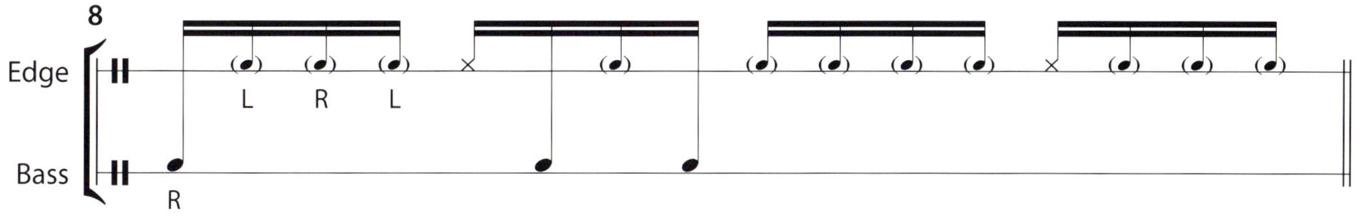

Funky Patterns

When you intersperse your playing with *accents with the left hand,* it can sound 'more angular' or *'funky'* which, in turn, makes your playing more interesting and colorful.

Online video 30

Funky patterns (hand-to-hand)

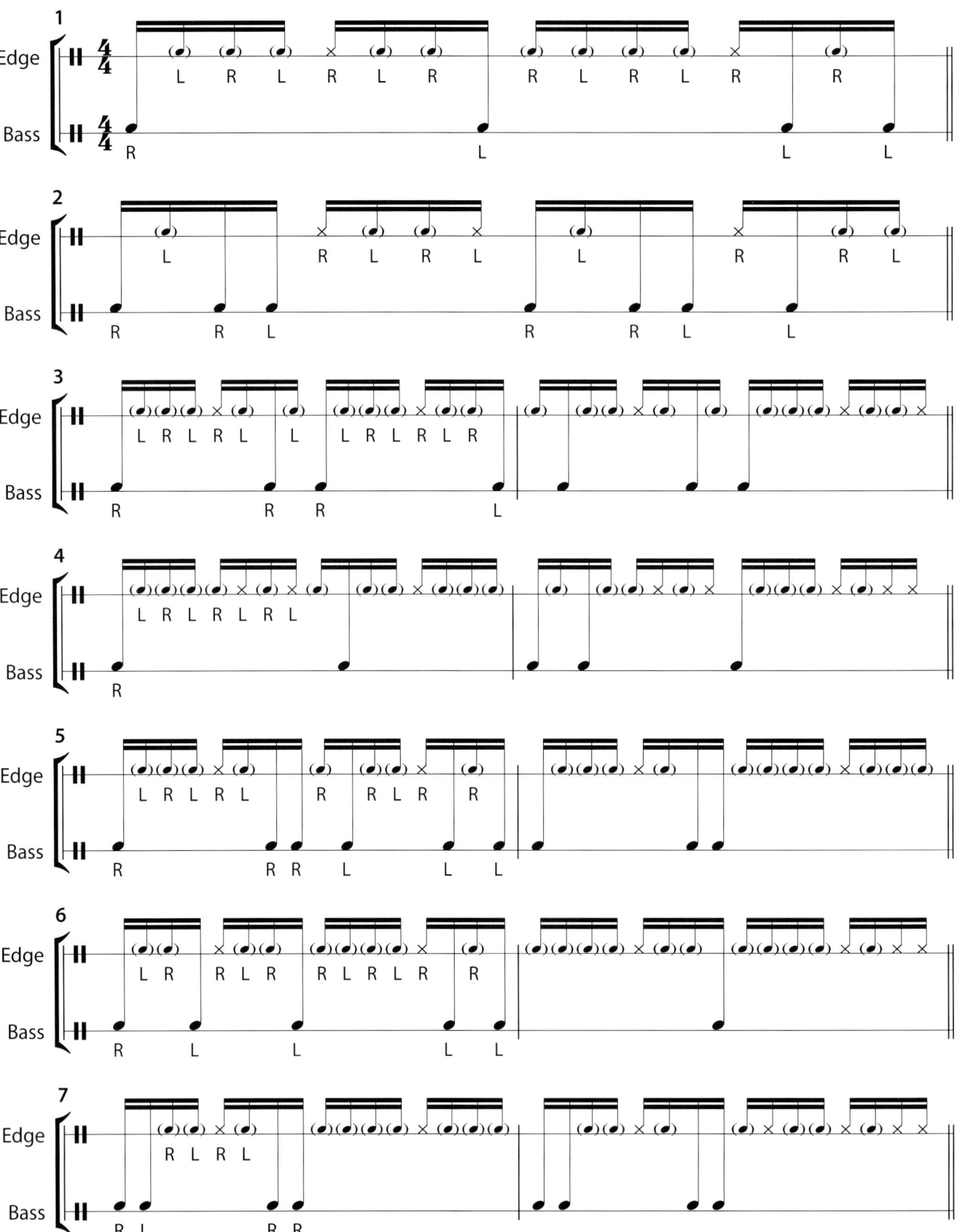

The Paradiddle as a module

Continue with the *paradiddle* (*see p. 26 and following*) as a new module. First practice the modules separately and try to make a sharp distinction between the loud and soft beats. Execute the *filling strokes* (*tips*) as quietly as possible. The quieter you play,, the more feeling you get for the *accents*. The goal is to omit the fill beats (**gray**) altogether.

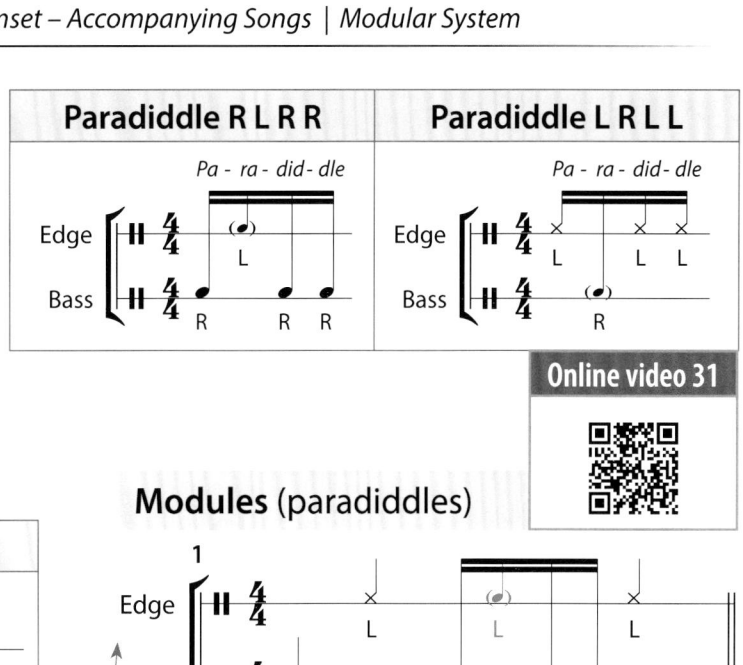

Paradiddle R L R R   **Paradiddle L R L L**

Online video 31

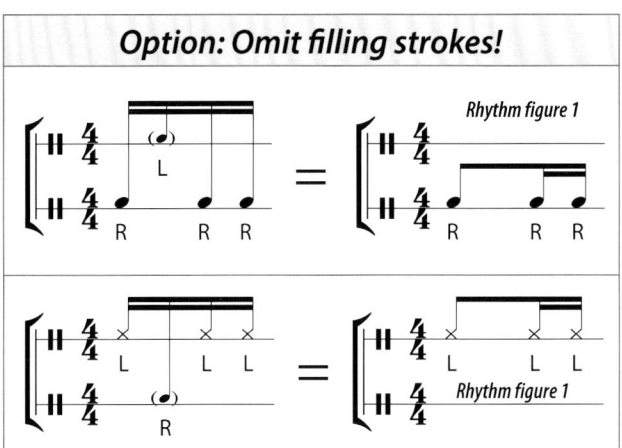

Option: Omit filling strokes!

Basic groove (bass | snare)

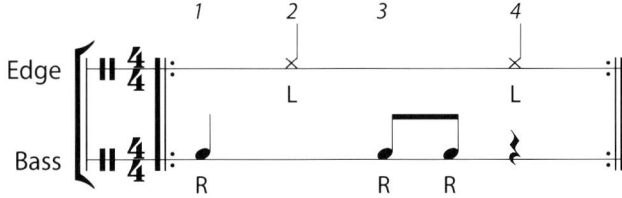

Modules (paradiddles)

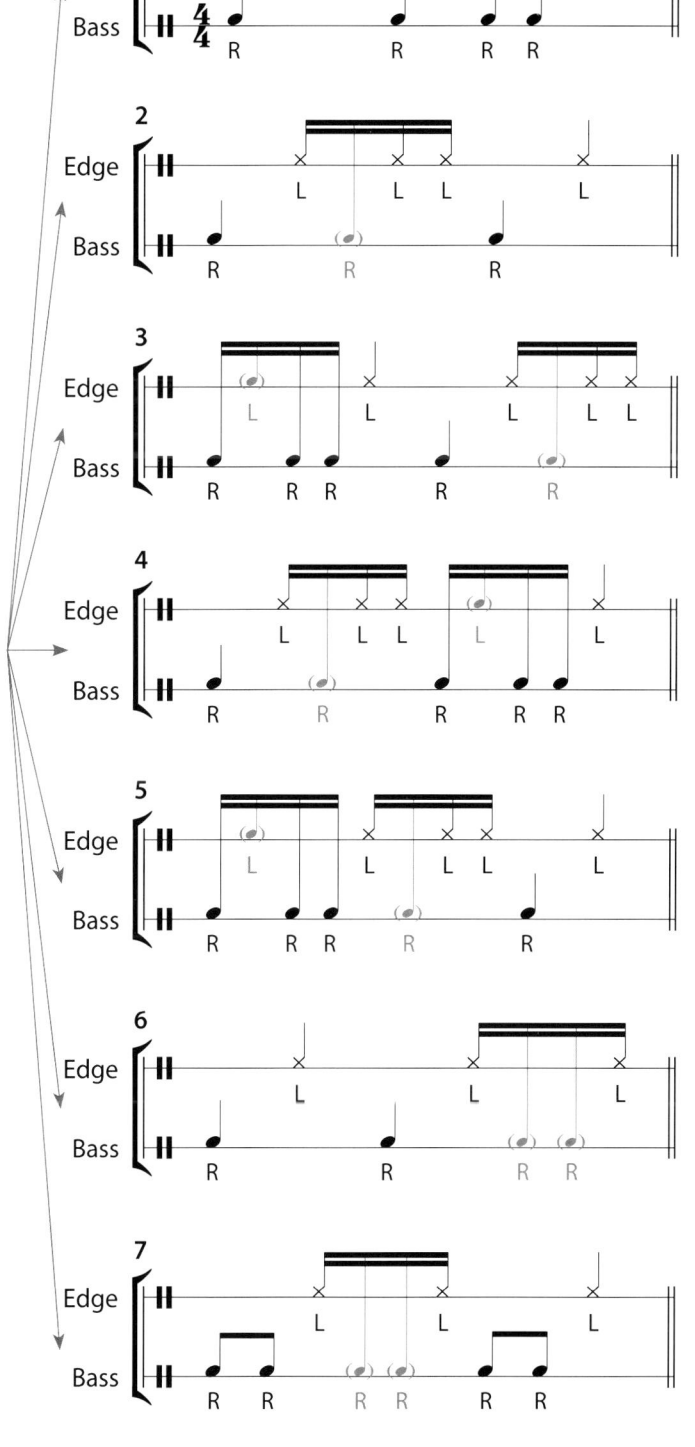

61

Now build the modules of the **Single** and the **Inverted Paraddiddle** (*see p. 27*) into a groove. Once again, you get numerous new variations that you can always play in alternation with the basic groove.

> ***Option: Omit filling strokes!***

Practice the variations with the *omitted filling strokes* (*gray*). They will still be a great help to you for understanding the *syncopations* in complex grooves ...

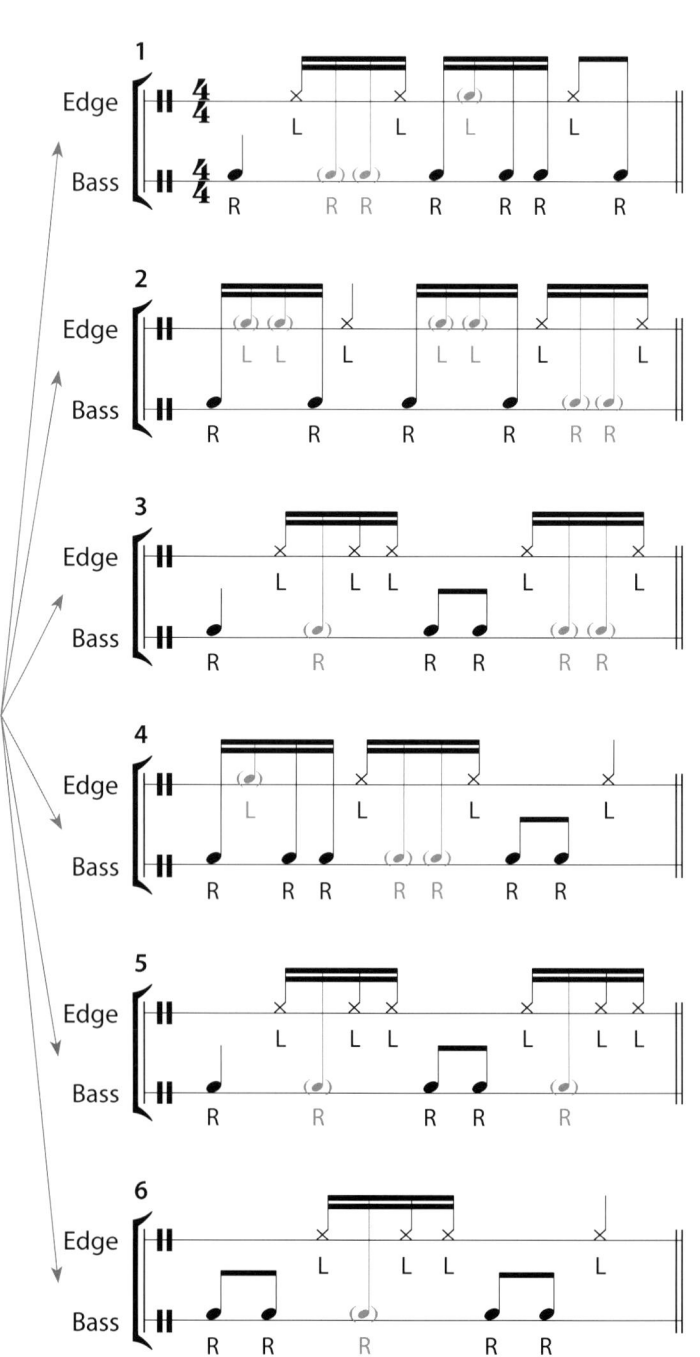

Modules (paradiddles)

12 Play-Along

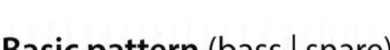

Basic pattern (bass | snare)

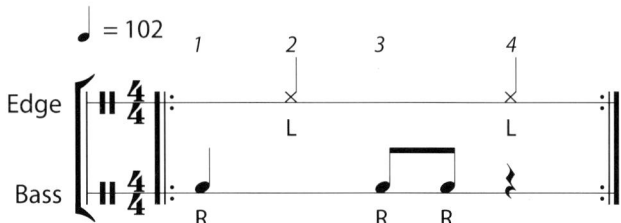

62

Grooves with Syncopation

With the omission of the filling strokes in the **Inverted Paradiddle** you have already enriched your rhythm repertoire with *syncopation*.

Syncopation [*Greek: syn = at the same time and kope = beat*] shifts the accents from usually *accented beats* to usually *unaccented beats*, i.e. syncopation occurs whenever a normally *unaccented beat* is *accented*.

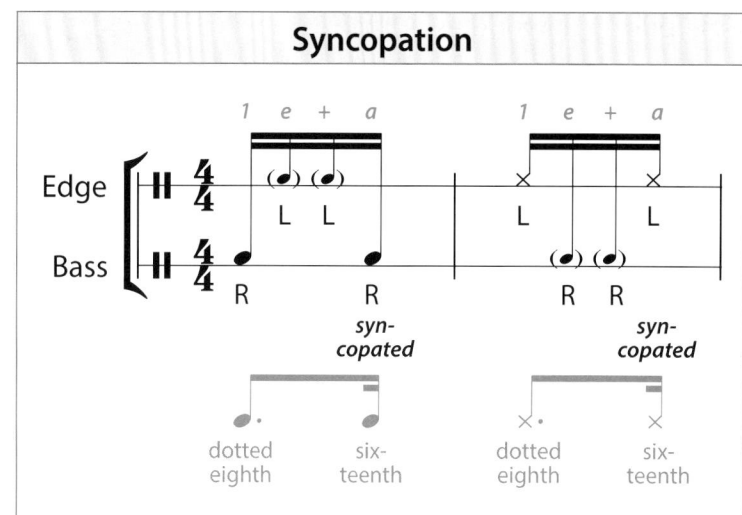

You can see this clearly in the example of the two modules of the **Inverted Paradiddle** at the top right:

The *first sixteenth note* in each case occurs on an accented beat (1, 2, 3, or 4). The *second* and *third sixteenth notes* are unaccented 'filling strokes' on counts 'e' and '+,' which should be performed as quietly as possible. The syncopation on the *fourth sixteenth*, — that is on the normally unaccented count 'a'—really comes into

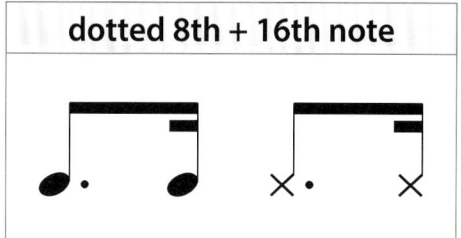

its own if you omit the filling strokes altogether. The result is a rhythm figure with a *dotted eighth note* followed by a *sixteenth note (syncopation)*.

Practice the two rhythm figures separately and divide the hands as before:

Strong hand in the bass, weaker hand on the edge of the cajón.

Online video 32

Syncopation 1 (Cuban bass & Peruvian tips)

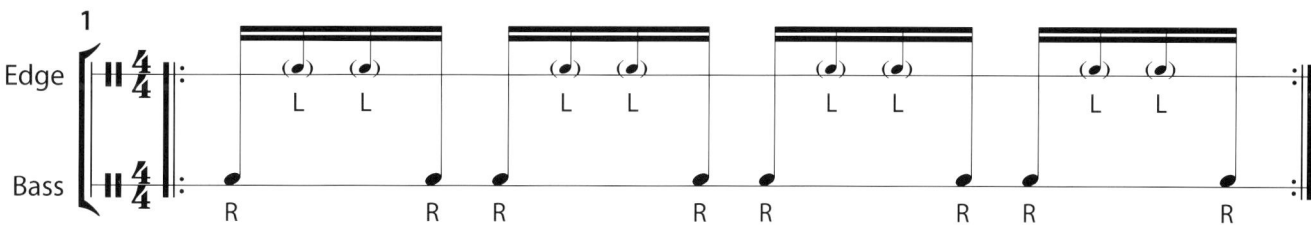

Online video 33

Syncopation 2 (Peruvian bass & Cuban slaps)

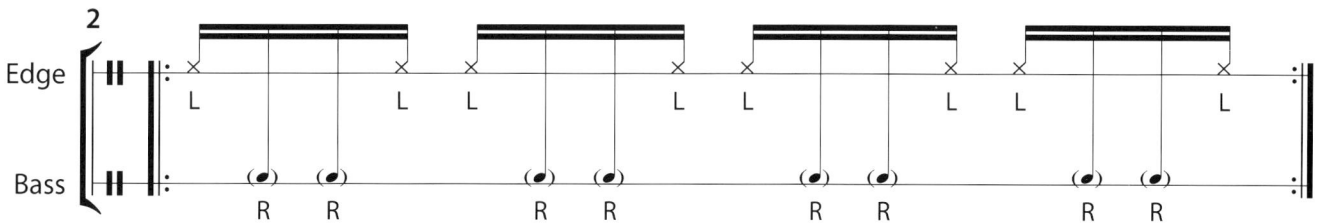

63

Singer/Songwriter and Independent Pop

Here's one of my favorite syncopation grooves, ideal for accompanying **singer/songwriter music** and **independent pop**. Just like the following syncopations in the modular system ...

Groove to accompany singer/songwriter and independent pop

11 Demo Track 12 Play-Along

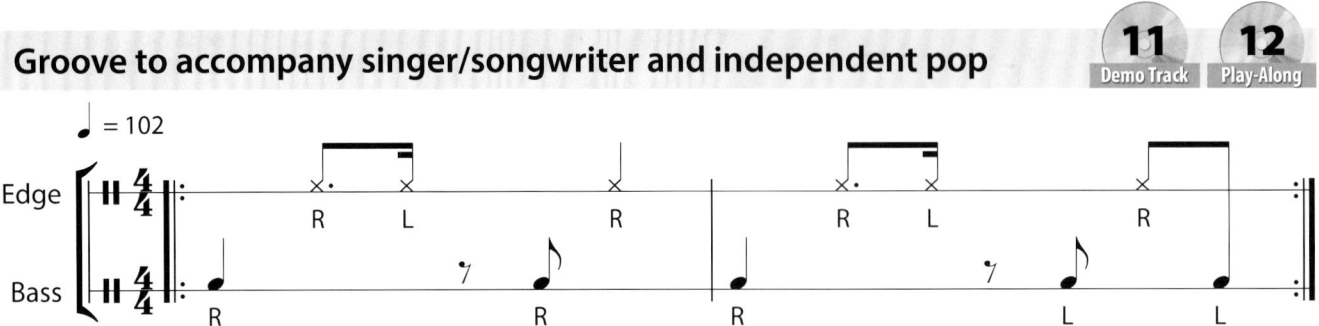

Modular System: Syncopation

First practice the following five syncopation modules in the *right column* separately and slowly. Then play the basic groove alternating with the rhythm modules. This will make your playing impressive. Play the filling strokes more and more softly until you completely abandon their execution.

Modules (Syncopation)

12 Play-Along

Basic groove (bass | snare)

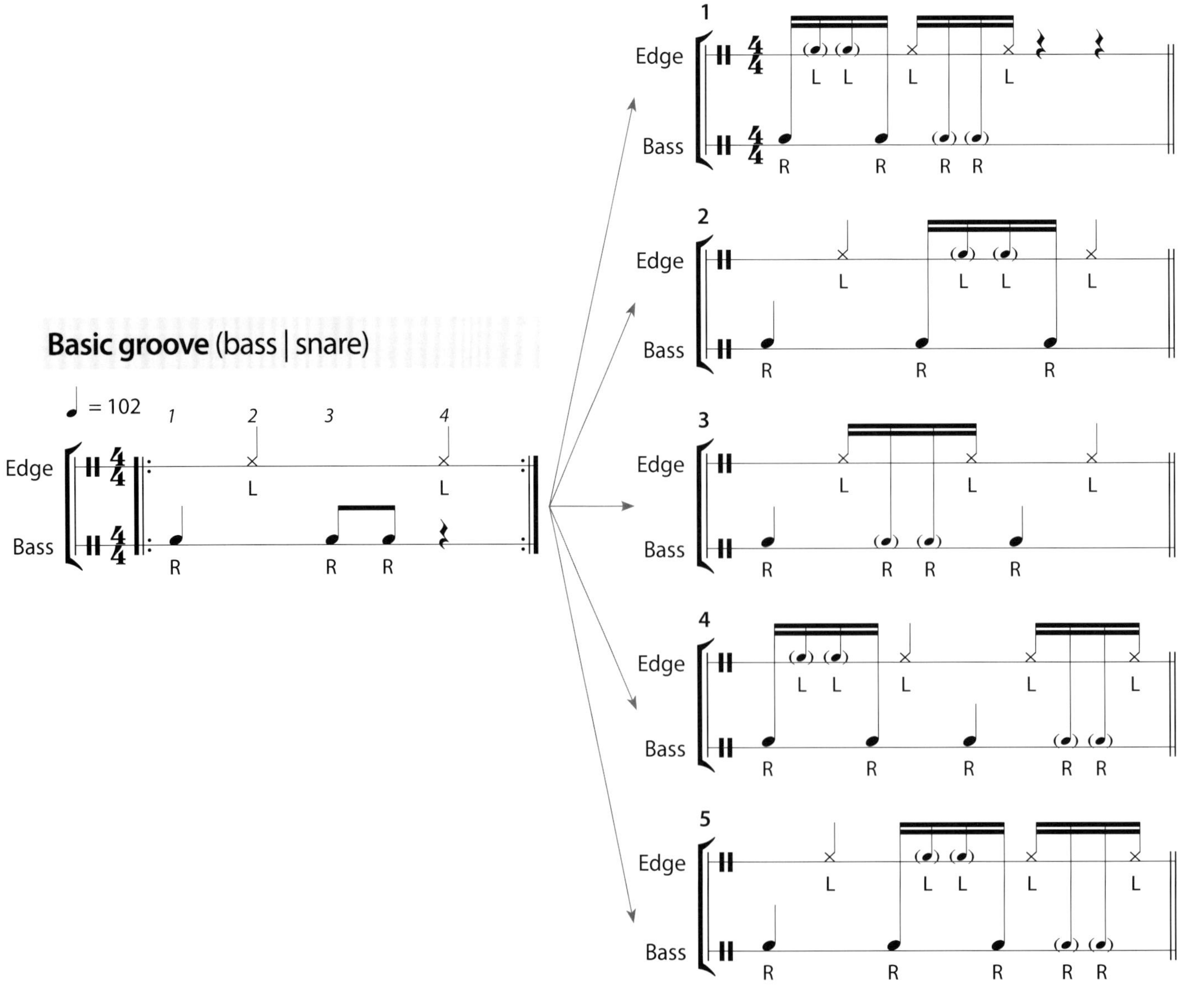

Drum-set imitation with Add-ons
Shaker patterns replace the hi-hat

Sounding like a complete drum set on the cajón requires *additional instruments* (*add-ons*) to replace the *cymbals* that are missing on the cajón.

The **hi-hat** can be imitated wonderfully with the shaker. To do this, divide your hands as follows:

LEFT-HANDERS (*leading left hand*):

RIGHT HAND (R) plays:
R alternates between **bass** and **edge**, imitating **bass drum** and **snare drum**.

LEFT HAND (L) plays the shaker:
L imitates the **hi-hat** with shaker.

RIGHT-HANDERS (*leading right hand*):

LEFT HAND (L) plays:
L alternates between **bass** and **edge**, imitating **bass drum** and **snare drum**..

RIGHT HAND (R) plays the shaker:
R imitates the **hi-hat** with shaker.

When playing the shaker watch out for:	Online video 34	
• *Stiff wrist* • *Horizontal movement from the forearm*		In the video I play all exercises one after the other (2 times each)!

IMPORTANT:
Unlike the previous modular systems, here you play SIMULTANEOUSLY:
- *L: basic pattern on cajón*
- *R: one shaker module each*

L: Basic pattern (cajón)

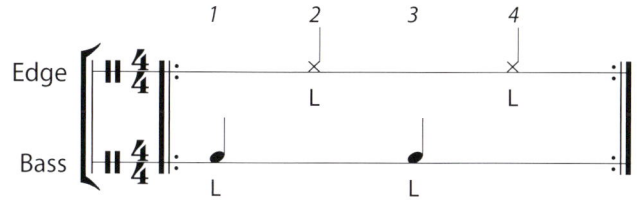

R: Shaker modules

65

Rods as hand replacement for Hi-hat or Ride cymbal

Rods are preferred over drum sticks by drummers for quiet, fast playing. When playing the cajón, they are ideal for imitating **hi-hat** or **ride cymbals**.

With a rod in the lead hand, you take over a *softly played ostinato pattern*, which is usually played on the hi-hat or ride cymbal at the drum set. You create the *bright sound* on the outer edge of the cajón. I have written down the commonly used figures. Once you master them, get creative and combine them within a modular bar.

The **other hand** continues to play—as with the *Shaker Grooves*—the bass drum/snare basic pattern with bass and and edge tone in alternation. Of course, you can also vary the basic pattern, e.g. with an additional bass stroke on the last eighth note (**4+**).

NEVER use sticks on your cajón—rods and brushes only!

Combine **Basic pattern for the left-hand** with:
R: Rod modules

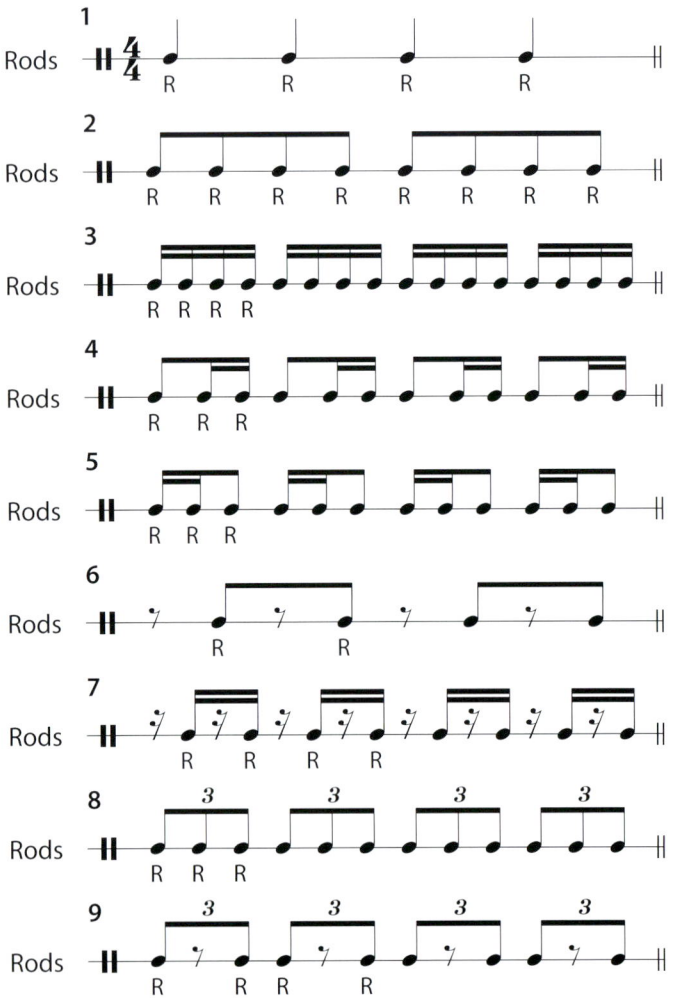

Material: bundled wooden or plastic sticks that are flexible and soft enough not to damage the face. *NEVER use drum sticks* on the cajón, please!

Online video 35

Sound: soft attack, replaces hi-hat and ride, softer than drum sticks, louder than brushes.

66

Timbres and variations in the leading hand

Online video 36

Always sound interesting and extraordinary, even if you are playing the same or similar rhythms because the music demands it. The *add-ons* are ideal for bringing other timbres into play.

If you replace the rods with other instruments with your leading hand (*R for right-handed players; L for left-handed players*), you convey a different sound to the listener. You can hear and see some helpful examples on the videos. As always, be creative and find your own 'colors.'

Sizzle Board replaces Hi-hat

The **Sizzle Board** is an interesting sound option because you can also use it to create vibrating and longer-lasting sounds by stroking it with a rod or brush—like on a washboard. In the score I have shown this sound effect with a *vibrato* (⌇⌇⌇). The ➣-symbol stands for a *stress accent*.

In addition to the hi-hat effect, the Sizzle Board also enables vibrato and sustain effects by stroking the board like you do it on a washboard.

Combine **Basic pattern for the left-hand** with:
R: Sizzle Board modules

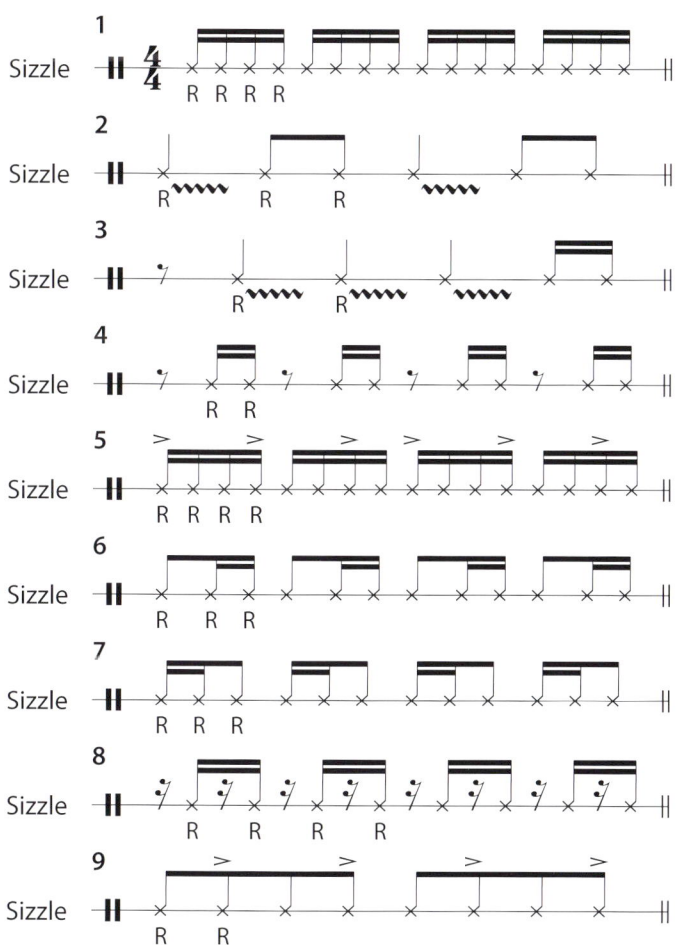

Proceed in the same way with the modules for the next add-ons.

Buzz Board

Online video 37

Material: wooden plate with metal snare spirals you glue onto the cajón surface as an add-on like a playable snare carpet. This gives you more new sounds on the surface.

Sound: sidesnare effect

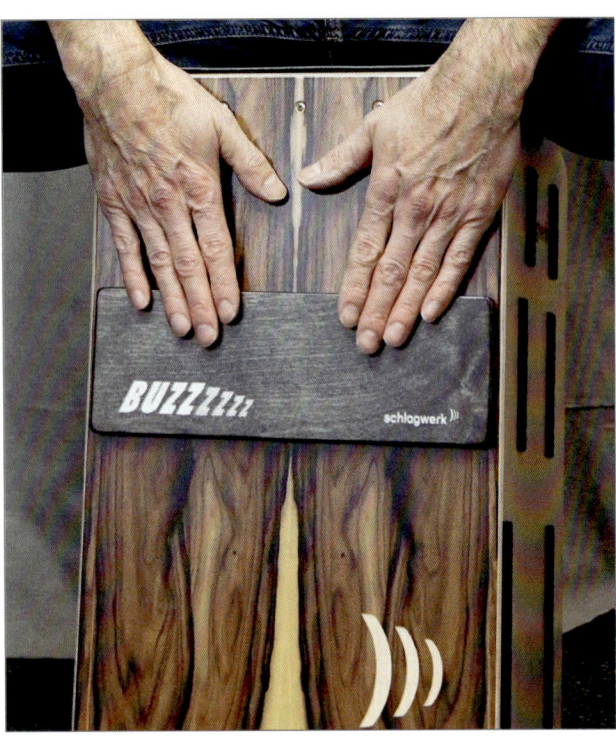

The Buzz Board is hit by the hands.

Brushes

Online video 38

Material: Please ONLY use plastic brushes, NEVER metal brushes! They destroy the surface of your cajón.

Sound: softer than drum sticks, quieter than rods, wipe and stroke effects

The brush sound is quieter than that of rods.
Their playing style also allows for stroked sounds.
Use the Sizzle Board modules for this (page 67)!

68

Cabasa (Cabaça)

Online video 39

Material: folk instrument from Cuba (orig.: *bottle gourd*), cylindrical head, spanned with a profiled sheet metal, which is covered with close-fitting chains of metal pearls. Fixed (*without handle*) with Velcro on the side of your strong hand (guide hand).

Sound: fine pearly, rustling sounds

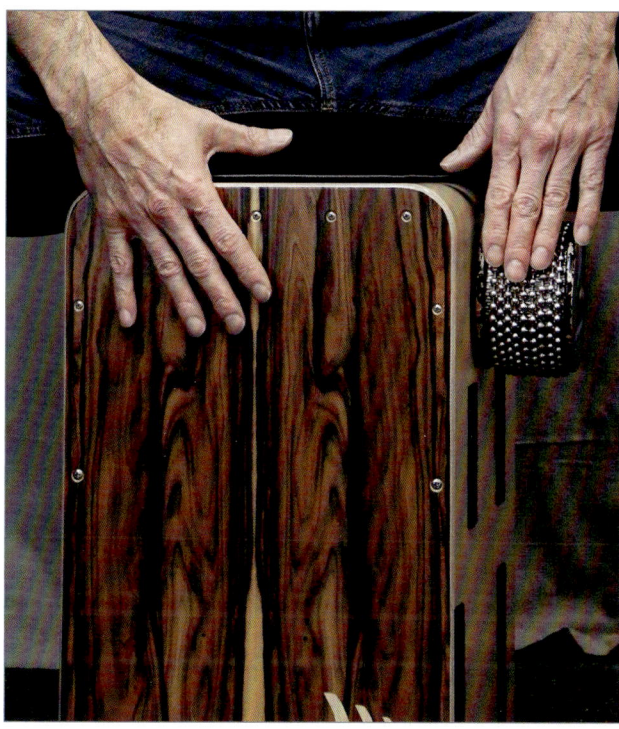

The Cabasa is particularly suitable for Latin rhythms.

Flaps

Online video 40

Material: wooden panels to be fixed to the side of the cajón with a Velcro fastener —always on the side of the strong hand. I am left-handed, so shown on the left in the photo.

Sound: concise castanets sound

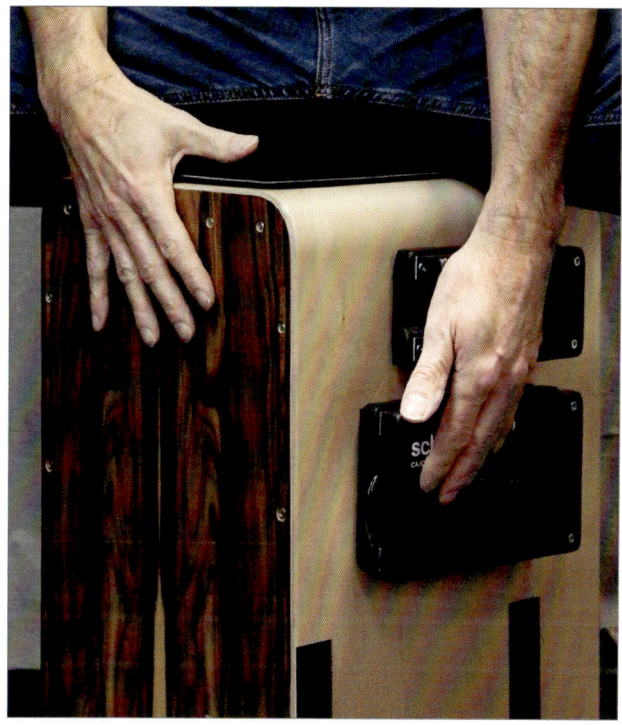

The castanets sound is characteristic for flamenco music.

69

Scratchboard & Cowbell

Online video 41

Material: Two more sounds from Cuba. With the *scratchboard (metal grate)* you imitate the *guiro/cucumber*, with the *cowbell* you complete your Cuban percussion set-up.
Sound: scratch effects (guiro) and cowbell

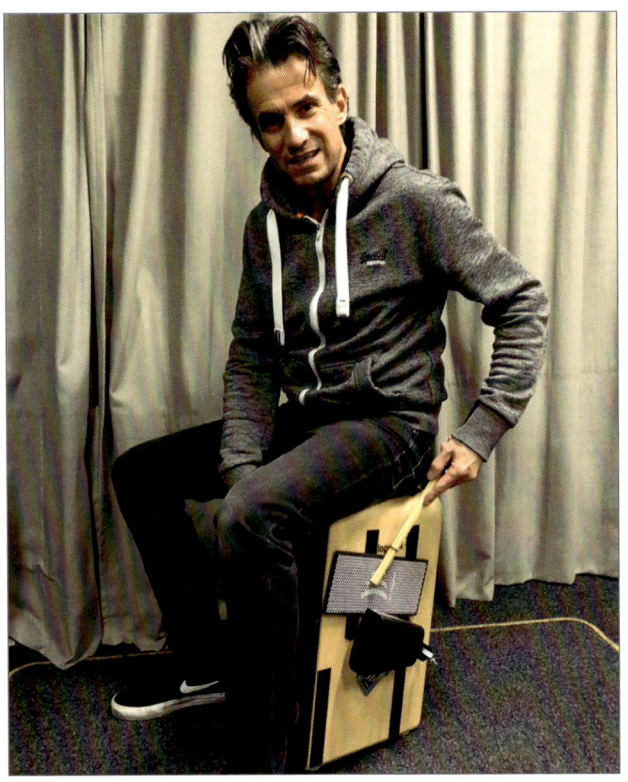

The Scratchboard imitates the Guiro, ...

... the Cowbell is its original sound.

Cha Cha

The *Cha-Cha-Chá* is one of the most popular rhythms in Cuba. It evolved from the *Danzón-Mambo* at the end of the 1940s. The introduction of singing gave rise to a new, independent musical genre that has established itself as one of the Latin American standard dances to this day.

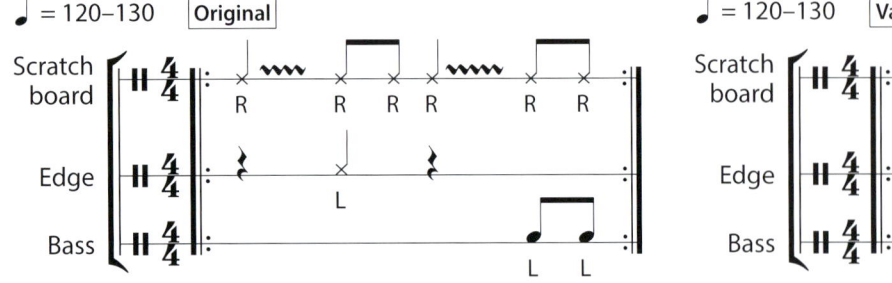

Cha Cha (scratchboard | cajón)

Cascara and Son Clave 2/3

The *Cascara* [*Spanish: shell*], which is usually played on the side of the kettle of the timbale, and the *Son Clave 2/3* (see page 36) are among the most important basic elements of Cuban rhythm. Their combination is extremely effective:

Play the *Cascara pattern* on the **cowbell** with your leading hand. The other hand divides the *Son Clave 2/3 imitation* between the bass and the edge of the cajón.

Online video 42

Cascara (cowbell | cajón)

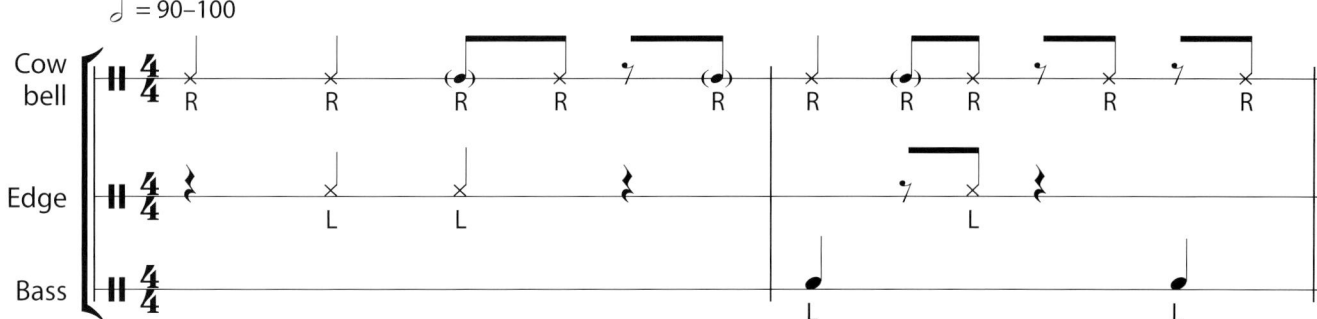

Mambo on the Cajón

As soon as you have mastered the Cascara pattern, you can combine it with new 'melodies,' such as with a *mambo pattern* on the cajón.

Mambo on Cajón (cowbell | cajón)

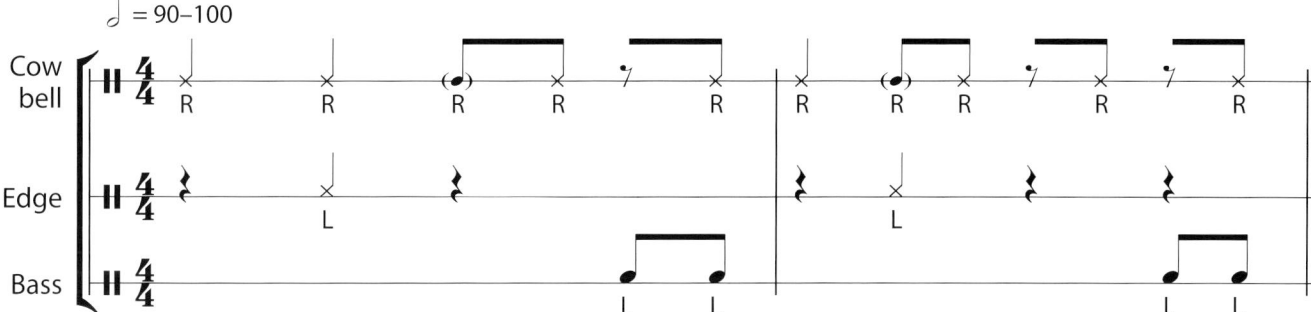

Now you move back and forth between cowbell and scratchboard.

Online video 43

Grooves with Cowbell and Scratchboard

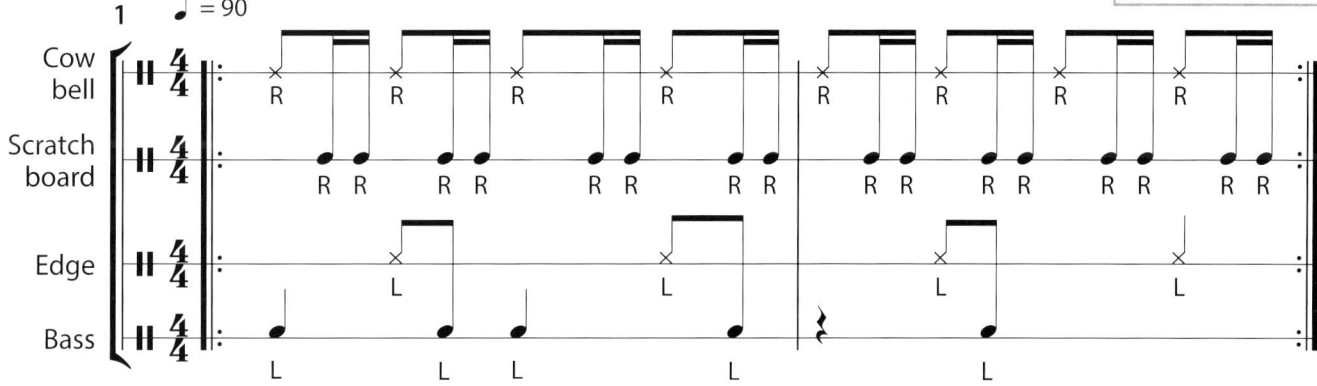

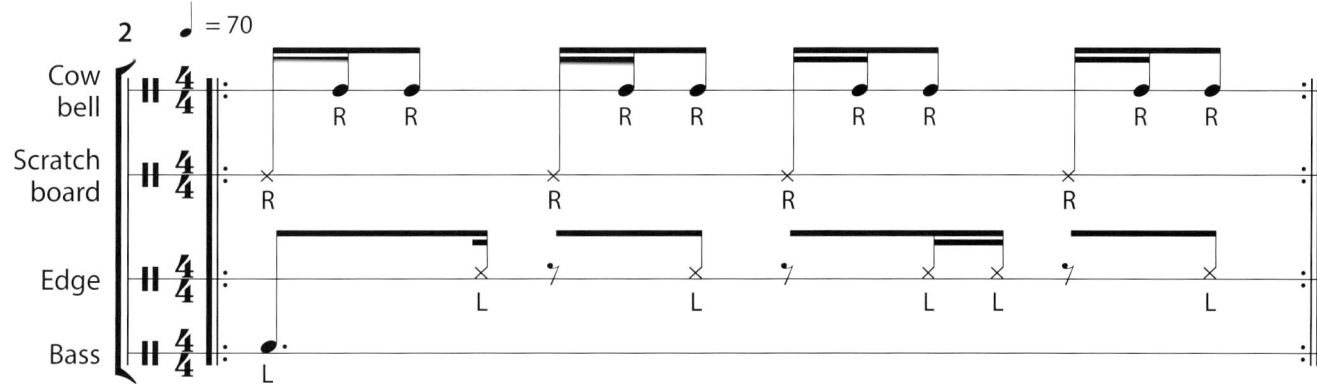

Pop Grooves for song accompaniment

Here I have summarized some very concise grooves for you accompanying songs. Every listener will immediately think of a small drum kit. You can play them both with the Cajón's own sounds and with add-ons of your choice. I recorded the *upper part* for Rods.

Pop Grooves (Rod in the leading hand)

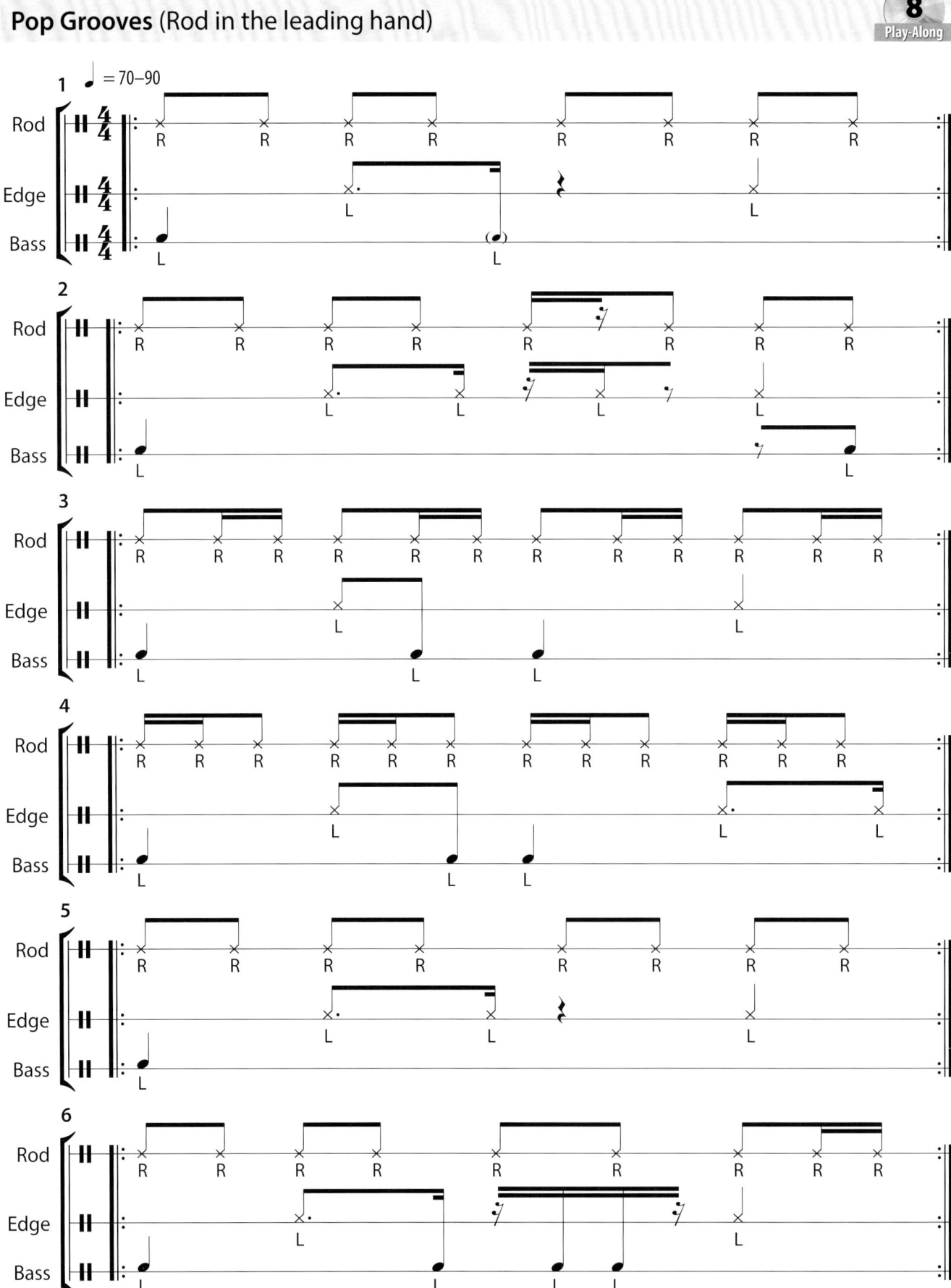

Latin Pop Grooves for song accompaniment

Mixing the elements of *pop* with *Latin music* can create the following rhythms. Make sure to pay attention to the tempo information and use a *metronome*. The previous concept is used again here. The leading hand imitates the *cymbal pattern* of the drum set with a rod on the edge of the cajón.

Latin Pop Grooves (Rod in the leading hand)

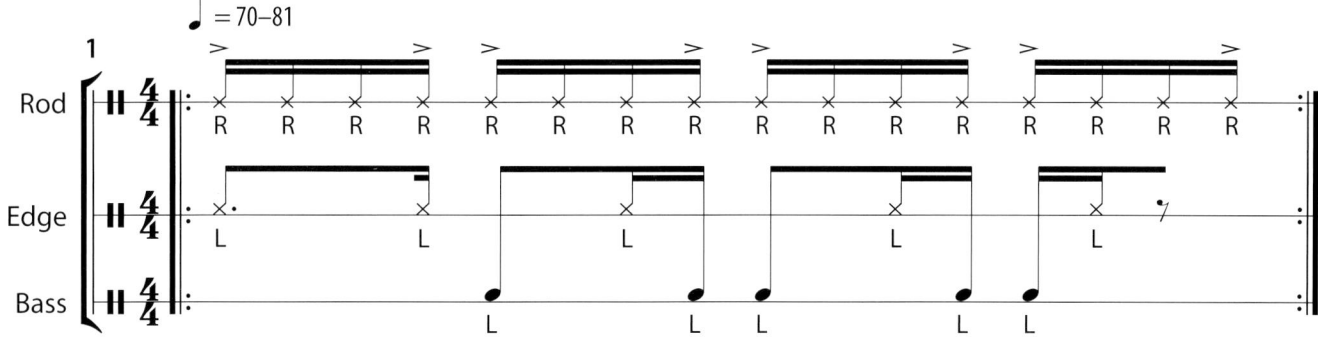

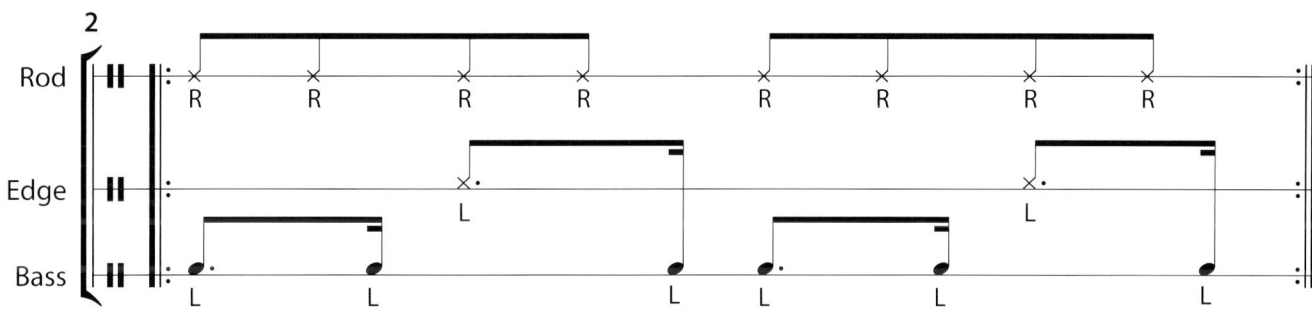

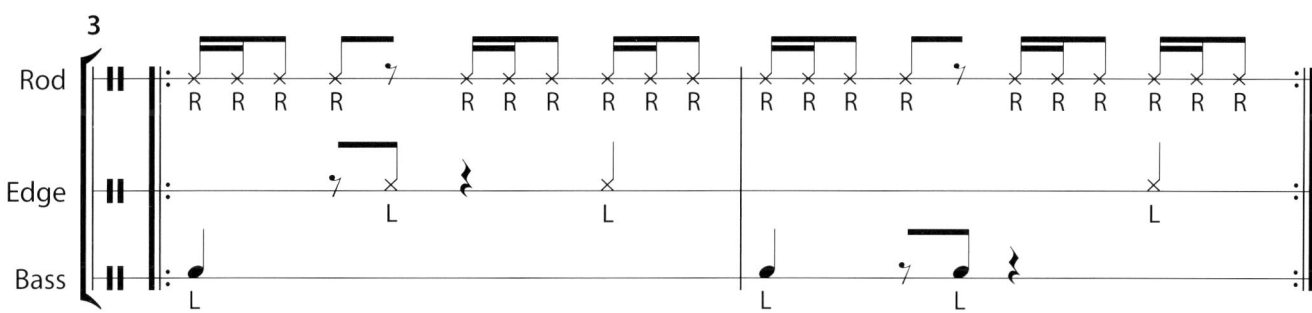

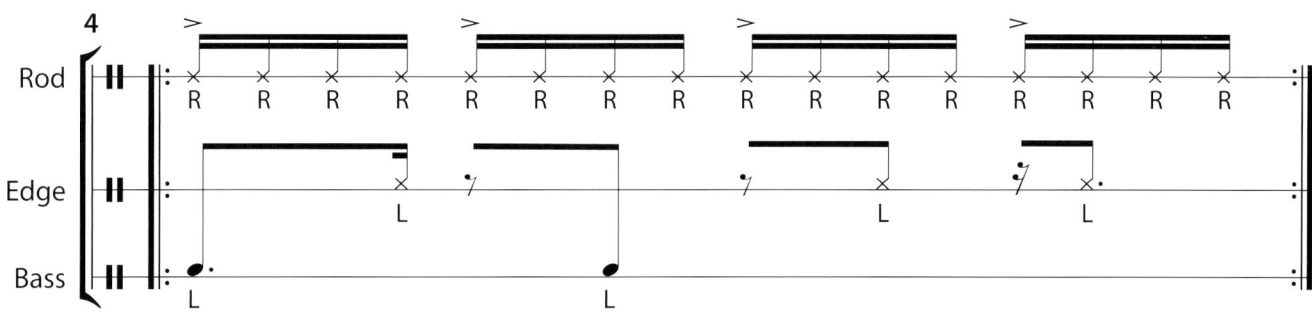

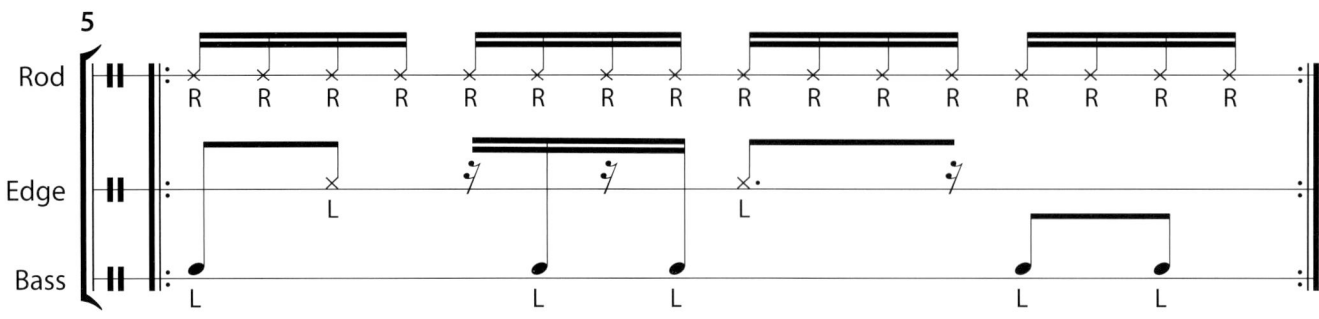

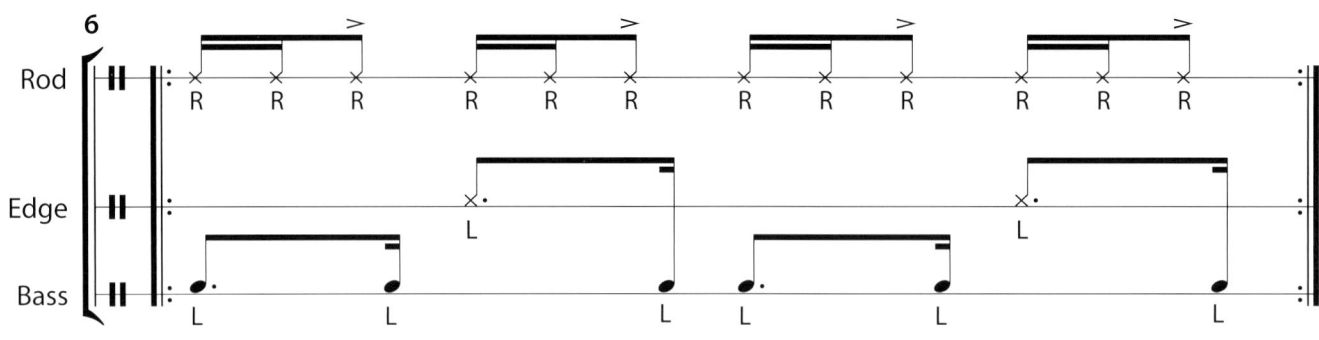

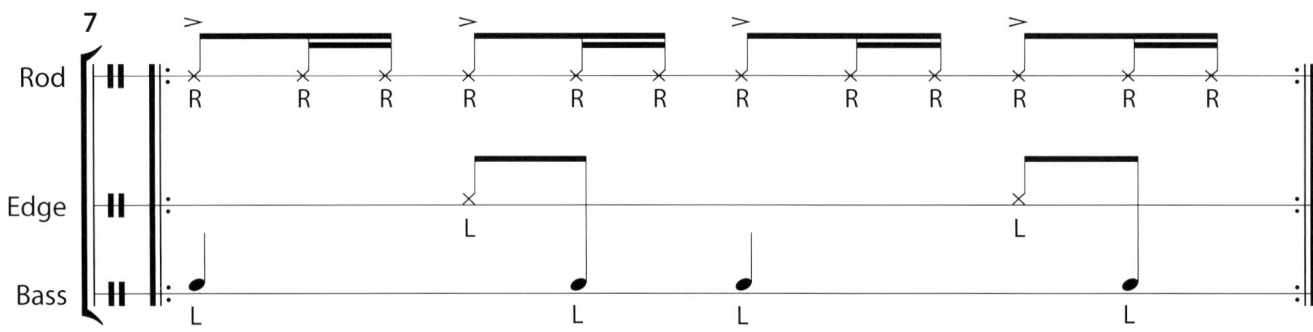

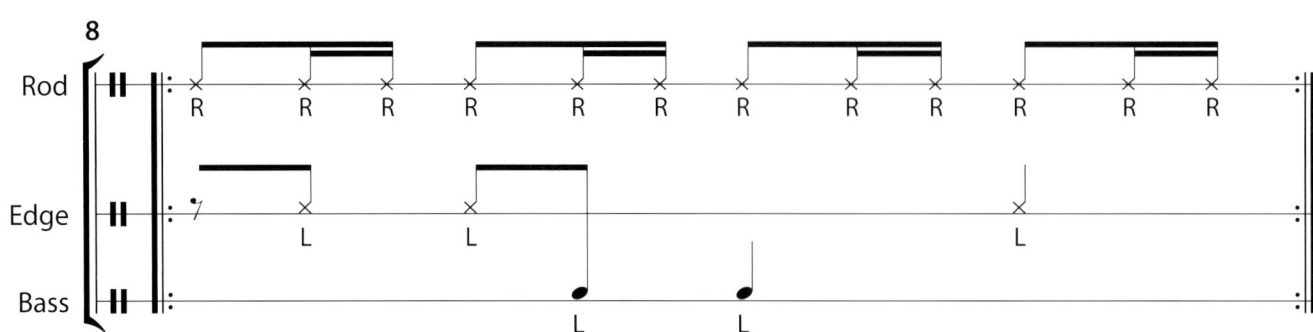

Ternary Grooves for song accompaniment

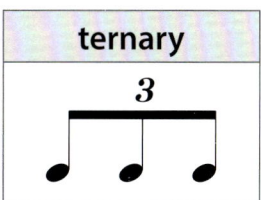

So far, in PART 2, you've only played *binary* styles, i.e. patterns with one, two or even four beats per pulse. Here we start with *three beats per pulse* (*ternary, see also page 48*) in the modular system:

The *leading hand* plays the modules with the rod on the outer edge of the cajón to the basic groove of the *other hand*.

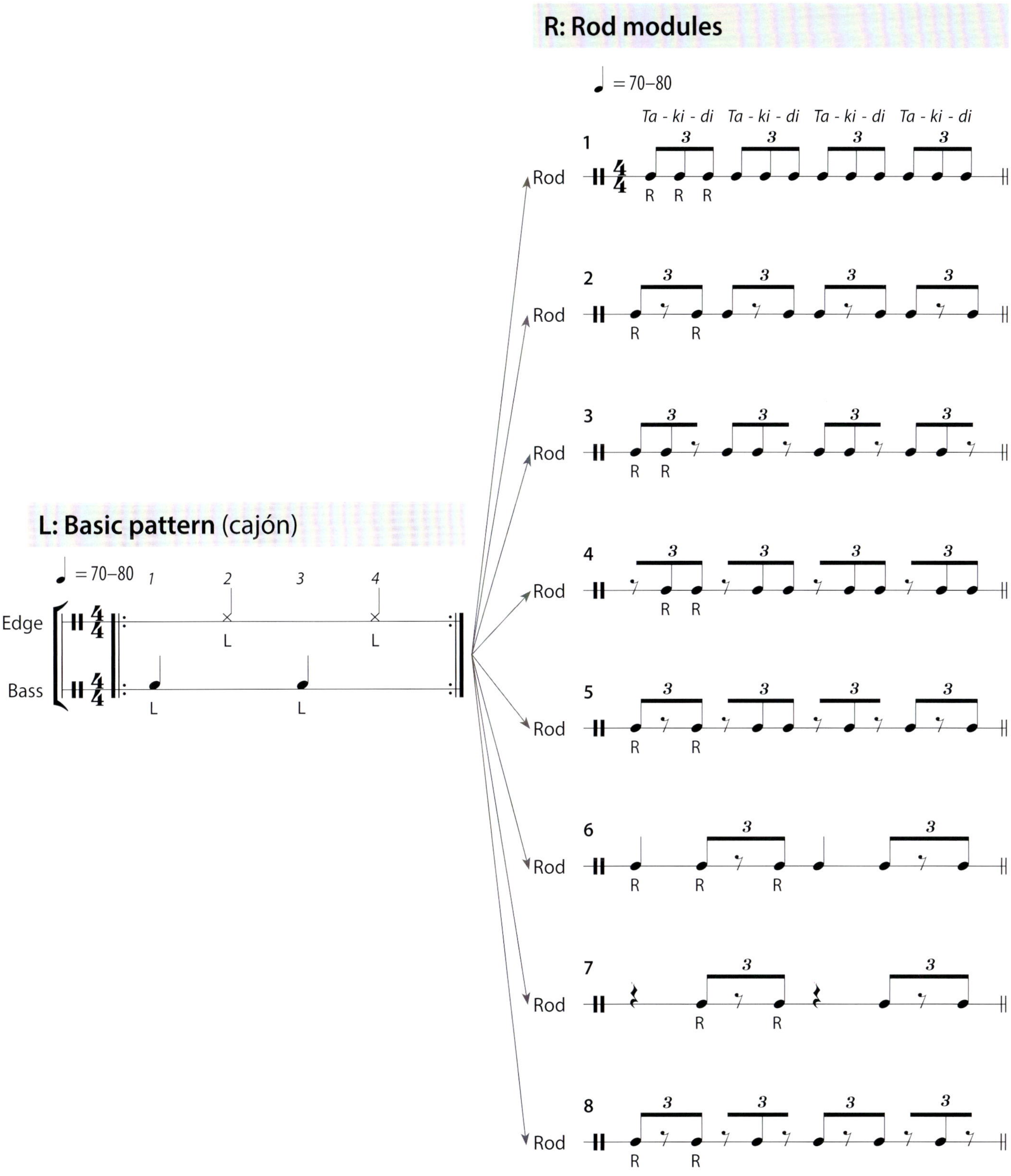

R: Rod modules

L: Basic pattern (cajón)

Here are some very popular ternary rhythms presented in three parts. Choose *example 1* as the basic pattern and play it alternately with one of the other five patterns.

Popular ternary Grooves (Rod in the leading hand)

Shuffle Grooves for song accompaniment

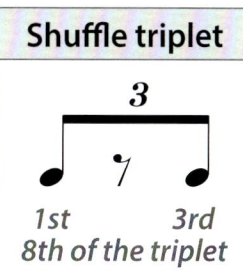

Shuffle triplet

1st — 3rd
8th of the triplet

The **Shuffle** is one of the *ternary rhythms* and is mainly used in blues and jazz. Basically, the binary rhythm is transferred to the ternary rhythm. In the shuffle, only two eighths of the triplet are played: **the first and the third**! Eighth or sixteenth notes that are to be played as a shuffle are often written in the usual eighth or sixteenth notation, but with the additional note:

 *(see page 101)*

Start by practicing the shuffle groove individually. It is important to have a *slow tempo (approx. 80 bpm)* and then add the basic groove.

Online video 44

Basic Shuffle groove

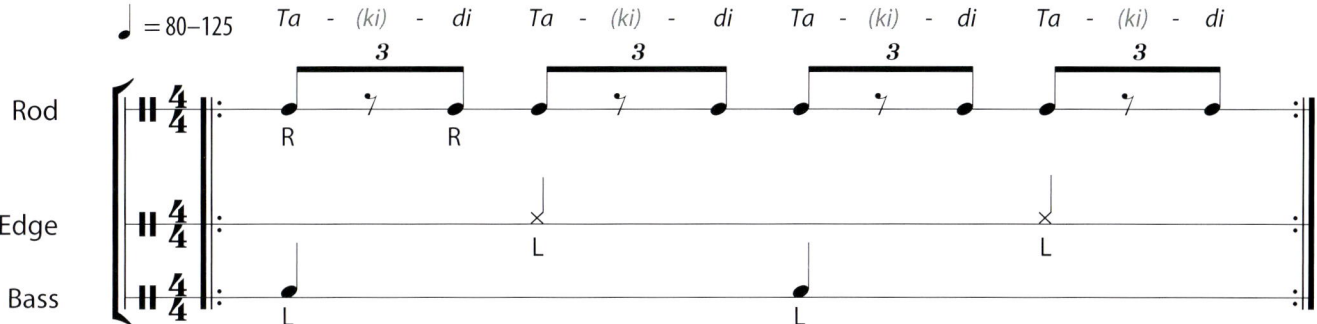

Complete the triplet by dividing between the add-on and the edge of the cajón. The *leading hand* plays the *shuffle triplet* and the *other hand a soft tip* on the edge of the second triplet eighth.

Online video 45

Shuffle triplet 1 (R: shuffle triplet | L: tip on the 2nd eighth of the triplet)

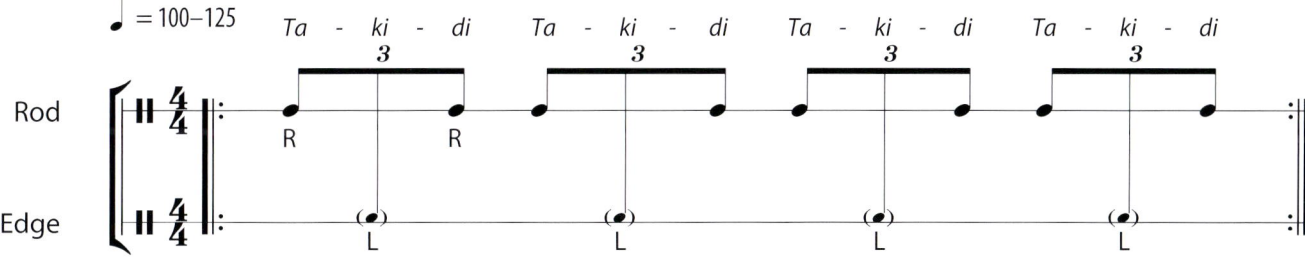

Now add a *slap* in your left hand on the *first triplet eighth*.

Shuffle triplet 2 (R: shuffle triplet | L: slap – tip – rest)

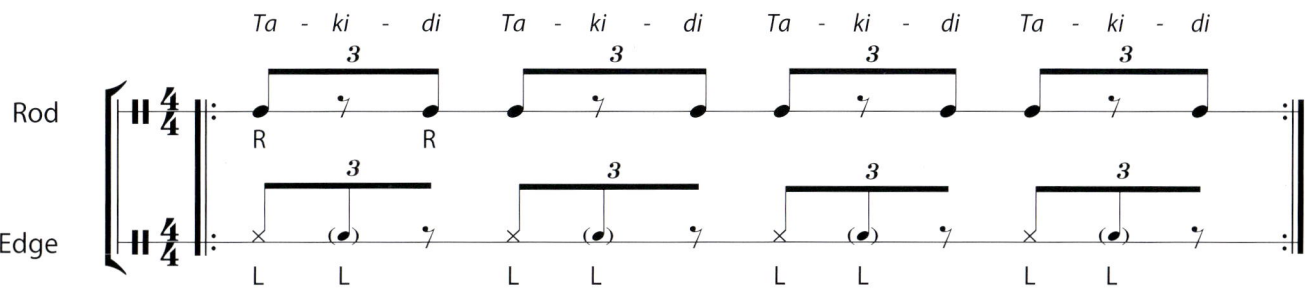

77

Here the *slap* moves on to the *last eighth* of the triplet.

Shuffle triplet 3 (R: shuffle triplet | L: rest – tip – slap)

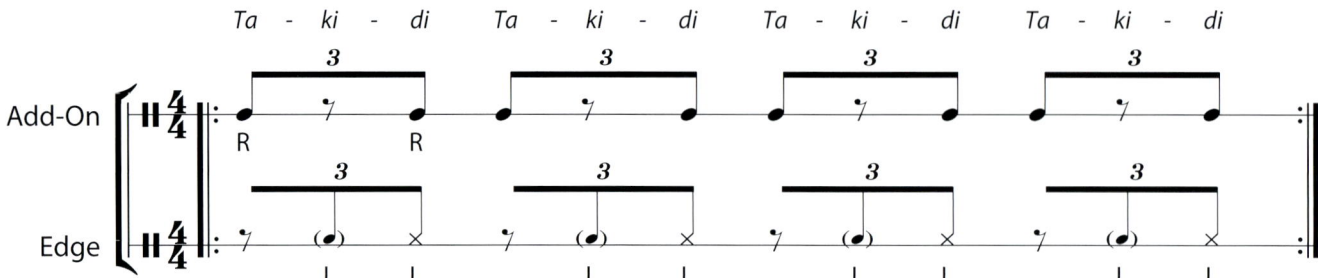

Now you integrate the divided *shuffles 1 to 3* into the basic groove.

Shuffle triplet 4 (combination of Shuffle triplet 1 and basic groove)

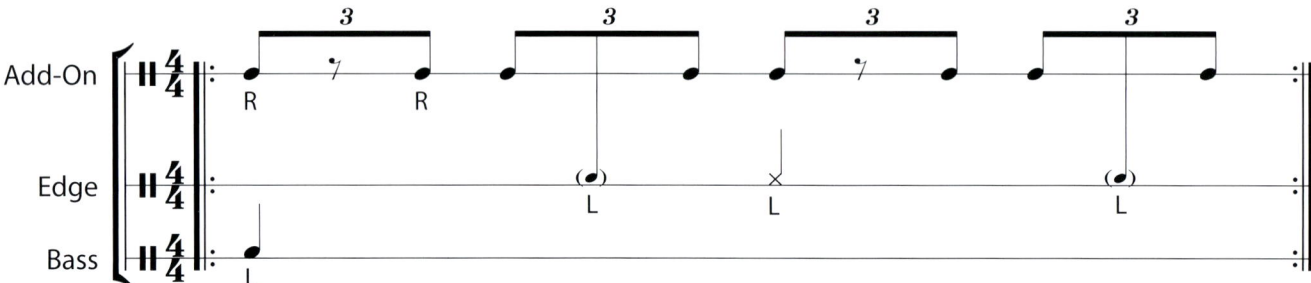

Shuffle triplet 5 (combination of Shuffle triplet 2 and basic groove)

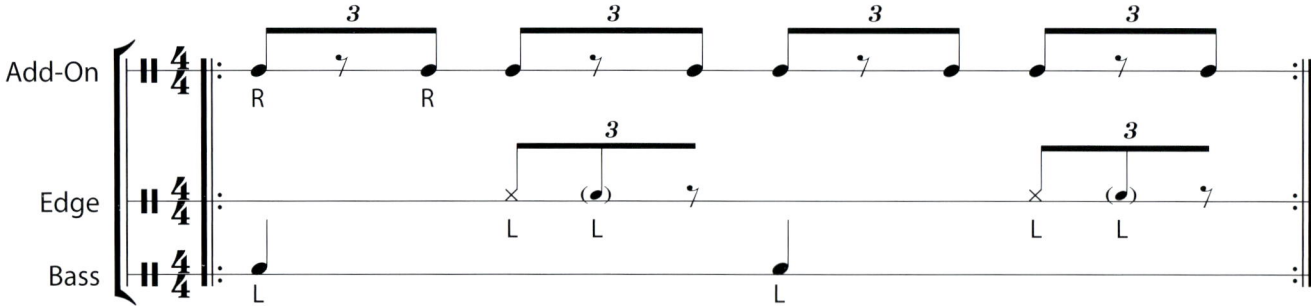

Shuffle triplet 6 (combination of Shuffle triplet 3 and basic groove)

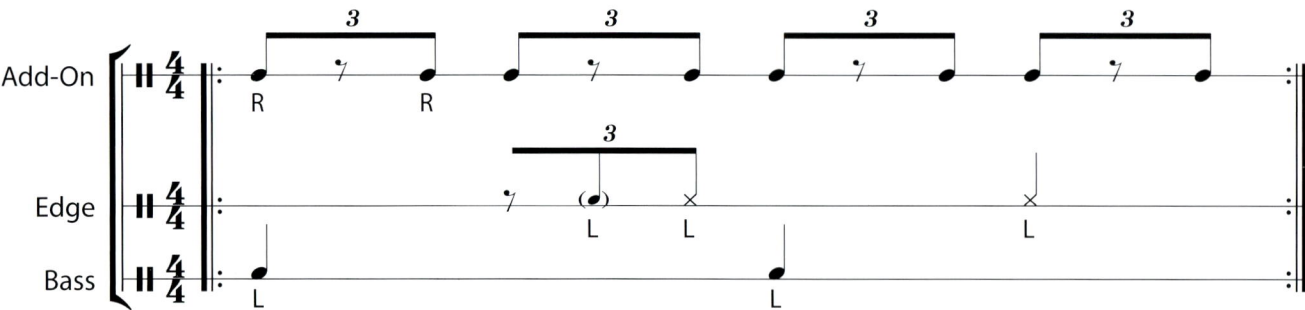

Mix the three modules in the groove.

Shuffle triplet 7

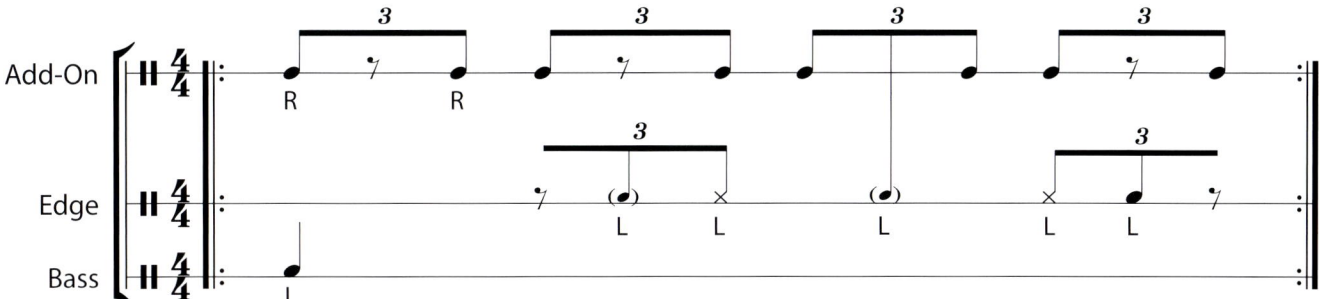

Shuffle triplet 8

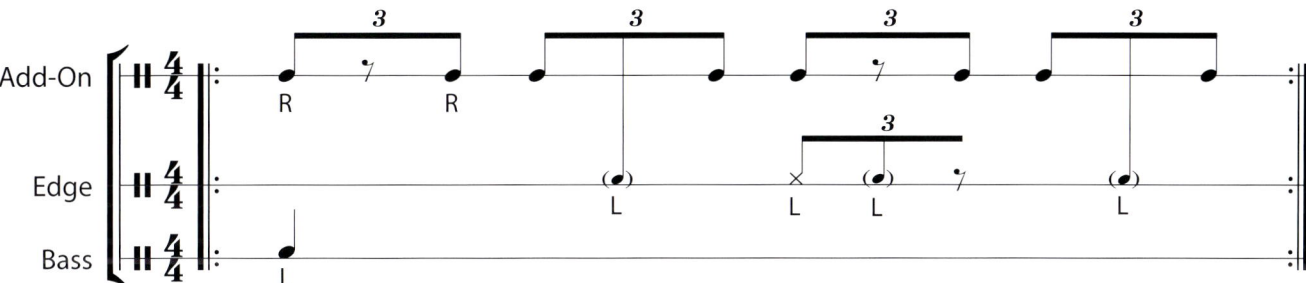

Shuffle triplet 9

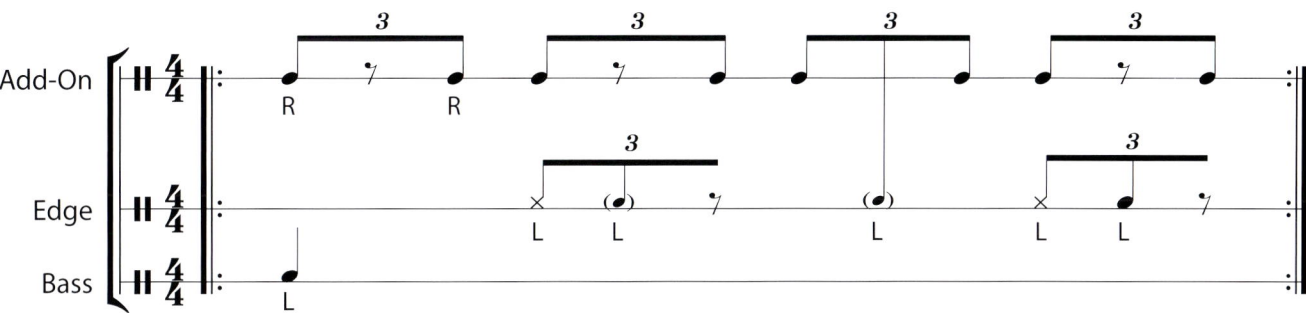

Blues Grooves for song accompaniment

Blues music comes from the rural Southern United States. Slaves from Africa had to work on the cotton fields of the large landowners. In these fields, they sang 'work songs' which helped them better endure their monotonous and strenuous work. The work provided the rhythm, the sequence of the same movements over and over again. Love, sorrow and longing – that was what the cotton pickers sang about. The songs reminded them of their home on the other side of the Atlantic.

From this the blues developed, which owes its name to the melancholy mood:

Anyone who feels 'blue' is melancholy or even sad. Music meant a lot to the field workers. It enabled them to feel free even in captivity. It gave them a cultural identity, although the white tribes in the USA despised this music. But the simple melodies prevailed. The blues revolutionized the music world – and still influences rock and pop music to this day.

Blues patterns (ternary)

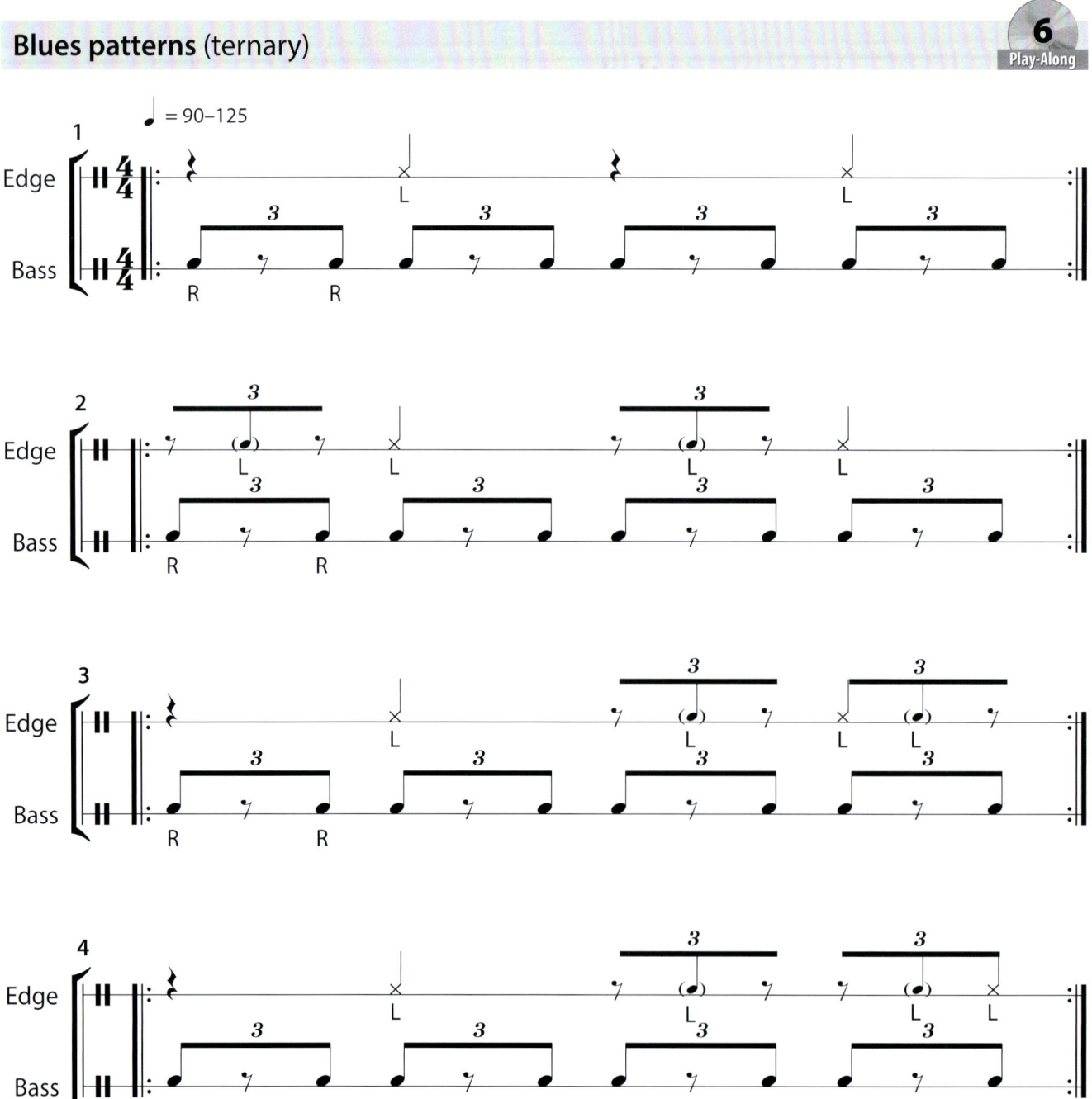

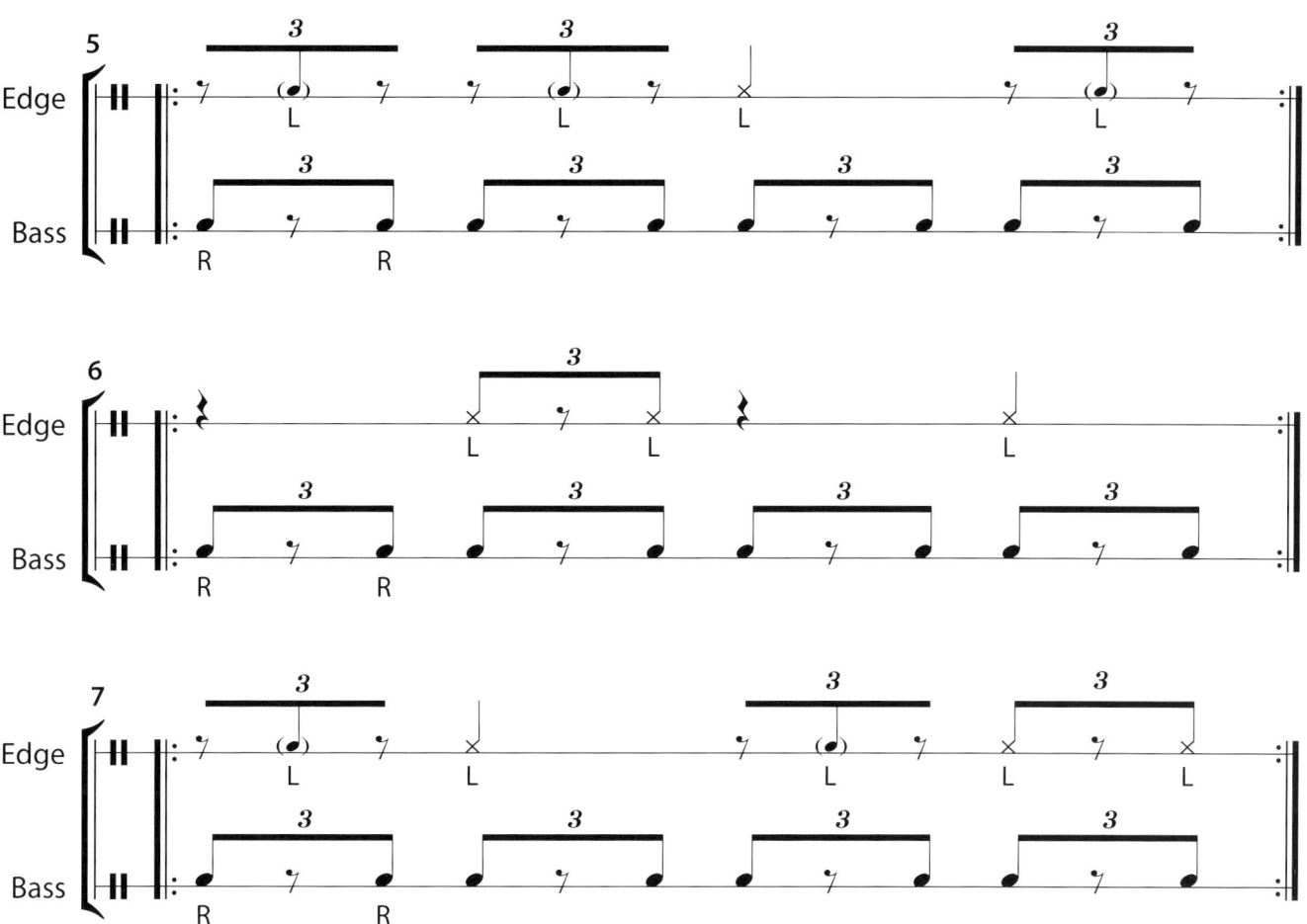

Matthias and Rob Collomb at the 'Colors of Percussion Festival' in Freistadt Austria 2009

Rhythms from Brazil

On the following pages I will give you an insight into the rhythmic world of Brazil and its diversity. Use the grooves shown in your music as well. This is no longer unusual today and often leads to surprising new interpretations of well-known themes and melodies. Ultimately, the cajón is also hard to find as a rhythm instrument in Brazil, but that shouldn't prevent you from playing these rhythms on it.

Baião

The **Baião** is a dance rhythm from the Brazilian northeast. Very lively and mostly performed with the pandeiro, accordion, triangle, and guitar, with the triangle pushing the tempo. Its basic pattern consists of two *groups of 3*, followed by a *group of 2*.

The *Baião rhythm* also forms the basis for other, now well-known styles of the Northeast such as *Forró* (*see page 83*) or *Côco* (*see page 84*).

Baião basic pattern

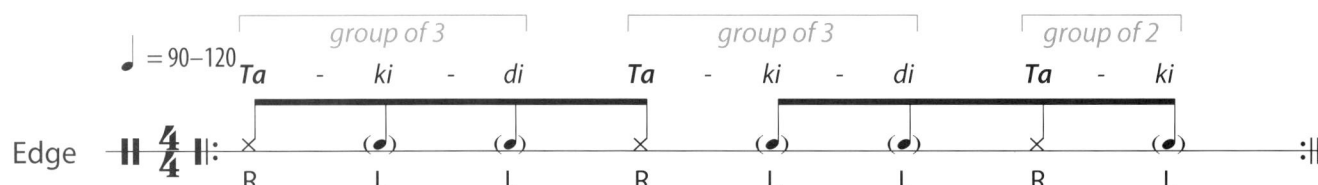

Online video 46

Baião patterns (orchestrated)

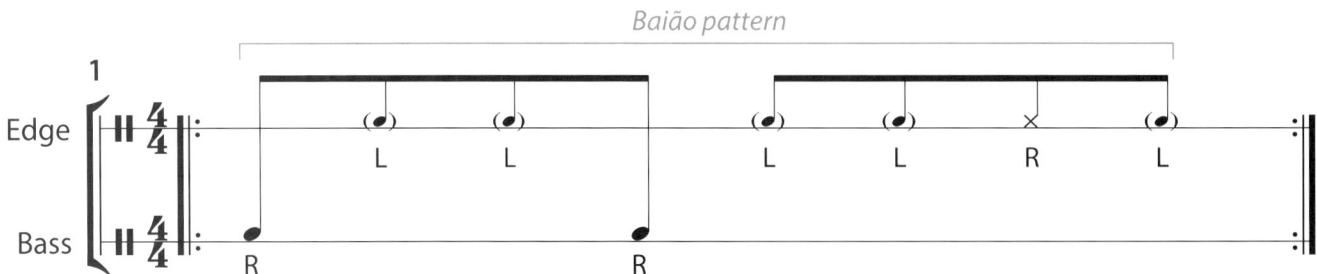

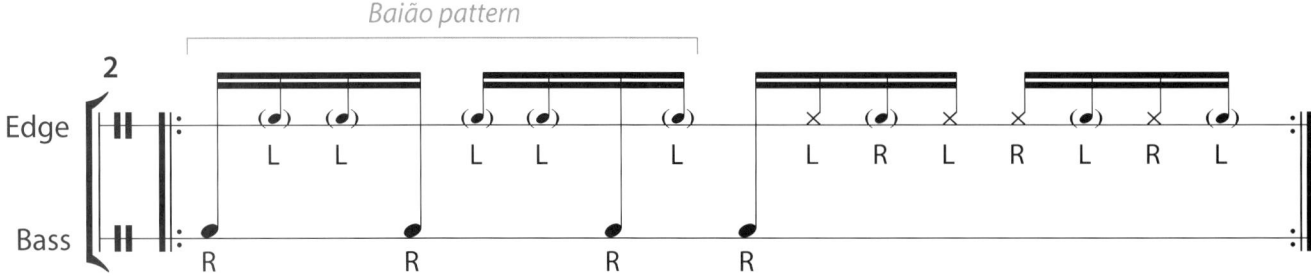

82

If the *right hand* takes over the pattern of the triangle (*rhythm figure 1, see page 17*) with a *rod* on the edge of the cajón and the *bass* takes over the *dotted 8th + 16th figure* (*see page 63*), the following adaptation is created on the cajón:

dotted 8th + 16thl	Rhythm figure 1

Baião pattern (played with Rod)

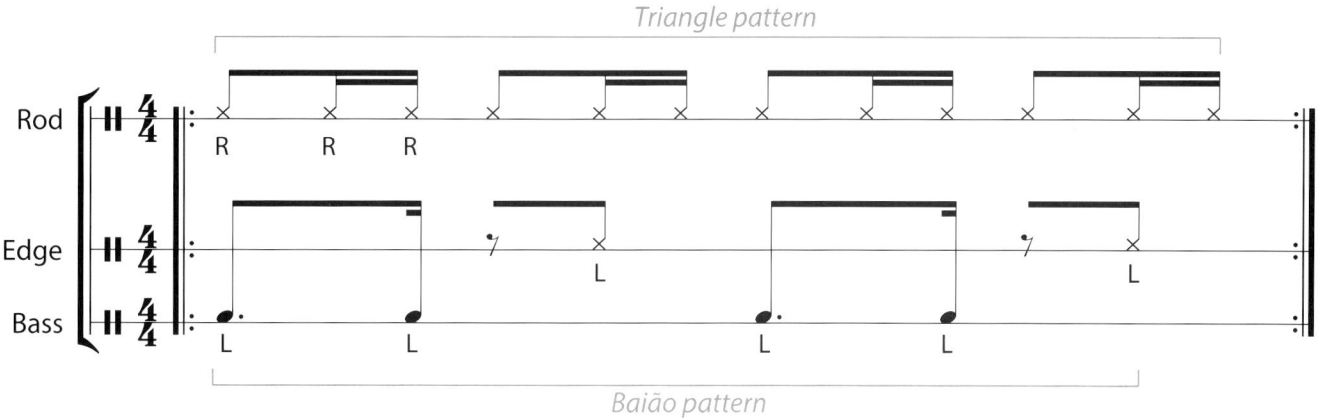

Forró

As a musical genre, the **Forró** can be seen as the son of the *Baião*. The name *Forró* was originally only used to denote the place where the dance events took place. Later, the name was also referred to a musical style, as the successor to the *Baião*.

Divide the hands as follows:
R: bass
L: edge

Forró basic groove

$\quad$ = 80–99

... or a Forró variation with accents on the edge played with the right hand.

Forró variation

$\quad$ = 80–99

83

... or as a drum interpretation with the right hand playing a hi-hat pattern with a rod (*rhythm figure 2, see page 20*):

dotted 8thl + 16th	Rhythm figure 2

Forró pattern (Rod)

16 Play-Along

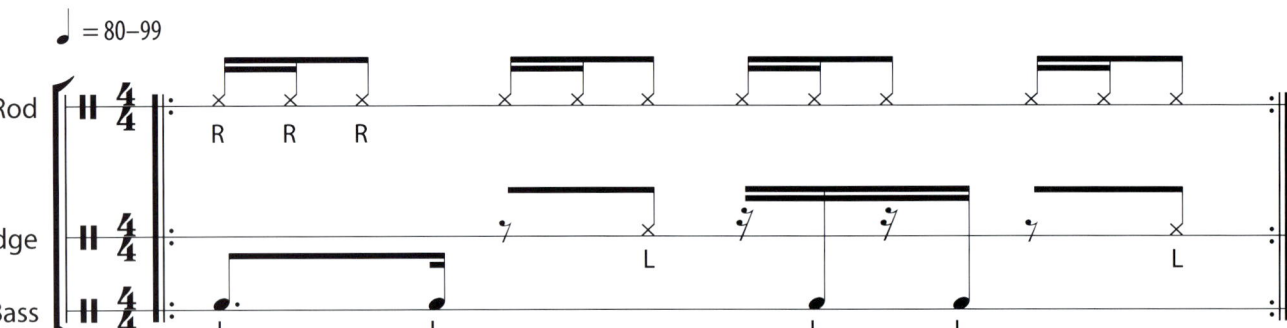

Cóco

The **Cóco**, also known as *Samba de Cóco*, is a Brazilian dance rhythm and belongs to the '*Musica Nordestina*', the regional music of the northeast. This couple dance is based on the *Baião* and was first mentioned in the second half of the 18th century.

Cóco basic pattern

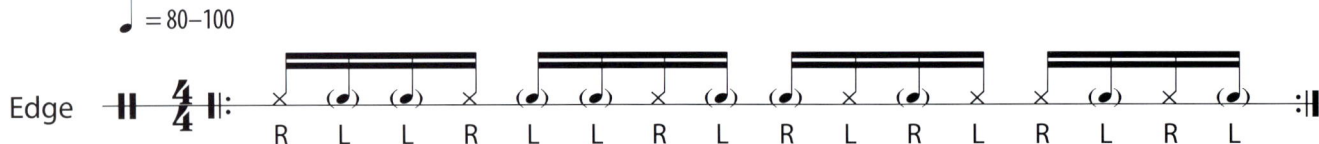

Cóco pattern on the cajón

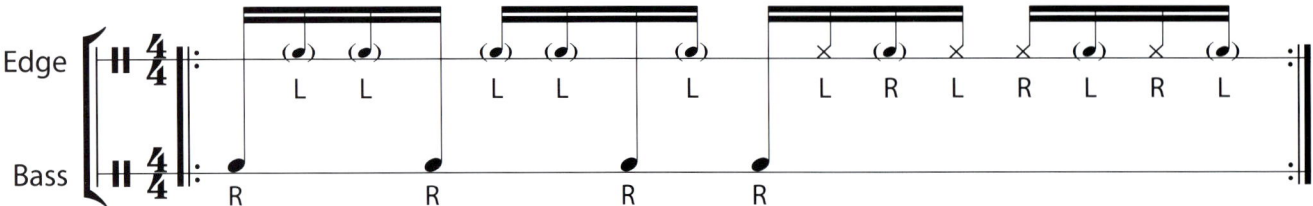

84

Bossa Nova

Bossa Nova is probably Brazil's most popular rhythm, along with the samba (*see also page 87*). Its tempo is slower than the samba, and it became known worldwide through the title *The Girl from Ipanema*, a composition by Antonio Carlos Jobim from 1962. Significant here is the accent figure of the *surdo* (*a deep bass drum*). You make the accents sound like a heartbeat, i.e., the sixteenth is somewhat quieter than the dotted eighth note, similar to an upbeat.

Bossa bass pattern (surdo)

Now 'fill up' with soft tips on the edge in the 'weak' hand and divide your hands as follows:

R in the bass

L on the edge

Play the tips as softly as possible until you omit them completely.

Bossa bass pattern (surdo pattern filled up with tips)

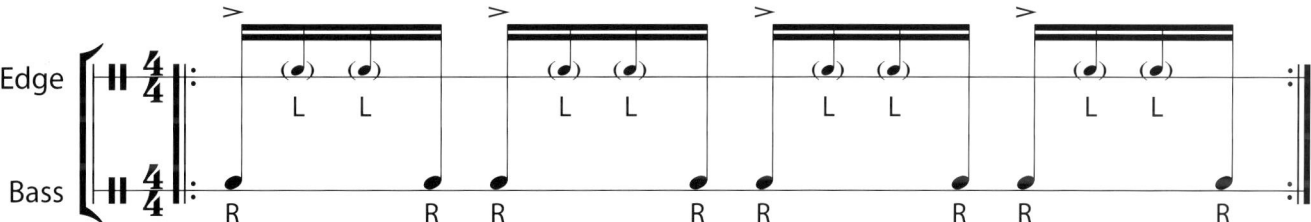

This bass pattern includes the 'bossa melody,' which is normally played by the *claves*. You already know it from the *bossa clave* – here with dotted eighth notes instead of dotted quarter notes (*see page 39*).

Bossa clave pattern (with dotted eighth notes)

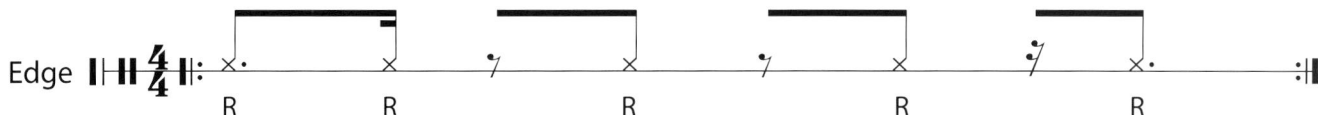

'Fill up' here, too, in the left hand with soft tips on the edge of the cajón.

Bossa clave pattern (filled up with tips on the edge)

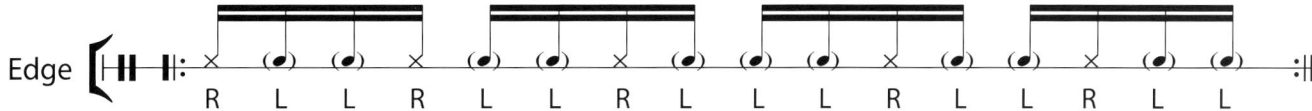

85

Matthias at the Musicfest in Moscow, Russia

Now join bass and 'melody' in a groove. The *right hand* plays the accents of the *surdo pattern* and the *left hand* plays the *bossa clave*:

Online video 47

Bossa basic pattern (bass: surdo pattern | edge: claves)

14 Play-Along

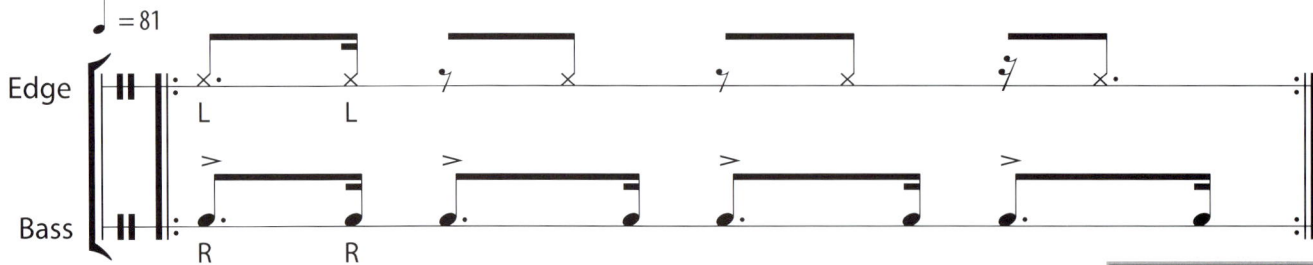

Online video 48

Here's a **hand-to-hand** sticking variation:

Bossa pattern (hand-to-hand)

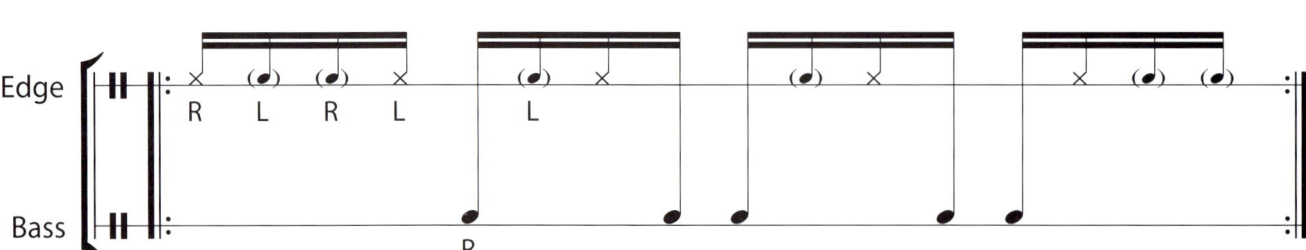

Samba

The term **samba** (*see also Samba Clave on page 40*) describes both a musical genre and a dance from Brazil. Along with the *bossa nova* (*see page 85/86*), it is probably the best-known Brazilian rhythm. It was originally brought to Brazil by African slaves from West Africa and is particularly familiar to us through the carnival in Rio de Janeiro.

Played on the cajón, the samba offers a variety of possibilities, and you should again try to combine the fluid dance-like ease of this groove with other styles (*see also the chapters **Playing Technique and Phrasing** starting on page 106 as well as **Latin Pop** on page 73*).

First, play the same surdo accents as the bass beat like you already did in the bossa nova. Remember to make the accents sound like a heartbeat (*see page 85*).

Samba bass pattern (surdo)

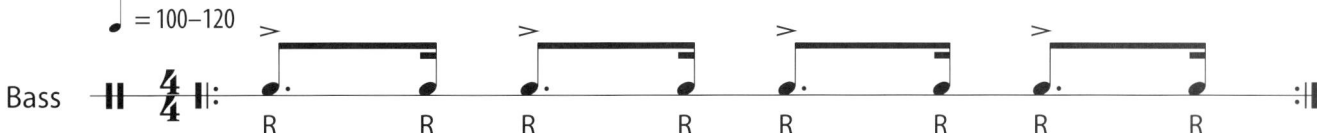

This bass pattern includes the 'samba melody,' which is usually played by the *claves* you already know from the *samba clave* played in eighth notes on *page 40*. Transferred to the *sixteenth-note grid*, it looks like this:

Samba clave (accents in sixteenth notes)

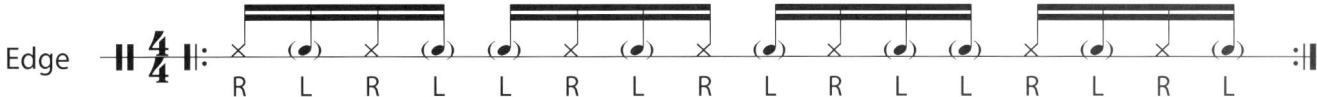

Now try to combine both components step by step in a groove. The idea here is that the *right hand* plays the accents of the surdo pattern and the *left hand* fills up with tips. Start in the 'weak' hand with a light eighth-note figure running over the pulse and divide your hands as follows:

R in the bass
L on the edge

Samba pattern (derivation with tip eighth figure on the edge of the cajón)

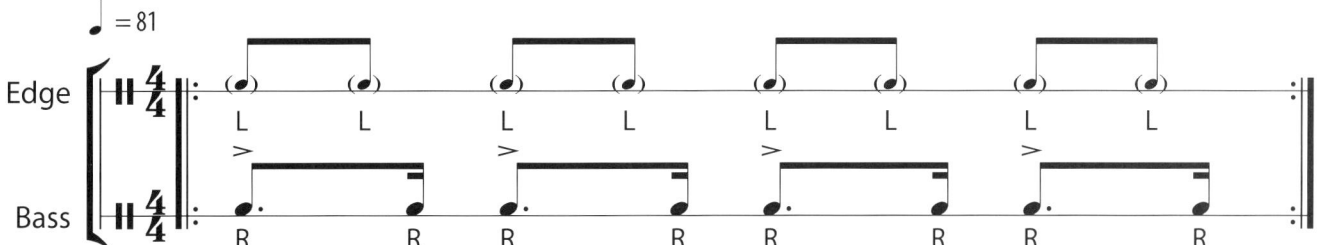

87

You have already covered the two pairs of eighth notes on the first and last beats.

Now replace the eighth-note tips with slap accents, and shift the eighth notes on the second and third beats by a sixteenth note:

Samba clave (slap accents in sixteenth notes)

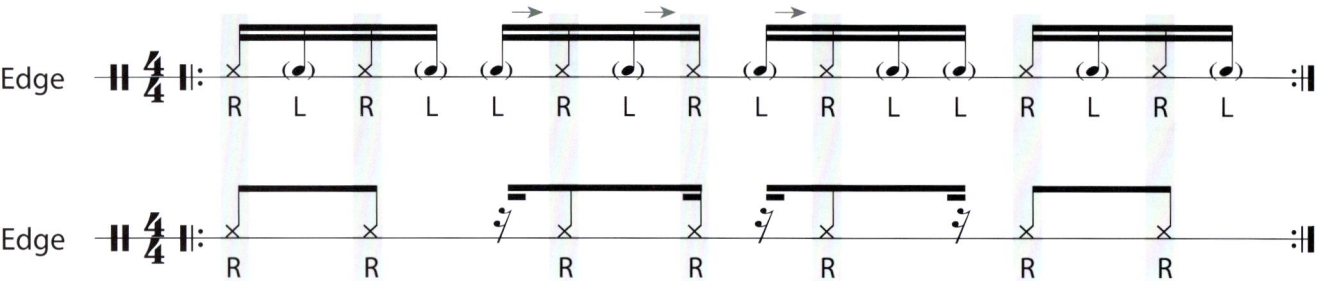

Finally, bring both samba original figures together to create the complete samba groove:

Online video 49

13 Demo Track **14** Play-Along

Samba groove (original)

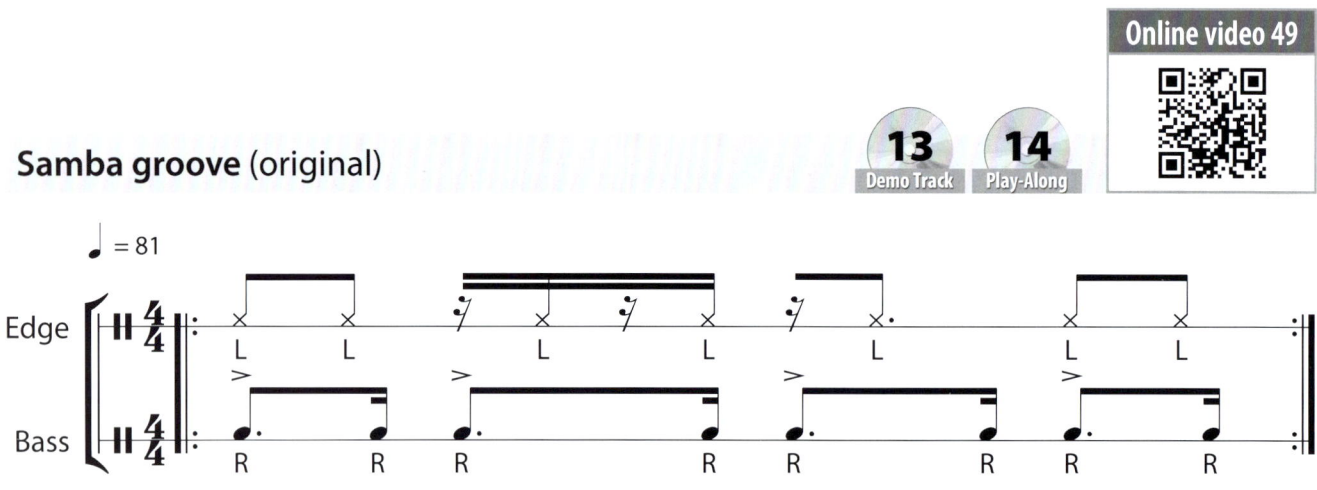

A wonderful adaptation is this 1980s pop samba in the style of Matt Bianco's *Half a Minute*:

Pop Samba (in the style of Matt Bianco)

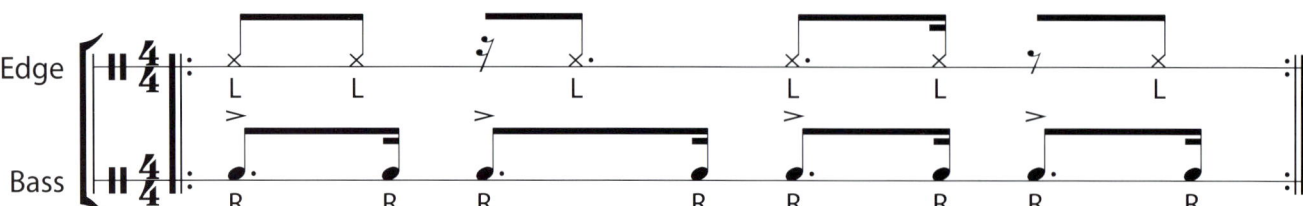

Samba Flow

I call **Samba Flow** the flowing, light and never 'straight,' rather dance-like way of playing samba. You can do this best with the sticking **R L**:

Samba Flow patterns

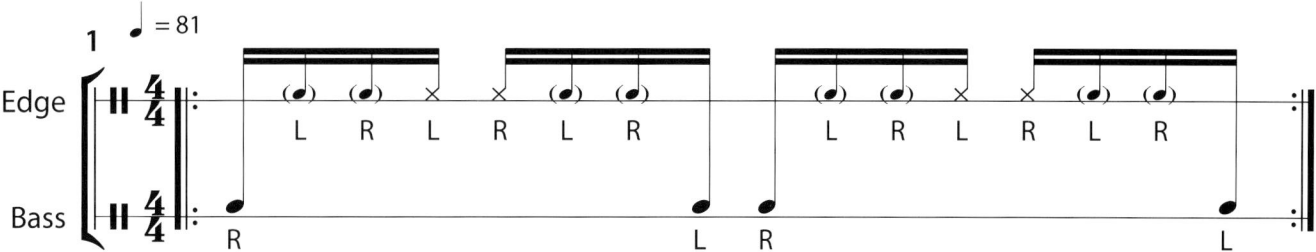

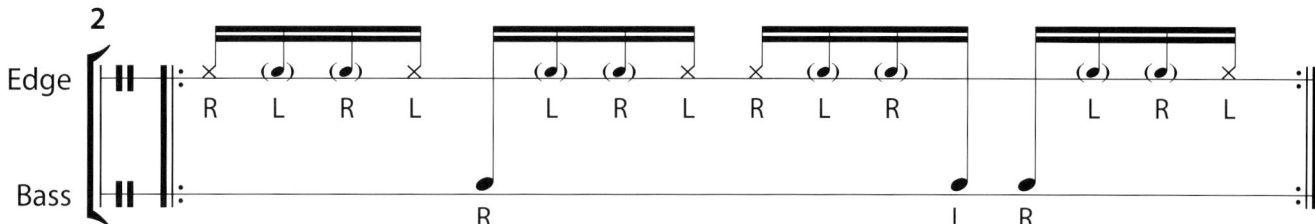

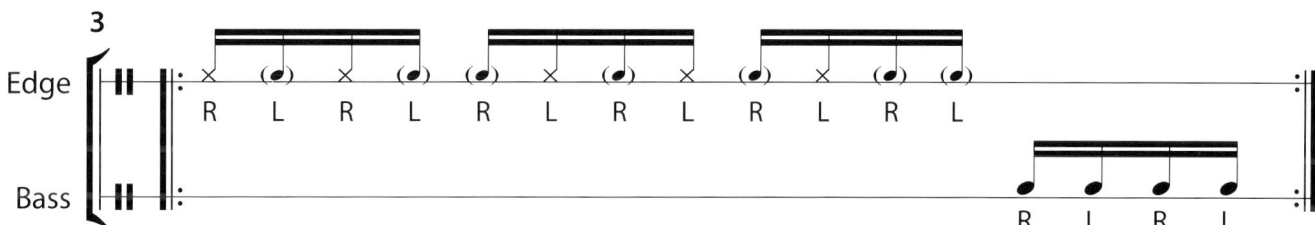

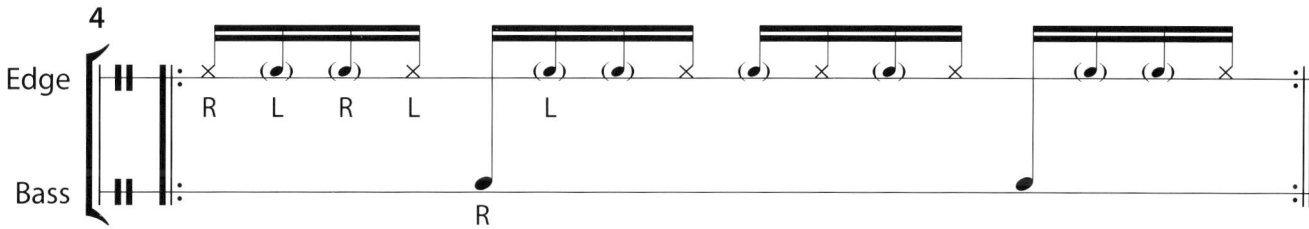

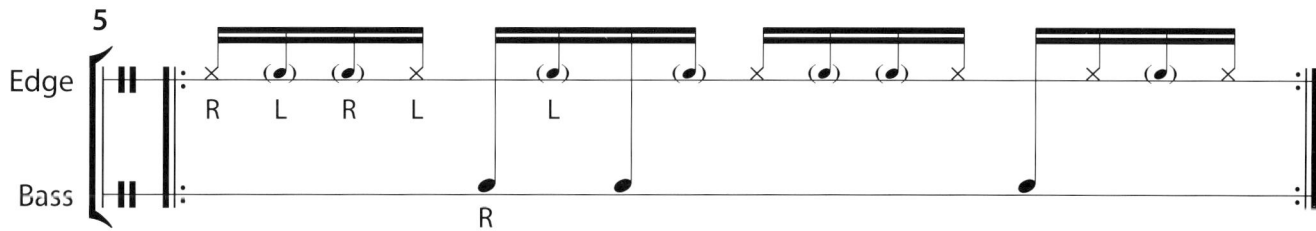

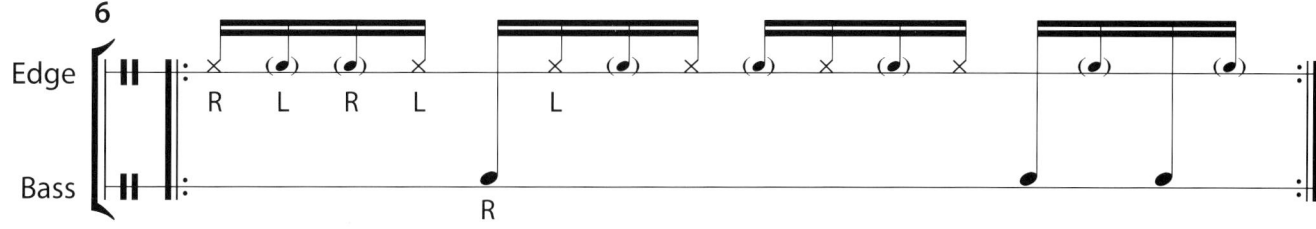

Samba Reggae

Samba Reggae is a mixture of samba and reggae and was first played in the region of Bahia. It is particularly attractive if you always *combine two patterns* with each other according to the **modular system**. The resulting two-bar grooves are used very often.

Online video 51

Samba Reggae patterns

17 Demo Track **18** Play-Along

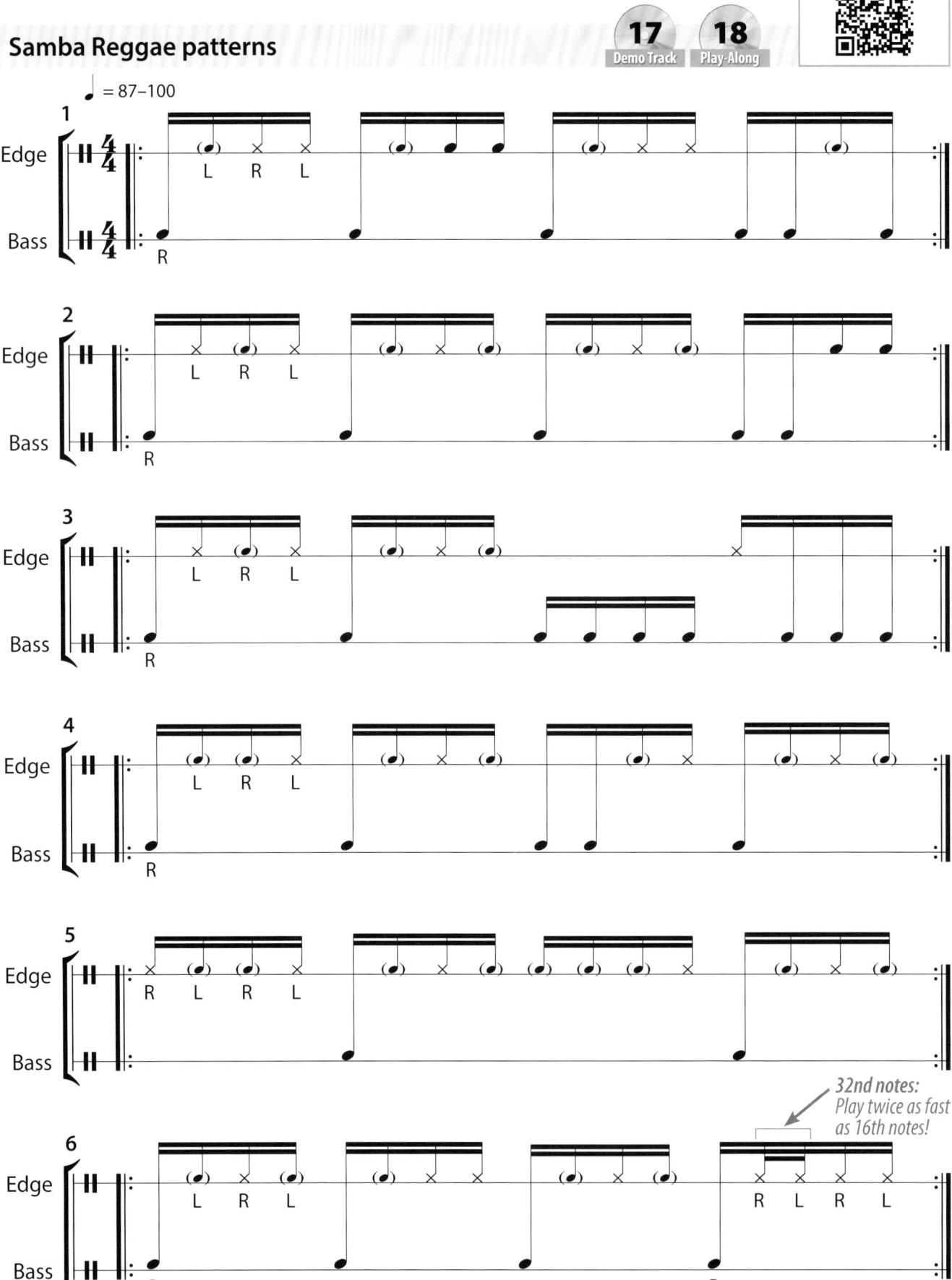

32nd notes:
Play twice as fast as 16th notes!

Partido Alto

The **Partido Alto** belongs to the genre of the *samba* in its rhythmic structure. Musically, it is a dialogue between several singers, in which the accents are particularly emphasized. Originally from Africa, the *Partido Alto* goes back to a dance, the *Jongo*, which was performed in the southeast of Brazil on the coffee plantations between Rio de Janeiro and São Paulo.

Its integration into jazz and also pop music is very appealing. Some more examples of this later. But first the **accent pattern** with the 'weak' hand, combined with a **shaker** in the leading hand at the edge of the cajón:

Online video 52

Partido Alto accent pattern (edge | shaker)

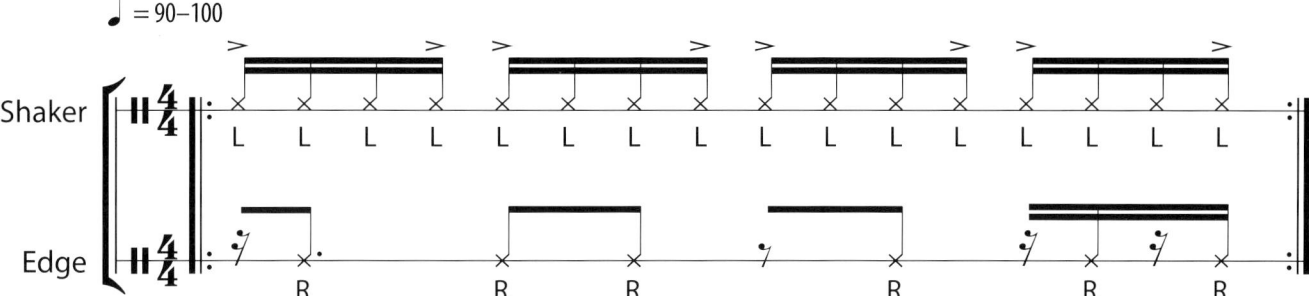

Start varying the accents in the 'weak' hand between edge and bass. If you play the pattern *hand-to-hand* and split between bass and edge tone, you'll get the following funky groove:

Online video 53

Partido Alto funky patterns (hand-to-hand)

Rhythms from Peru

Peru is the birthplace of the cajón. 200 years ago, this instrument was 'misappropriated' as a commodity. *Boxes* of various sizes became drums, the inner workings (*the snares*) were added later to complete the distinctive sound (you can learn more details about the history of the cajón from the wonderful work *El Cajón – Afro Peruano* written by Rafael Santa Cruz.)

The African rhythms of the slaves on the cajónes merged with native melodies and harmonies. The result is *Musica Criolla*, a unique music with very special grooves of the West African slaves, mixed with the Spanish influenced musical tradition of Peru. Here are some of the most important rhythms of Peru, which can be easily transferred to today.

Zamacueca

Zamacueca is a dance from the 16th century at the time of Spanish and Portuguese rule in South America. It consists of African, Spanish but also native elements. The $\frac{6}{8}$ time (*see page 52*) is a very inspiring suggestion for me to play *three- and six-beat rhythms*. Again you divide the hands:

R in the bass
L on the edge

Time signature

$$\frac{6}{8}$$

Online video 54

Zamacueca basic pattern (6/8 time)

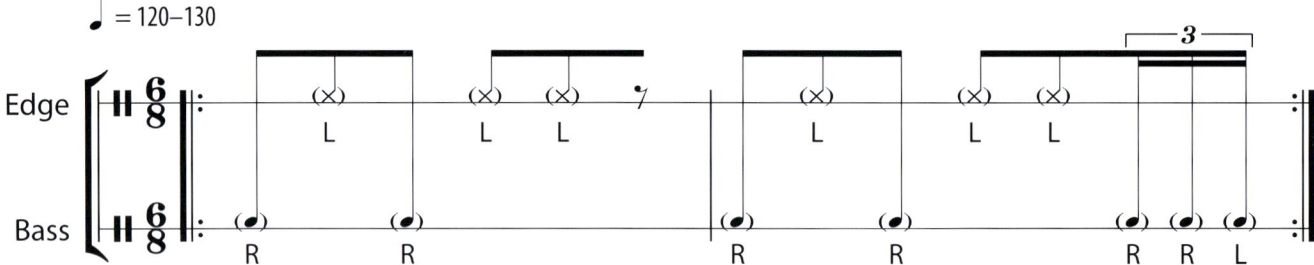

This variation of the **Zamacueca** can be used well in an ensemble as *second part*:

Zamacueca variation (6/8 time)

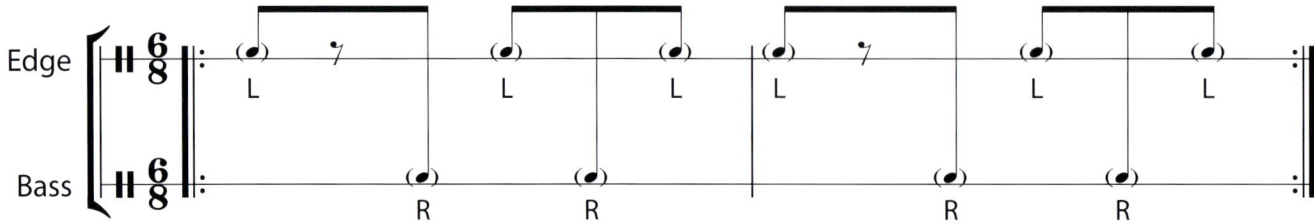

The corresponding *clap pattern* is:

Zamacueca clap pattern (6/8 time)

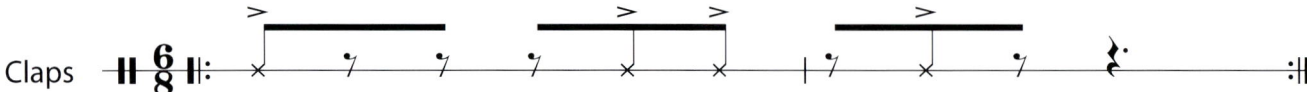

92

Lando

The **Lando**, also called *londo* in Brazil, is a very popular music whose basic pattern in $\frac{6}{4}$ time is often played in the following way:

Time signature

$\frac{6}{4}$

Lando basic pattern (6/4 time)

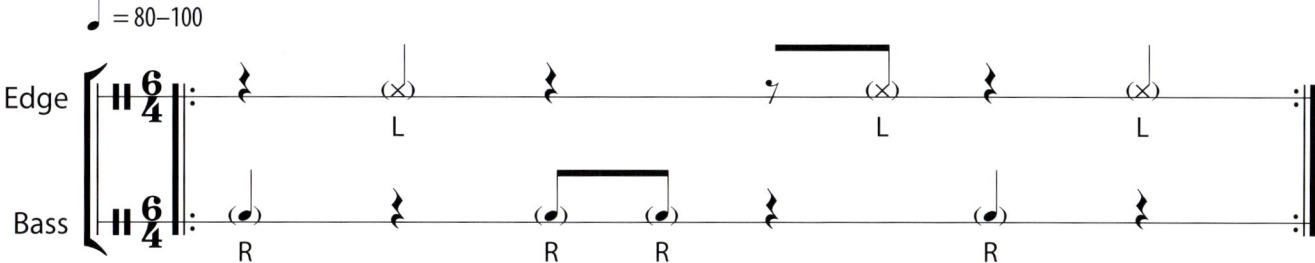

Very often, the lando is also interpreted in eighth notes in $\frac{12}{8}$ time.

Time signature

$\frac{12}{8}$

Lando basic pattern (12/8 with claps)

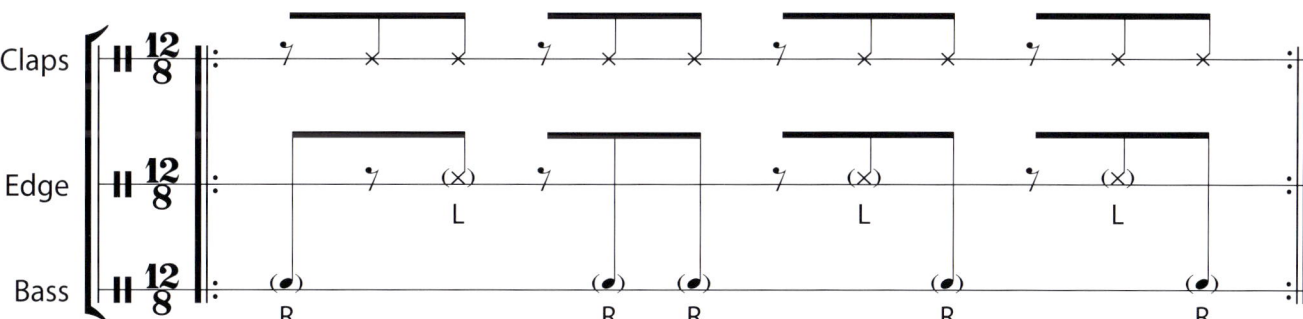

Festejo

The **Festejo** is a dance rhythm originally influenced by the African slaves from the Congo, Mozambique and Angola. It expressed the desire to achieve the end of slavery and is accordingly played with a lot of energy and tempo. The *Festejo* is the most popular and widespread rhythm of *Musica Criolla*. Its *three-beat feel* is created by the *triplets* in $\frac{4}{4}$.

Festejo basic pattern (4/4 ternary)

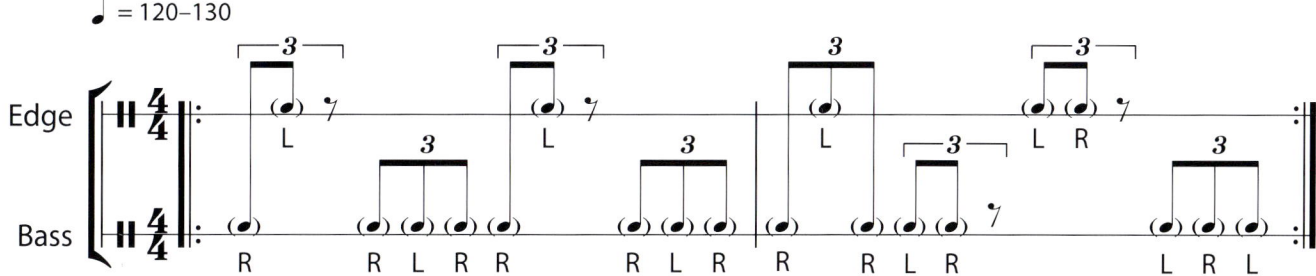

Festejo basic pattern (4/4 binary – Rafael Santa Cruz)

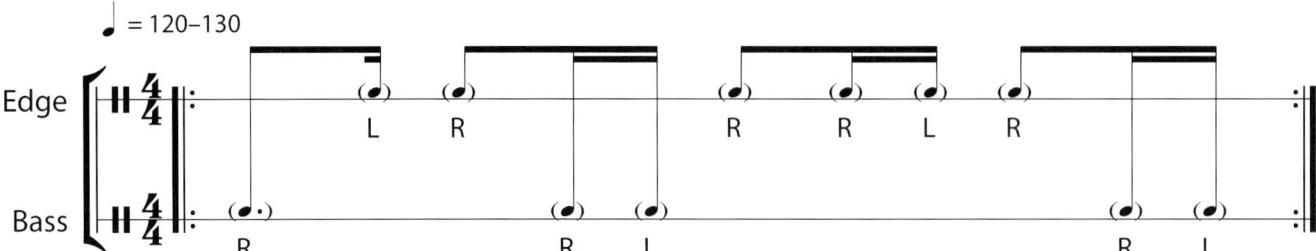

Vals Criollo (Peruvian Waltz)

The **Vals Criollo** – or Peruvian Waltz – is inspired by the influences of the Europeans, in this case the Spanish occupants of Peru. It was also very popular among the slaves and the natives.

It is interesting what can be created from a simple, familiar waltz in $\frac{3}{4}$ time ...!

Time signature

$$\frac{3}{4}$$

Online video 55

Vals Criollo basic pattern (3/4 time)

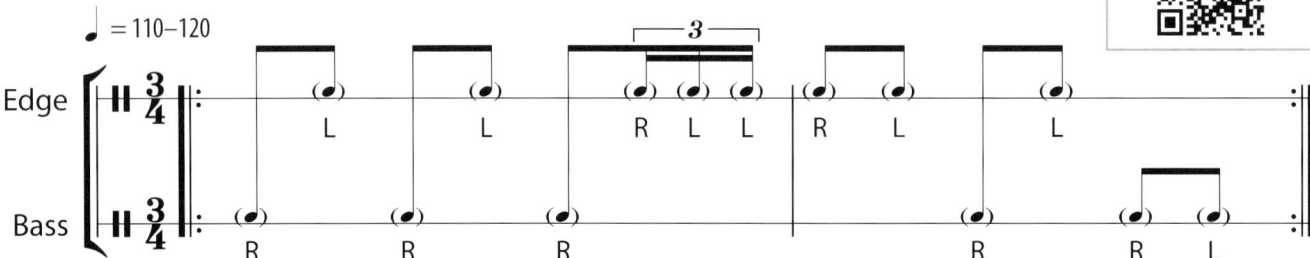

Matthias 2019 at the Colors of Percussion Festival in Freistadt, Austria

Modern Grooves

Trap Music

Trap Music is is a descendant of *hip hop* and originated in the early 1990s in the southern states of the USA. Rap musicians from Atlanta made this gritty and rhythmically very heavy music known worldwide, so that trap music has now become a recognized style in its own right.

In addition to the solid, very bass-heavy beats, bright and fast hi-hat patterns provide the necessary contrast from which this music lives.

When practicing, pay attention to the precise execution of the beat sequences and the dynamics as well as the tempo indications (*metronome*).

Trap basic groove 1

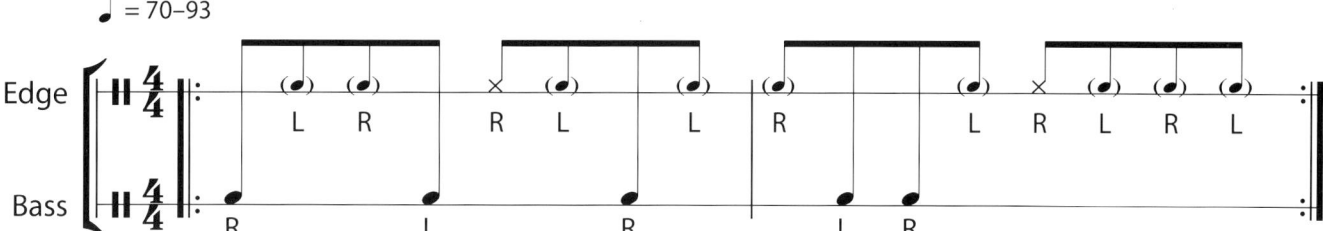

For the following *pattern variations* you proceed step by step according to the familiar *modular system*:

1. first practice the **basic trap groove** (*see above*) and learn it by heart.
2. then practice one of the following variations on the edge of the cajón and memorize it as well.
3. since the variations are played *twice as fast* (*doubletime*) as the basic groove, you should already be able to play them quickly but precisely. Be sure to watch the **video**!

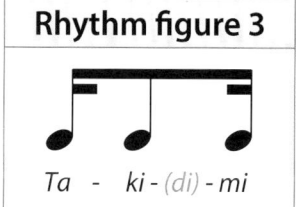

Trap –variation 1 (buzz board)

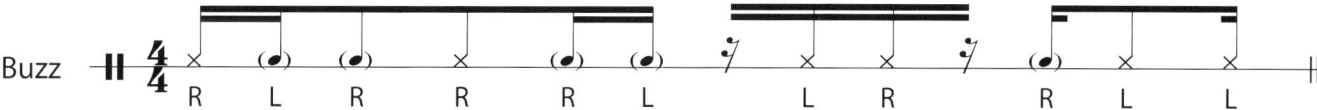

Trap variation 2 (buzz board)

Trap variation 3 (on the edge of the cajón)

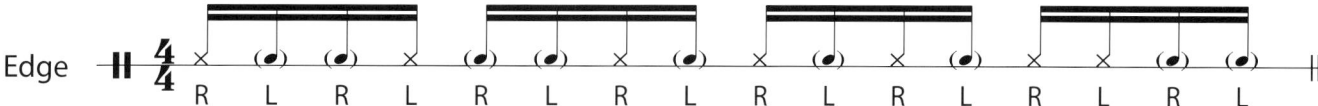

Trap variation (on the edge of the cajón)

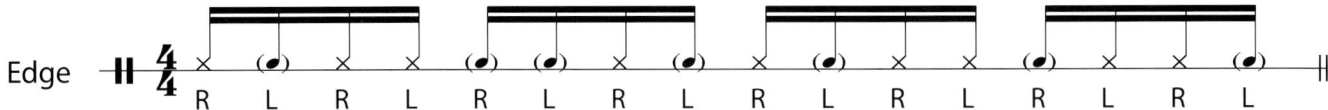

4. now add one of the three basic grooves to one of the four trap variations in the following way:

| 3x 2 bars basic groove | + | 1 bar basic groove | + | 1 bar variation 1, 2, 3, or 4 |

You get an authentic trap groove.

Option: Play the variations on a bright sound source such as the *buzz board* (*see page 68*).

5. Proceed in the same way with the other basic grooves and variations.

Sample (Trap basic groove 1 + variation 1)

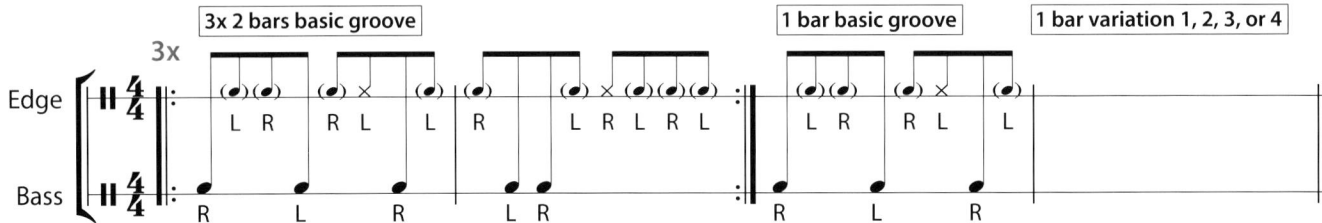

Trap basic groove 1 to 3 (cajón)

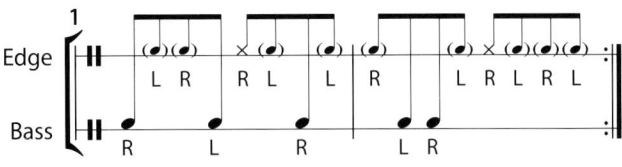

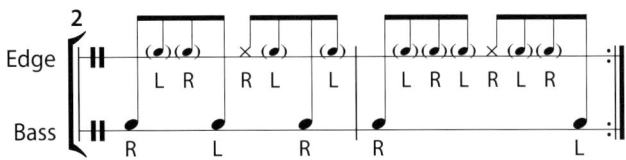

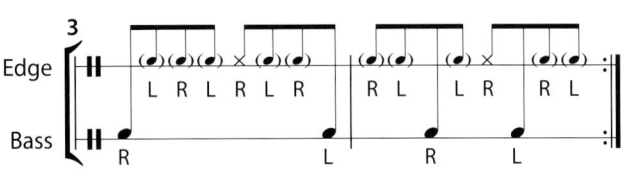

Trap variation 1 (edge or buzz board)

Trap variation 2 (edge or buzz board)

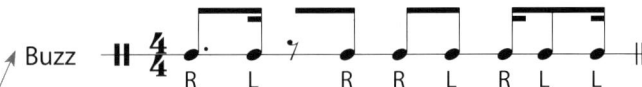

Trap variation 3 (edge or buzz board)

Trap variation 4 (edge or buzz board)

96

Trip Hop

Trip Hop is also derived from *hip hop*. It captivates by slow, almost tough beats (70–90 bpm), by sound carpets and atmospheres. Harmonies and melodies are in the foreground and the rap typical of hip hop is absent.

Bands and artists like **Portishead**, **Björk**, **Tricky**, and **Massive Attack** are among the pioneers of this genre.

Trip Hop basic groove

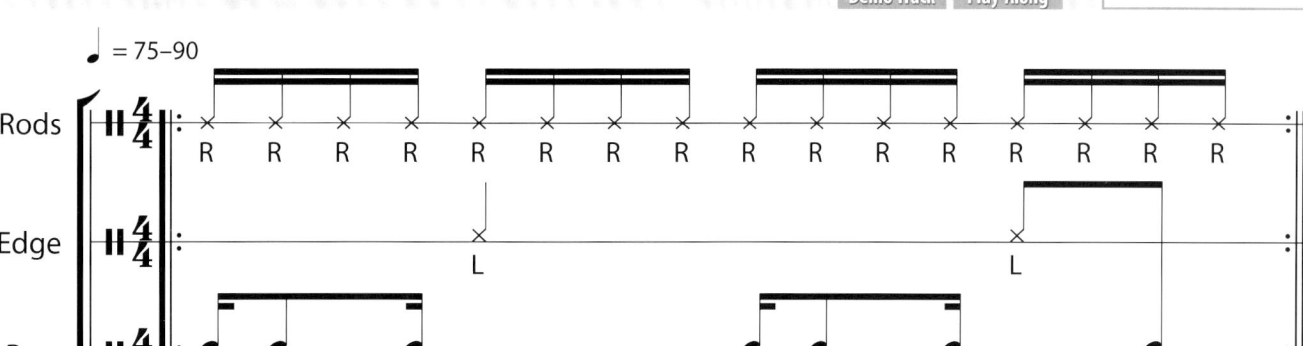

Lounge

This genre is wrongly called 'background music,' but lounge grooves are usually quite demanding. The following groove example can be played with a *heck stick* (*bell stick attached to the side of the cajón*) in combination with the cajón.

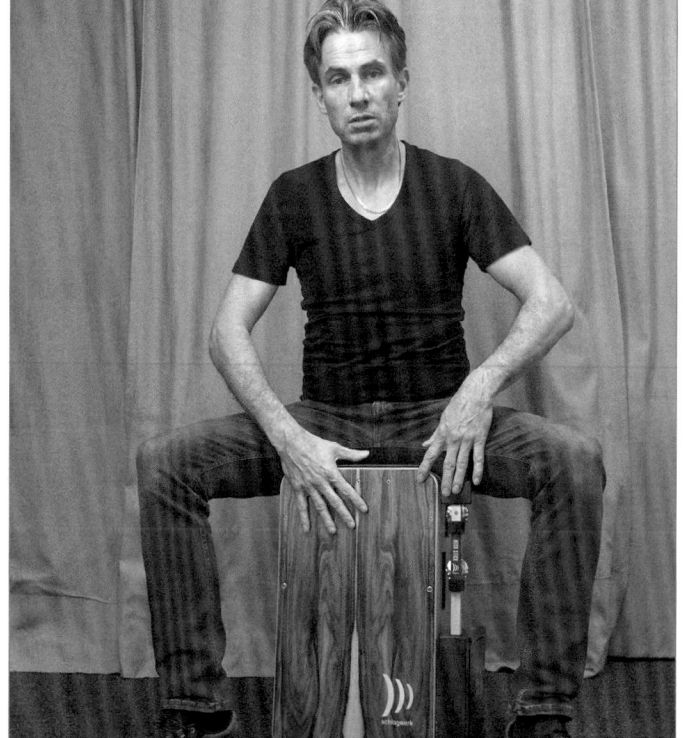

Heck stick

Material: jingle stick from metal whose sound imitates the hi-hat of the drum kit – for me one of the most innovative inventions of the last years!

Sound: Hi-Hat (bell sounds)

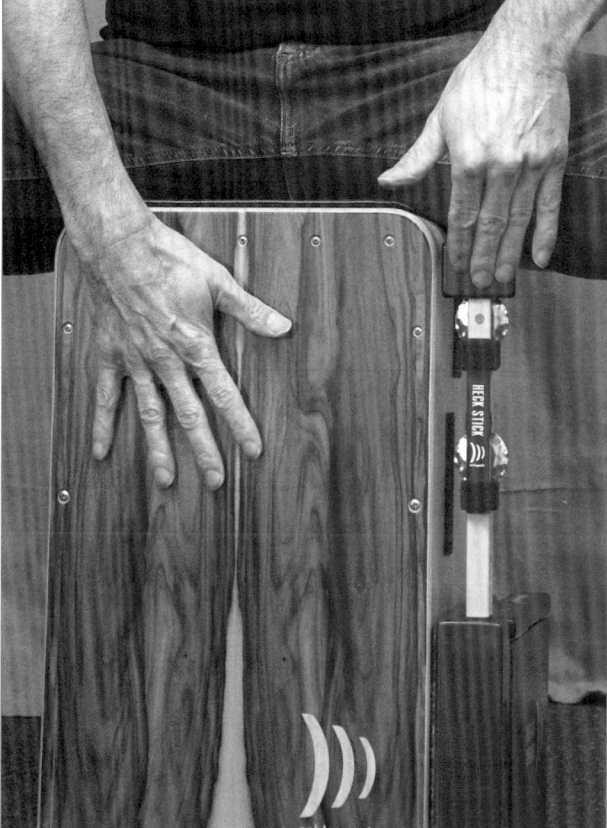

97

IMPORTANT: *First practice moving the right hand between bass and heck stick before adding the left hand.*

Lounge groove

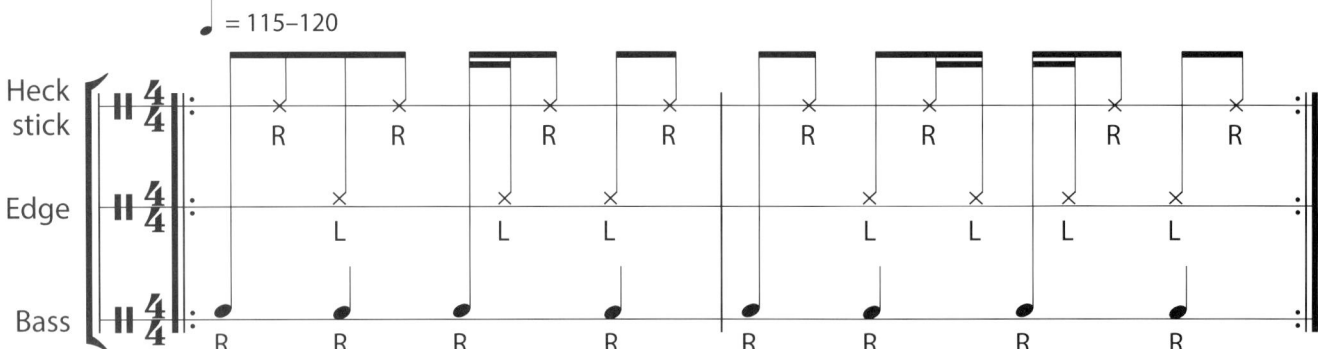

Matthias 2010 at the Bumfestival Zalec in Slovenia

Kuduro (also called Kuduru)

Kuduro refers to a style of music that originated in Angola in the late 1980s. Producers mixed African rhythms with the grooves of the Caribbean, like Soca or Calypso. The result was a very energetic, fast and danceable *mix of even (binary) and odd (ternary) elements*.

This is a big challenge to those of us that are new to playing both elements as a groove in one or two beats.

Consider the lead hand in the bass as a fixed point. Around this pulse revolve the accents and figures of the other hand on the edge of the cajón. Often this music is programmed. I find it very appealing to play it live and the cajón is great for that.

Split the hands:
R in the bass
L on the edge

Kuduro – preliminary exercise

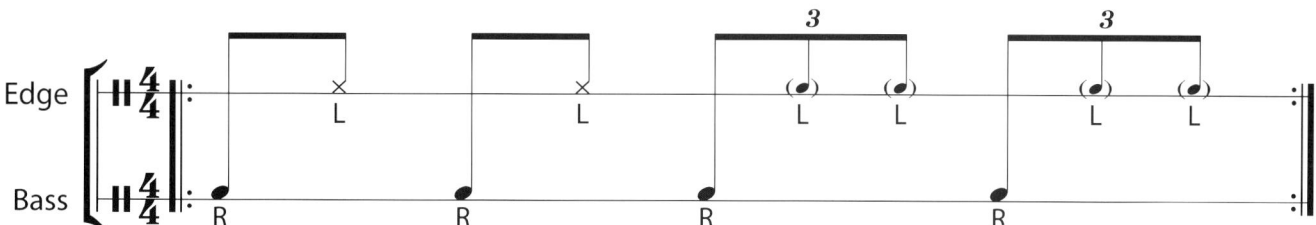

Practice the *one-bar basic groove* first, and then add to it to create a *two-bar basic groove* from which the following variations are derived.

Kuduro basic groove (one-bar)

25 Demo Track   **26** Play-Along

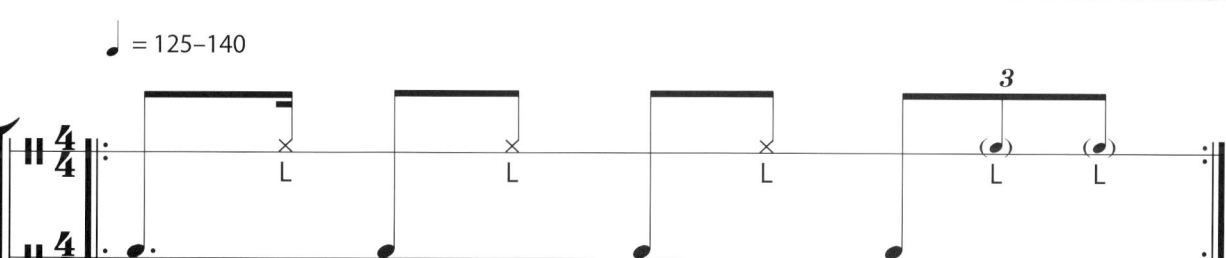

Kuduro basic groove (two-bar)

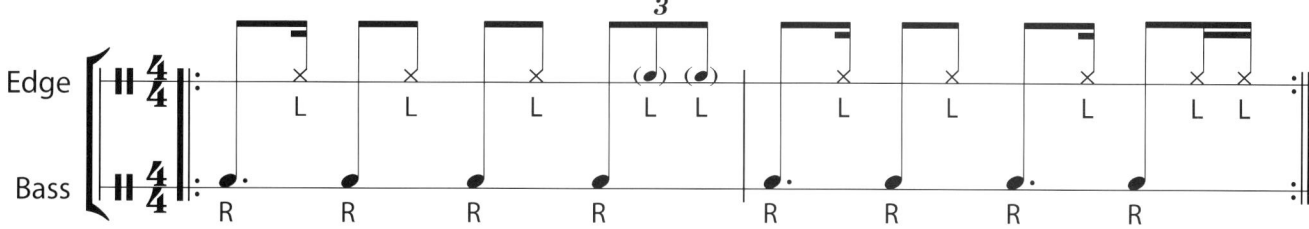

Kuduro variations (two-bar)

Kuduro is often played polyrhythmically. Here are four examples with a *split hand sticking*.

Kuduro variations (polyrhythmic)

27 Demo Track **28** Play-Along

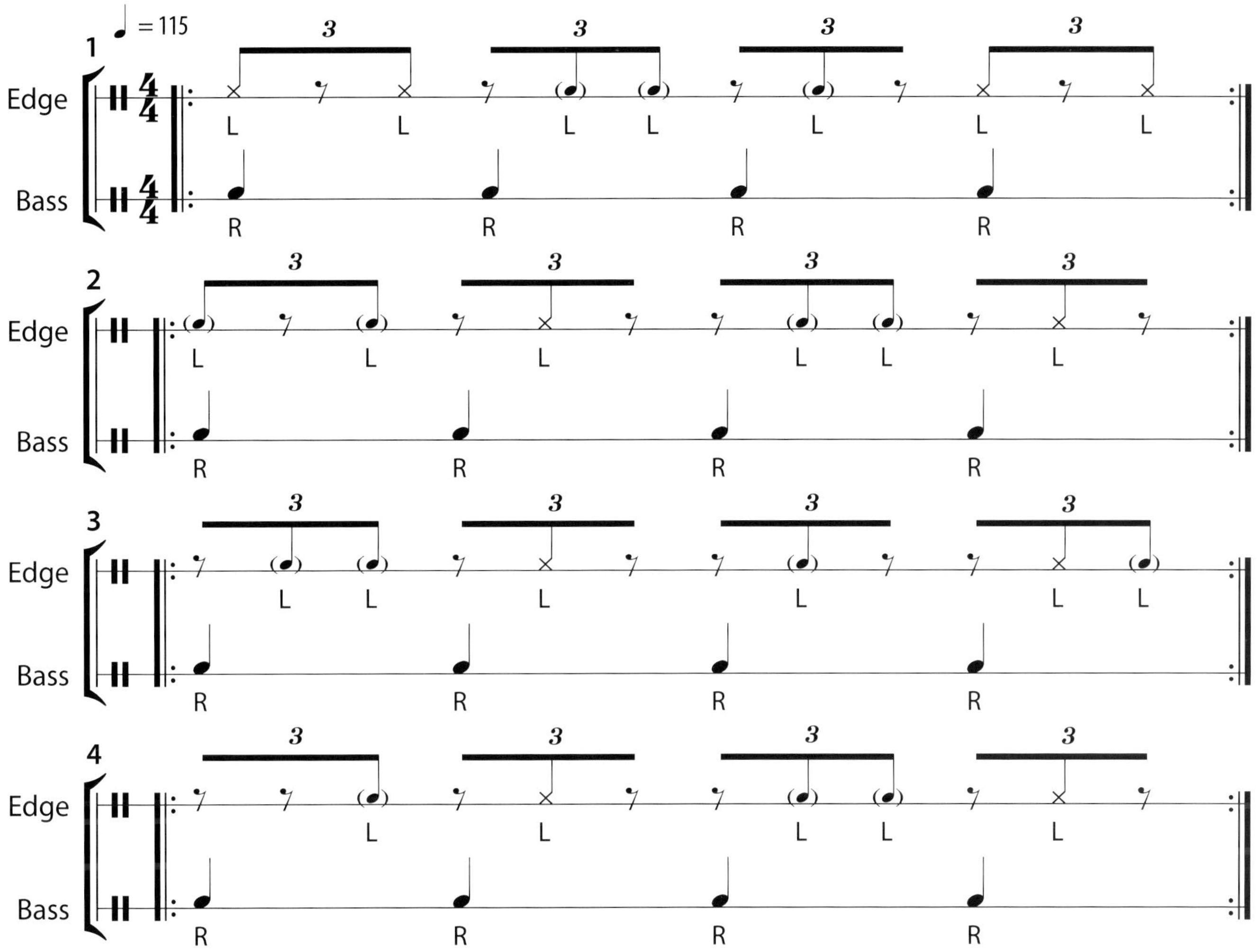

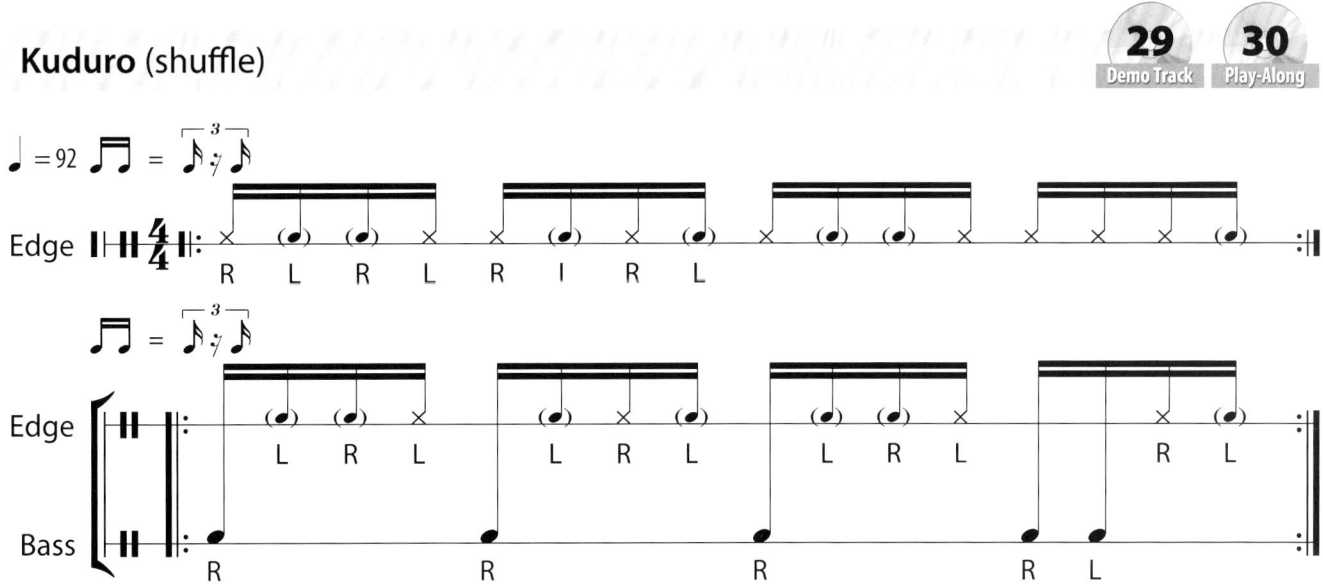

Kuduro Shuffle

Phrase the sixteenths in a *ternary way*, in this case as a *shuffle (see pages starting at p. 77)*. Practice the accent line first on the edge and then orchestrate between bass and edge:

Kuduro (shuffle)

29 Demo Track **30** Play-Along

Reggaeton

Reggaeton is a mixture of *Reggae, Hip Hop*, and *Merengue* (*dance originally from the Dominican Republic*), which has increasingly turned into electronic dance music. Puerto Rico, Panama, and Jamaica are considered to be the countries of origin. Later, Cuban elements and the electronic music of North America were added. *Reggaeton* has become very popular, especially in recent years, thanks to artists such as **Shakira**, **Alvaro Soler**, or **Enrique Iglesias**.

Its distinguishing feature from the *Moombahton* mentioned next page is the tempo with 96 bpm rather moderate and heavy.

Distinctive are a continuous $\frac{4}{4}$ bass pulse and *syncopated accents*.

Reggaeton grooves

31 Demo Track   **32** Play-Along

Moombahton

Moombahton is considered a mixture of *reggaeton* and *house*. Whilst rhythmically, it is hardly distinguishable, this style works with oriental sound collages (flutes and string instruments) as well as with various other percussion instruments. It has a soft and rhythmic bass (also called *wobble bass*) and the tempo is 109bpm.

Moombahton groove

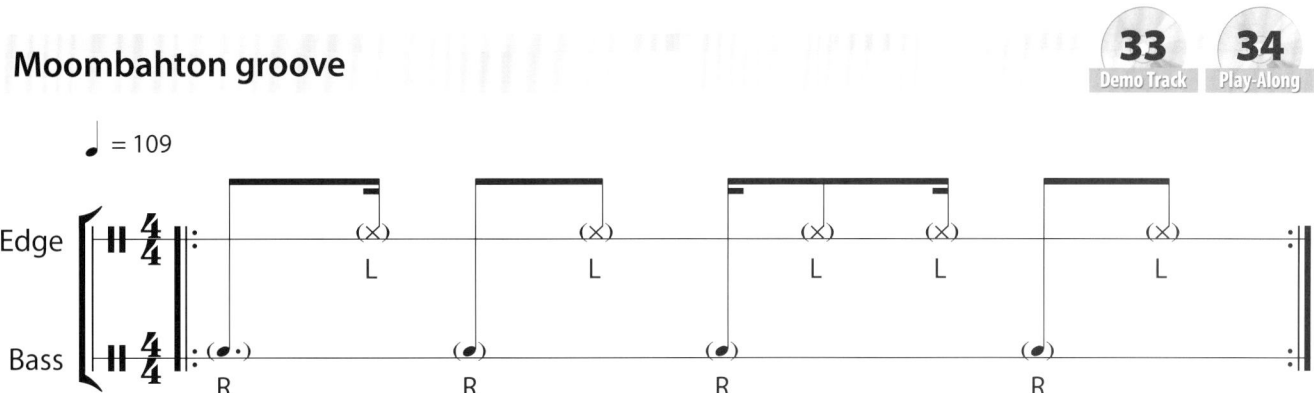

Dub

The name of this style originally comes from a recording medium, the *acetate record*, which is called *Dubplate*. At the end of the 1950s it was the 'mother' of the vinyl record in the record pressing plant. This dubplate could only be played on special sound systems, so the word *dub* can also be translated as 'outstanding' and 'special.'

A dubplate was only pressed in vinyl if it was successful. Musically, the origins and sequences of reggae music have merged with today's electro music, resulting in a pulsating *dance music*, the *dub*.

Pay attention to the repartition of your hands and play the accents of the *left hand more ternary*, 'reggae-like.' The *right hand* continues to play the *straight quarter pulse* in the bass.

Dub grooves

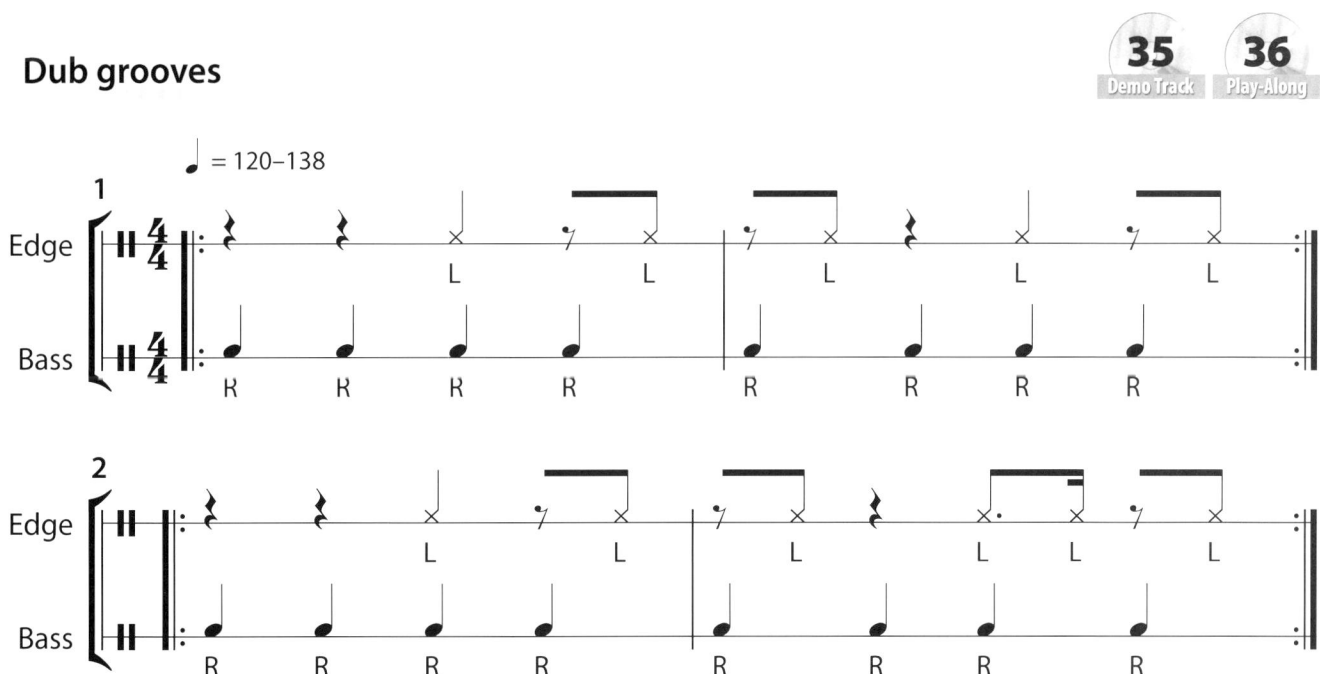

103

Rhythms from Spain

Spain, specifically the Andulsia region, may very well claim to have brought the cajón to Europe. *Flamenco* – a dance and its music that still have their home and tradition in the cities of Seville, Cadiz and Jerez – were the first stop of the cajón in Europe.

One of the stars of the flamenco scene **Paco de Lucia** brought back a cajón from a world tour in the early 1970s, which had also taken him to Peru. His percussionist **Rubem Dantas** recognized the advantages of the wooden box and appreciated its warm sound, which blended homogeneously with the instruments of flamenco such as classical guitar, flute, double bass, but also with the gaudy sound of the dancers' boot heels. Until that time, djembe, bongos, congas and also tablas were the percussion instruments preferred in flamenco. The cajón pushed them into the background and began its triumphal procession in Europe and worldwide.

I still know the cajón as the 'rumba box.' For a long time it lay dormant in the 'flamenco drawer' until its versatility and use in all imaginable styles was recognized. In my opinion, to this day, the accompanying instrumentation of a singer/songwriter – cajón meets acoustic guitar and bass – represents a wonderfully homogeneous unit in terms of sound that can hardly be surpassed.

Let's turn to some basic flamenco rhythms. I'll start with the **Rumba Flamenca** in $\frac{4}{4}$ time, which is not related to the South American Rumba. The **Gipsy Kings**, a French, Spanish-born *flamenco pop band* that was world famous in the 1980s and 1990s, introduced the timbres and atmosphere of flamenco with straight $\frac{4}{4}$ beats to a wide audience. They were undoubtedly the pop stars of flamenco that achieved world fame.

Rumba Flamenca

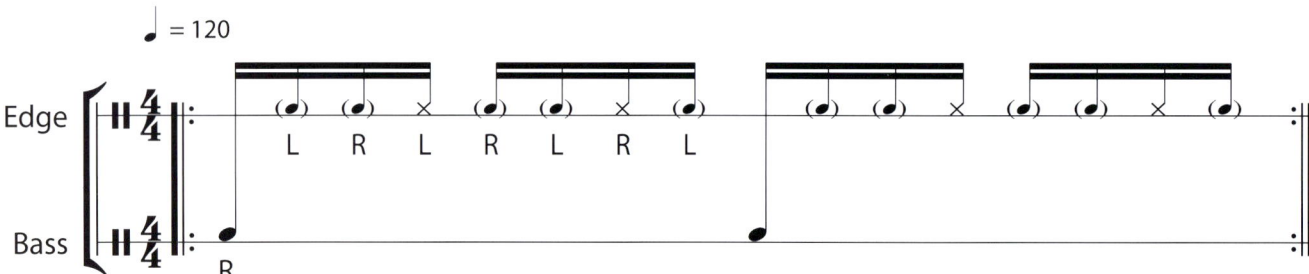

Also very popular is the **Tango Flamenco**, which is widely related to the *Argentine tango* of the same name because of the probable common roots. The biggest difference is in the dance. *Tango Flamenco* is a solo dance, while *Argentine Tango* is danced in pairs.

Tango Flamenco

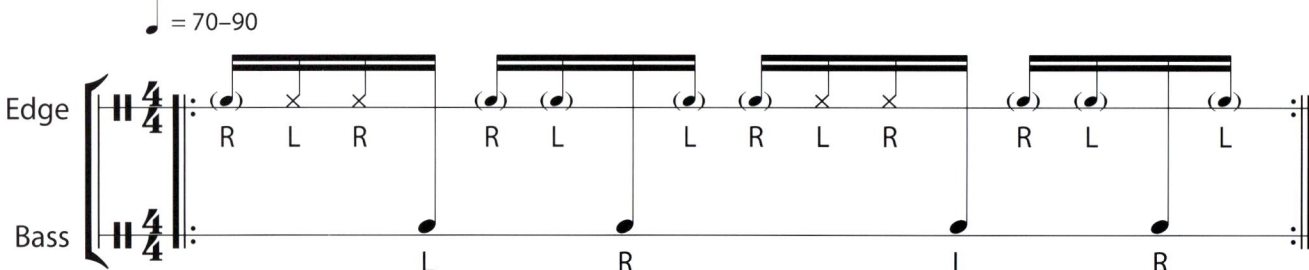

A dance in *triple meter* is the **Sevillanas**, which is often notated in $\frac{6}{4}$ time:

Sevillanas

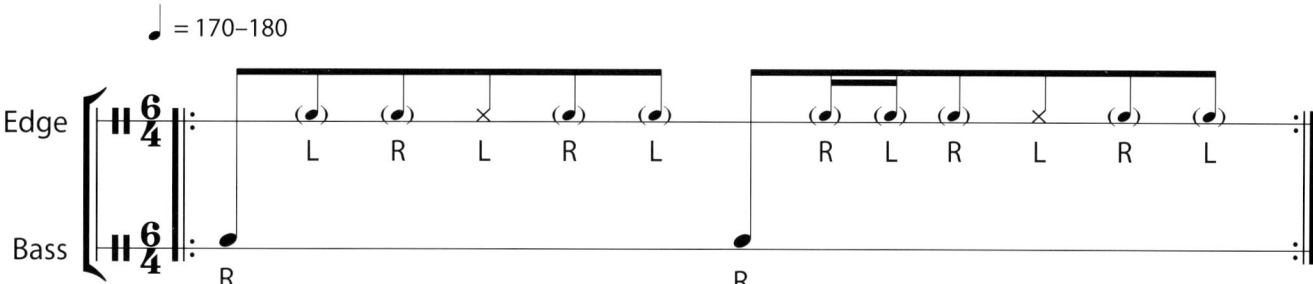

We will stay in the *triple meter*. I'll show you two of the original dance rhythms of flamenco.

In flamenco, we are very often oriented to a **12-beat cycle**, which looks like the *face of a clock*.

Compas

Let's start with the basic figure, the **Compas. Think in groups of 3 – 3 – 2 – 2 – 2:**

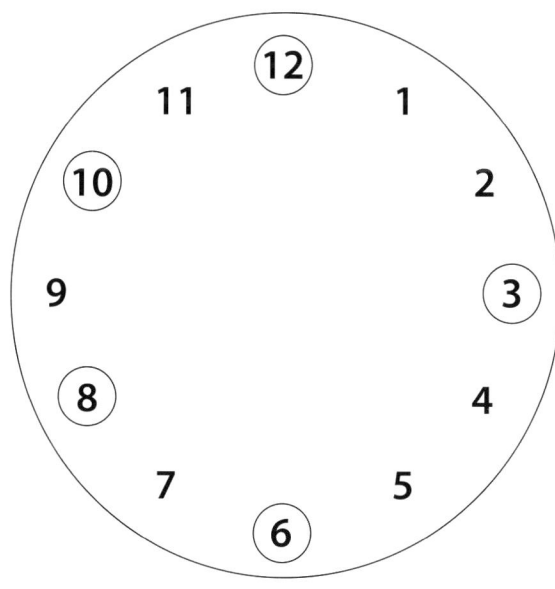

Buleria

Here is the **Buleria**:
Think in groups of 3 – 4 – 1 – 2 – 2:

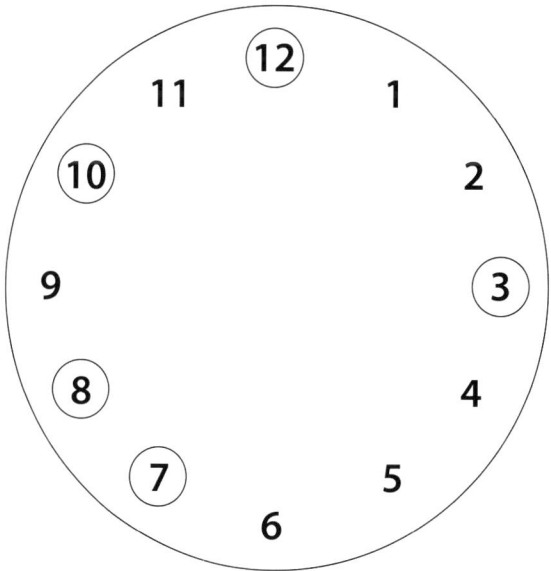

Always start at **12** and clap at *each of the 12 digits* until you reach the top of 12 again. Then clap the *accents* (*circled digits*) loudly (light) and the others softly (dark). Depending on the accent pattern, you will get different rhythms to accompany dances.

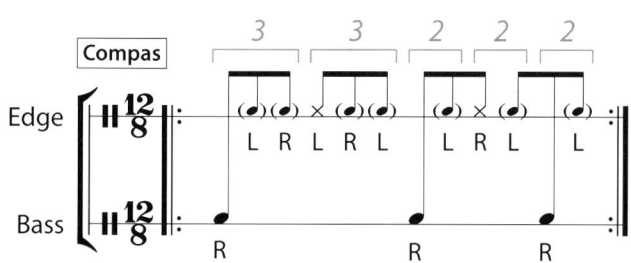

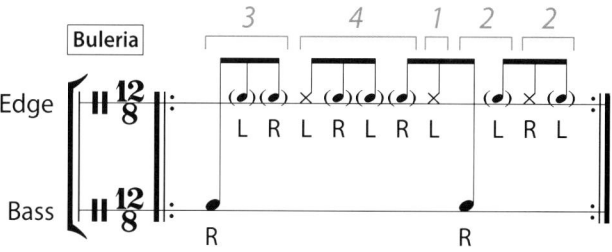

105

Part 3: Techniques & Phrasing

PART 3 is about playing techniques that have become established on the cajón, but originally come from other percussion instruments.

Floating Hand

This playing technique is adapted from the *conga*, the national instrument of Cuba. On the cajón, however, this technique is not performed with the hollow hand, but with the flat hand.

It is very important that you watch the **videos** to understand the exact movement and to practice correctly. Notes and symbols are only of limited help here – as they will be later with the split-hand technique (*see p. 115*).

Once you have internalized the sequence of movement, you will recognize the benefit of this technique very quickly, in the truest sense of the word a *flowing movement* that creates a smooth flow of movement – especially with fast stroke sequences. As with the tips, these are primarily *filling strokes*, which are important links between the more accented sounds of *bass tone, open tone*, and *slaps*. You're able to create *two strokes* with *one motion*, so you can effortlessly perform quick *double strokes*.

The **Floating Hand** (also called *Heel-Tip Motion* and *Heel-Beat Motion*) is a *rocking motion* from the palm to the fingertips. In a relaxed hand position, place your flat hand on the surface of the cajón with your thumb bent and fingers slightly spread. The movement sequence is as follows:

Online video 59

Step 1: Lift your **fingertips (T = tip)** from the surface, while your **palm (P = palm of your hand)** remains on the surface.

Step 2: Now drop the *fingertips* (T) onto the clubface. At the same time lift the *palm* (P) a little bit.

Step 3: Now tilt your *palm* (P) back onto the clubface. Your *fingertips* (T) return back to the starting position of *Step 1*.

In a figure-eight sequence, distribute the strokes as follows:

1, 2, 3, 4: The **palm (P)** strikes on the **main count times**.

1+, 2+, 3+, 4+: The **fingertips (T)** strike on the **minor counts**.

First, practice the *bass tone* in the floating hand technique with *right* and *left hand*.

If you don't have an instrument at hand, you can use a *flat playing surface (e.g. a tabletop)* to learn the movement.

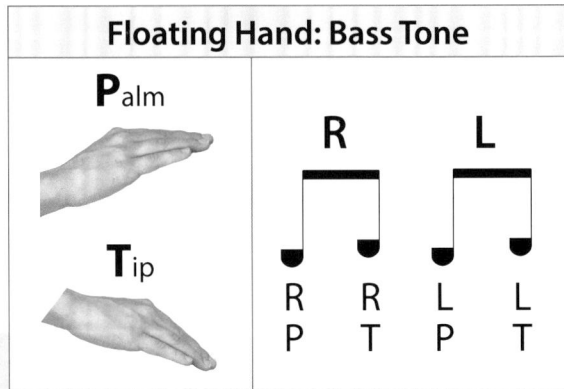

Floating Hand: Bass Tone

BASS Floating Hand: Basic exercise (R | L)

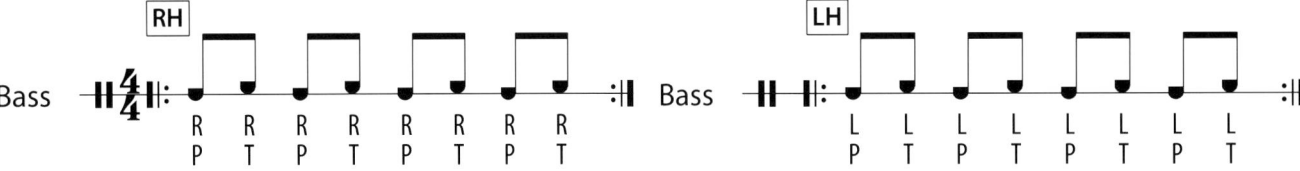

Now combine hand-to-hand strokes and floating hand in the bass:

BASS Floating Hand: R L and P T

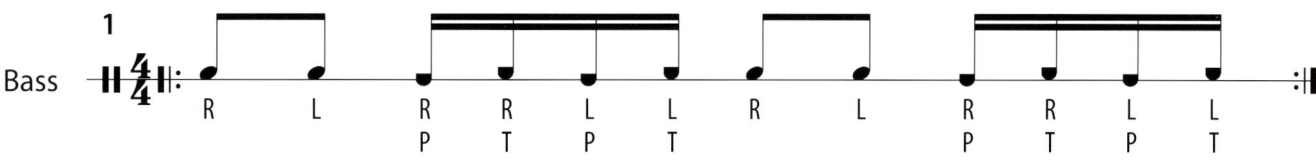

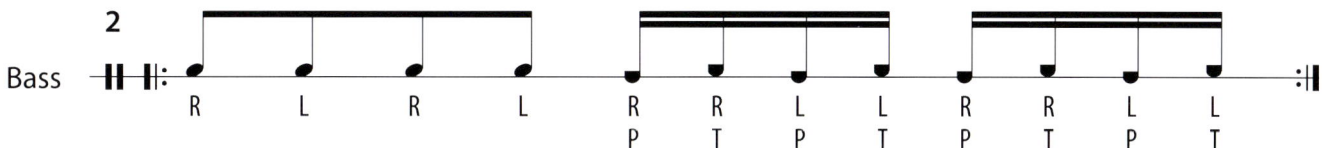

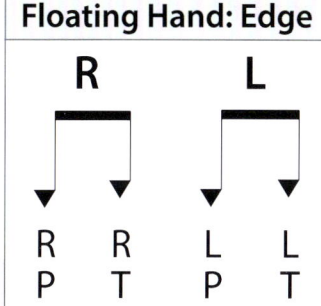

Now practice the *edge strokes* in the floating-hand technique with right and left hand.

Floating Hand at the EDGE: Basic exercise (R | L)

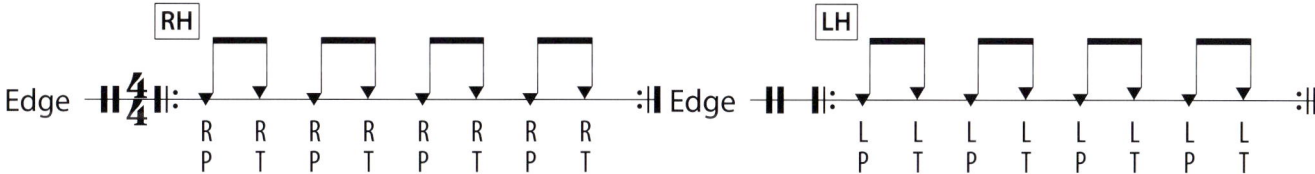

Here are two combinations of *hand-to-hand strokes* and *floating-hand double strokes* at the edge:

Floating Hand at the EDGE: R L and P T

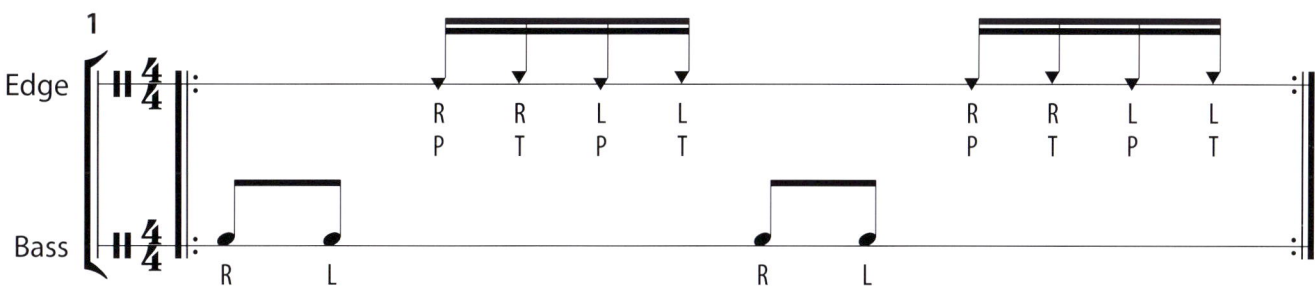

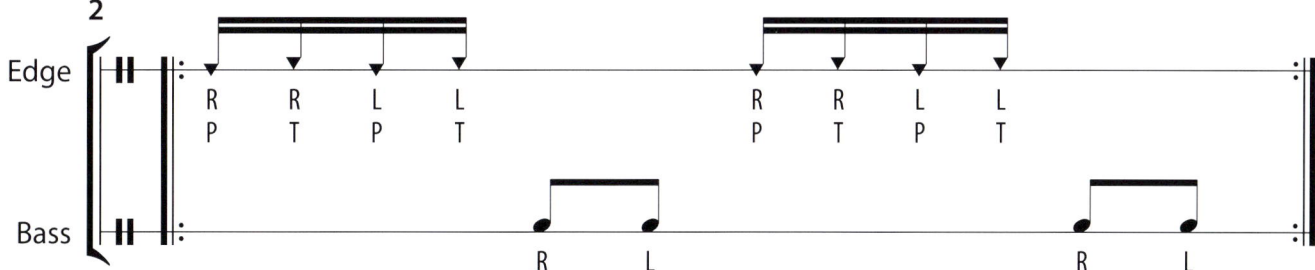

107

Now combine the basic groove with each of the floating-hand variations.

Play both modules once each:

Floating-Hand Variations 1–9

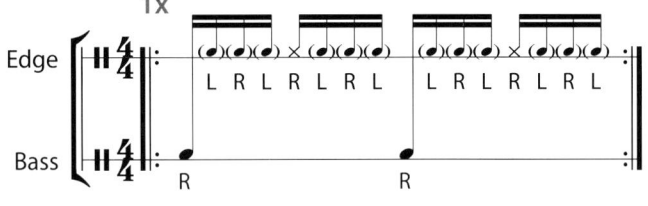

Basic groove

Choose an easy, clear 'melody' for the accents in the lead hand. Play around this accent melody with double strokes in the floating-hand technique – an idea that is especially suitable for solo playing or for discovering new fill variations.

Initial pattern (accent melody)

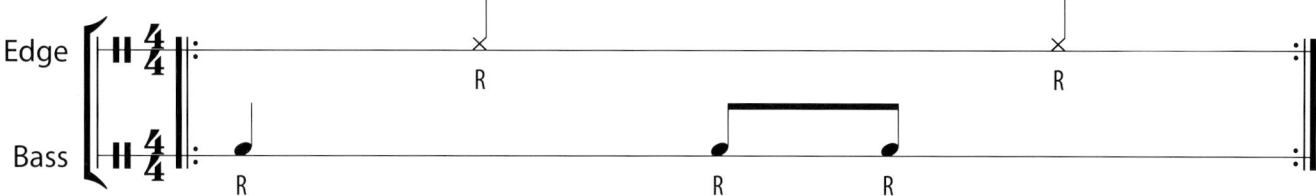

We choose *thirty-second notes* (*32nd notes, see also p. 90*) to play around the 'melody' by using fast double strokes. Two 32nd notes are exactly as long as a sixteenth note, and four are as long as an eighth note. Thus, thirty-two 32nd notes fit into one $\frac{4}{4}$ bar. The same applies, of course, to the thirty-second rests. Successive 32nd notes are connected with **three bars**.

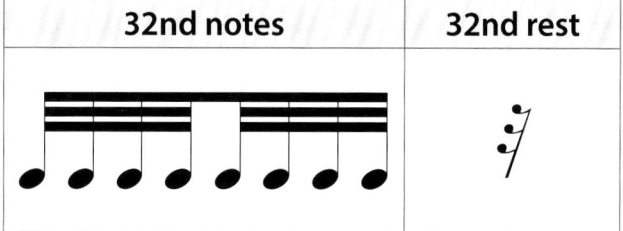

Now play around the accent melody with the 32nd note fills. Your left hand always stays at the edge of the cajón in this example:

Floating Hand using 32nd notes (Playing around the accent melody)

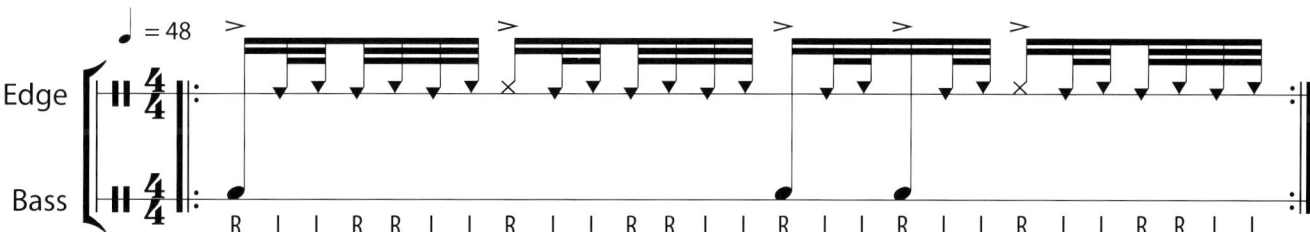

IMPORTANT:
Practice slowly (bpm = 48) and evenly!

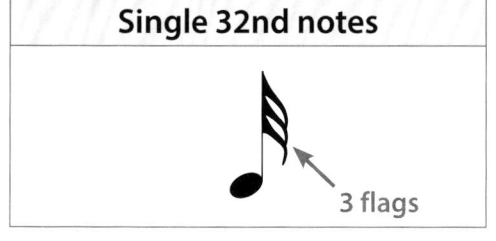

32nd notes that occur *singly* are notated with **three flags** instead of three bars.

Proceed in the same way with the following 'melodies'. Play around the eighth notes with thirty-second notes and the quarter notes with sixteenth notes in the bass and at the edge of the cajón:

Accent melodies with Floating Hand: Play-arounds (Initial patterns)

The *accented strokes* (bass and slaps) are always performed by your *leading hand*. The double strokes are always executed by one hand in the **P T** rocking motion.

Floating Hand: Playing around (Fill in your own play-arounds 2–7)

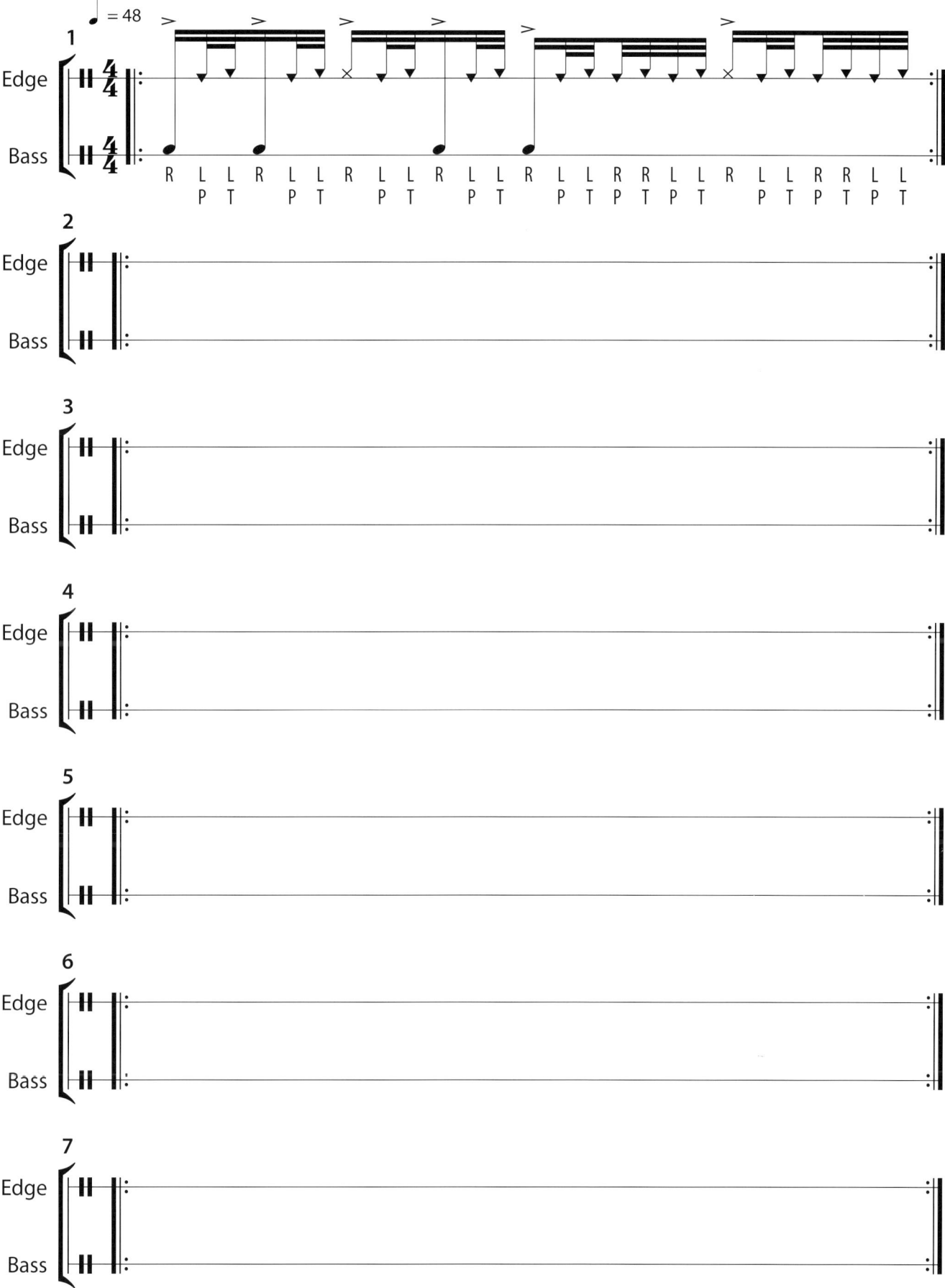

Now the stickings change. The hands run into each other, a different sound is created and especially for the *samba* (*see below*) a really authentic pattern is created. You can see how much stickings affect the movement and the sound when you play the two exercises **R R L L** and **R L R L** *in alternation*. First practice in the bass as it is easier to learn the movement:

Floating Hand: Play-arounds (R R L L | R L R L alternating)

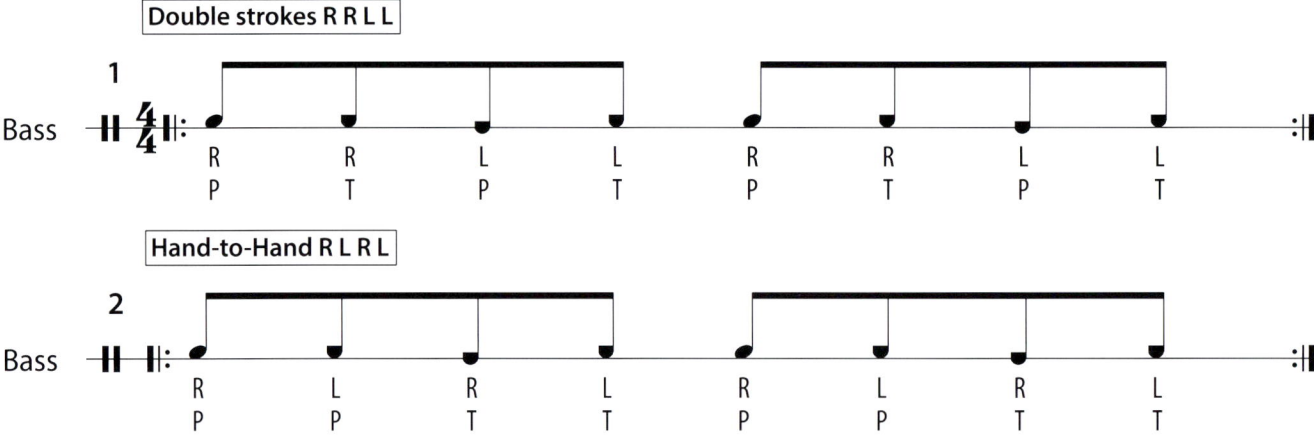

Integrate the new movement into your playing ...

... as a **groove**:

Floating Hand: Groove integration (R L R L)

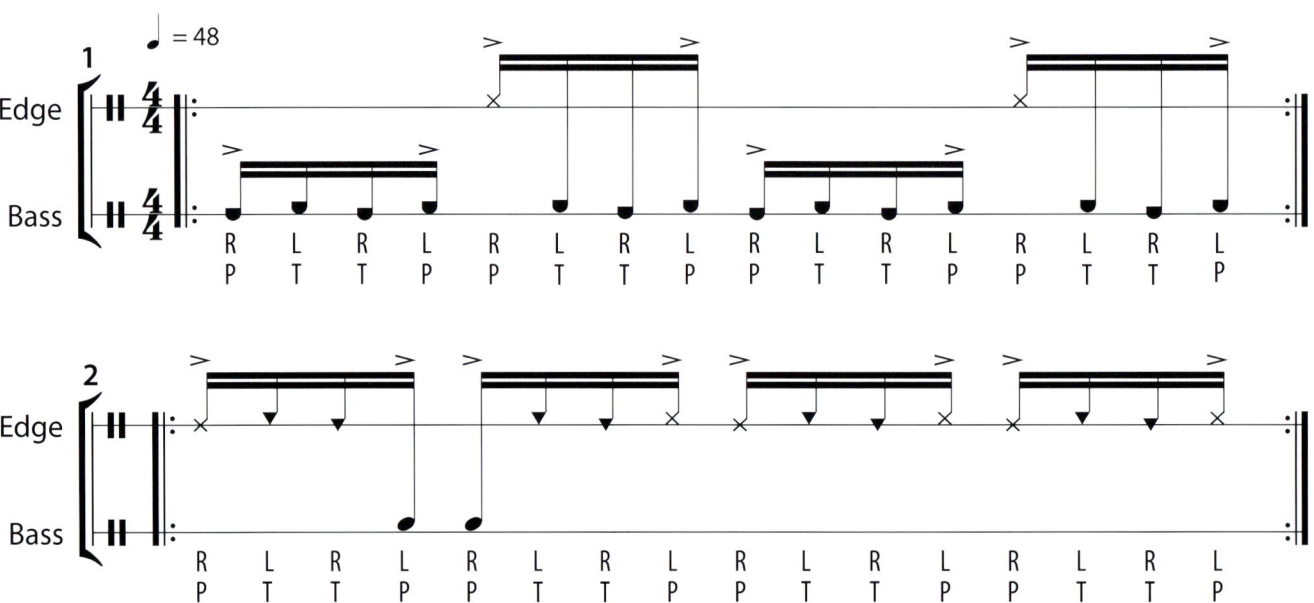

> **IMPORTANT:**
> *Practice slowly (bpm = 48) and evenly!*

... as traditional **samba pattern**:

Floating Hand: Samba

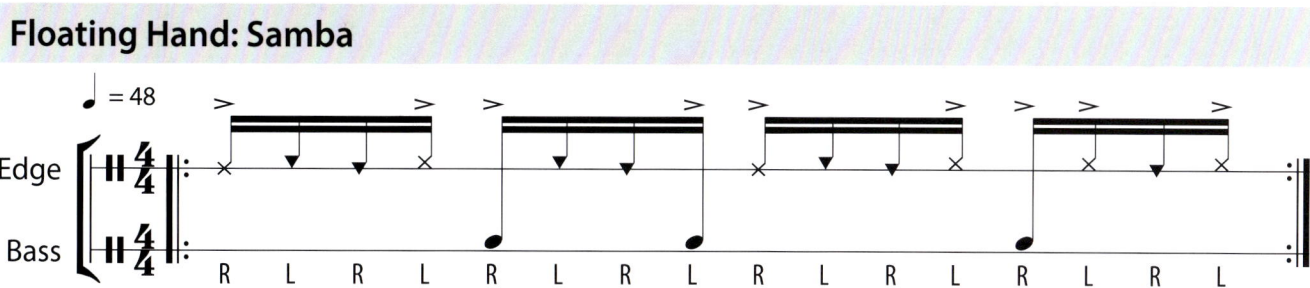

... as **Short Rolls**, here an example showing the adaption into rhythm:

Short Roll

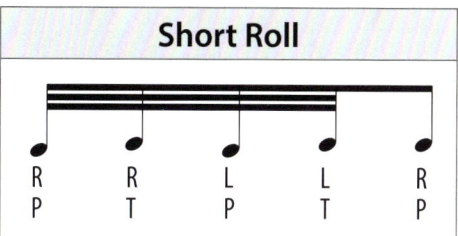

Floating Hand: Short Roll

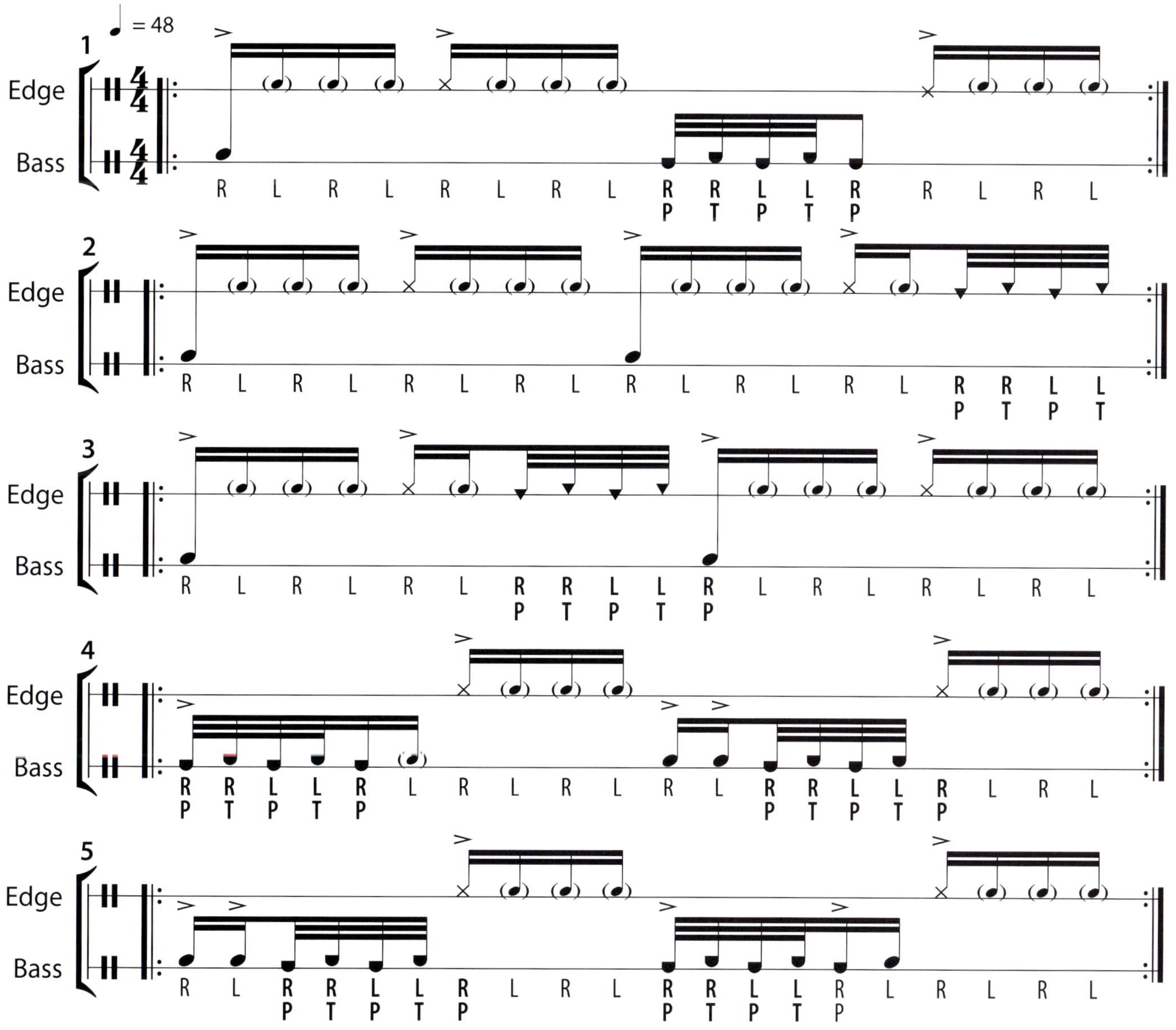

Floating Hand: Ternary

The *Floating Hand*, of course, also works in a *ternary* context, i.e. with triplets and sixtuplets and their adaptation into rhythms.

At first sight, the sixtuplet seems to consist of two triplets. The triplet, however, has an – albeit weak – accent on the first eighth of the triplet, so that you can distinguish between successive triplets. The sixtuplet does not have this accent on its fourth note.

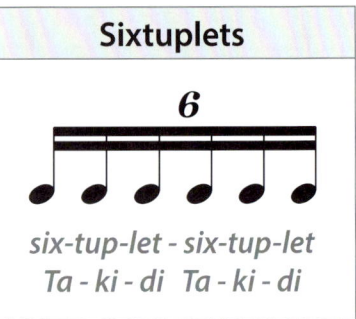

Sixtuplets

six-tup-let - six-tup-let
Ta - ki - di   Ta - ki - di

Practice the modules individually and then combine them with the starting pattern:

Floating Hand: Initial pattern (sixtuplet-double strokes)

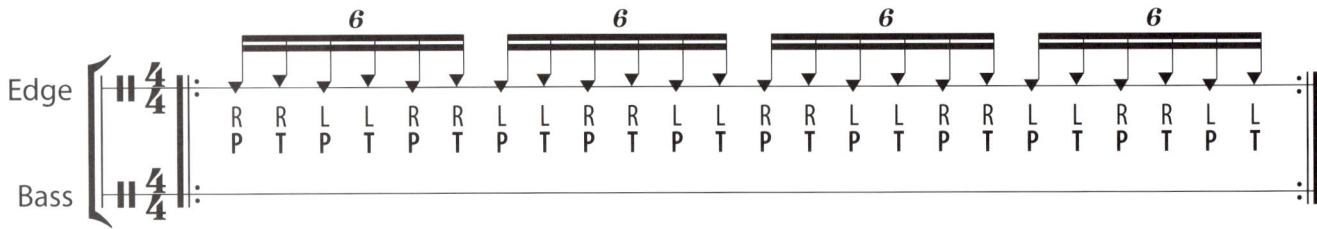

Floating Hand: Modules (ternary)

114

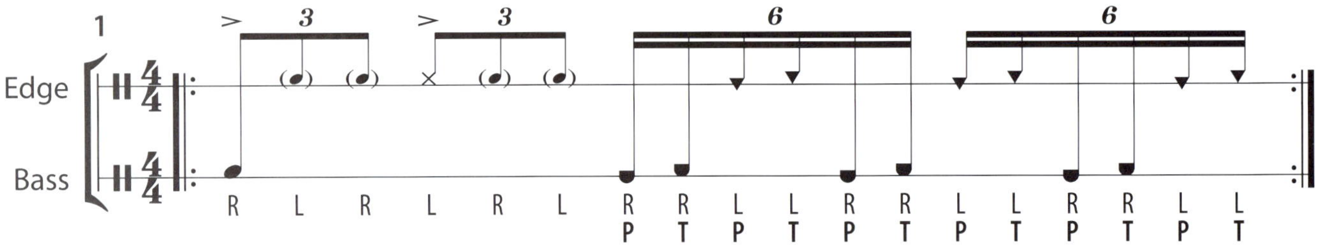

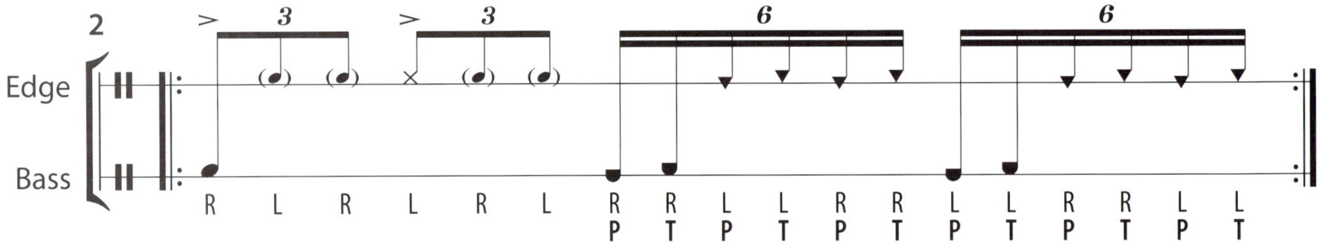

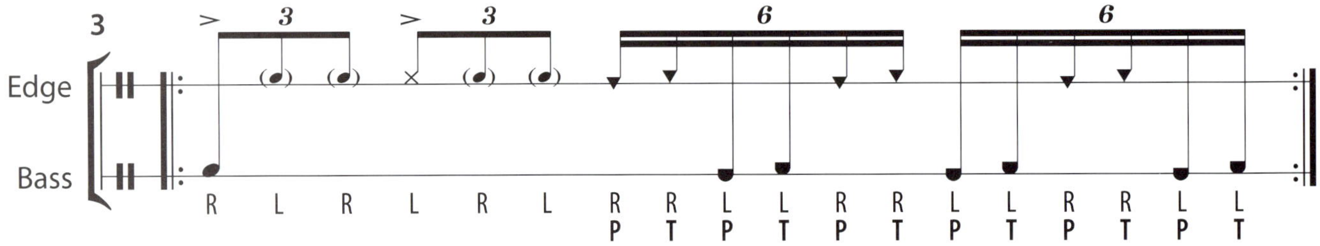

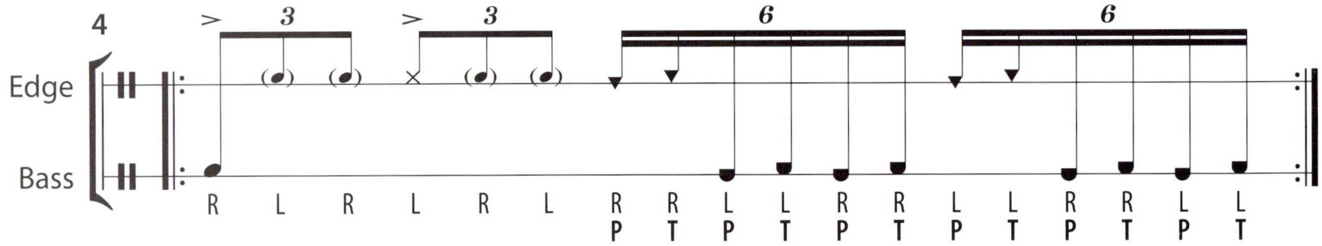

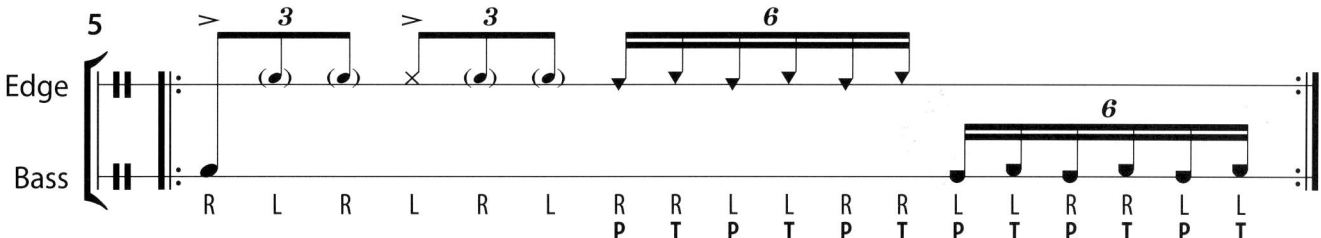

Split Hand

This very fine and virtuosic playing technique comes from the *frame drum* and the *Darabouka* (*cup drum from Arabic North Africa*) and was introduced to me by Jürgen Schuld, a fantastic percussionist and dear friend.

> **IMPORTANT:**
>
> *Watch the video first and then start the exercises.*

Online video 60

Basically, you can play all the exercises shown for the *Floating Hand* (*starting from p. 106*) with the Split Hand as well – with one big difference. The **Split Hand** only works if you have a *pivot point*, i.e. an edge or a skin edge. That's why you play this technique **only on the edge of the cajón**. Your hand is turned sideways in its longitudinal axis, so that you strike to one side with the *index finger* and to the other side with the *ring finger*. For this, your fingers must be *stretched* and your wrist must remain *stiff*.

Practice each line separately at a slow tempo (60 bpm).

Pay attention to even volume and always start with the turn to the *index finger* (i = *index finger*). The second stroke is on the *ring finger* (a = *anular finger*).

Then play all three lines one after the other in one go.

Split Hand: Edge

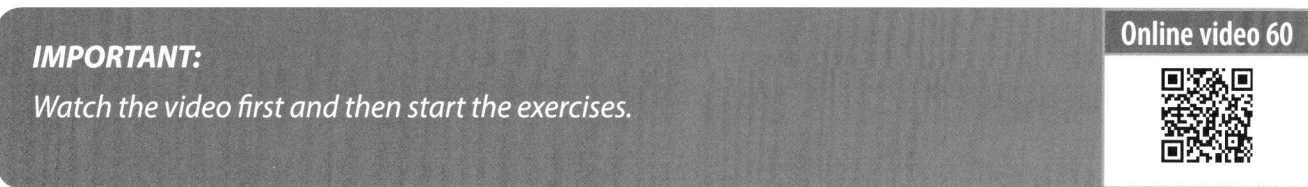

Split Hand: Preliminary exercises

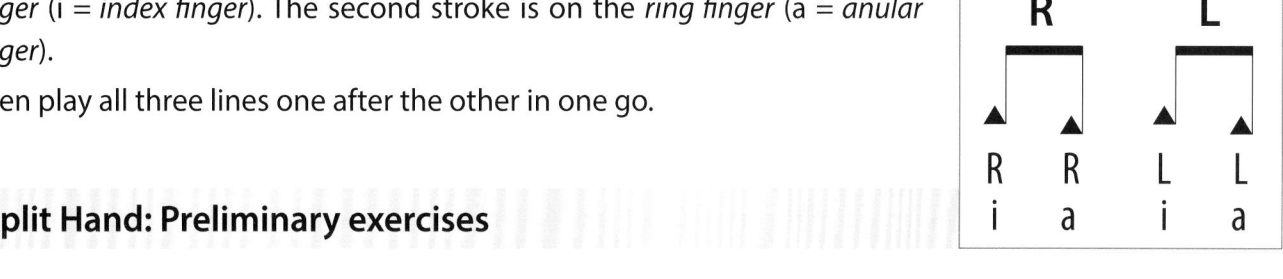

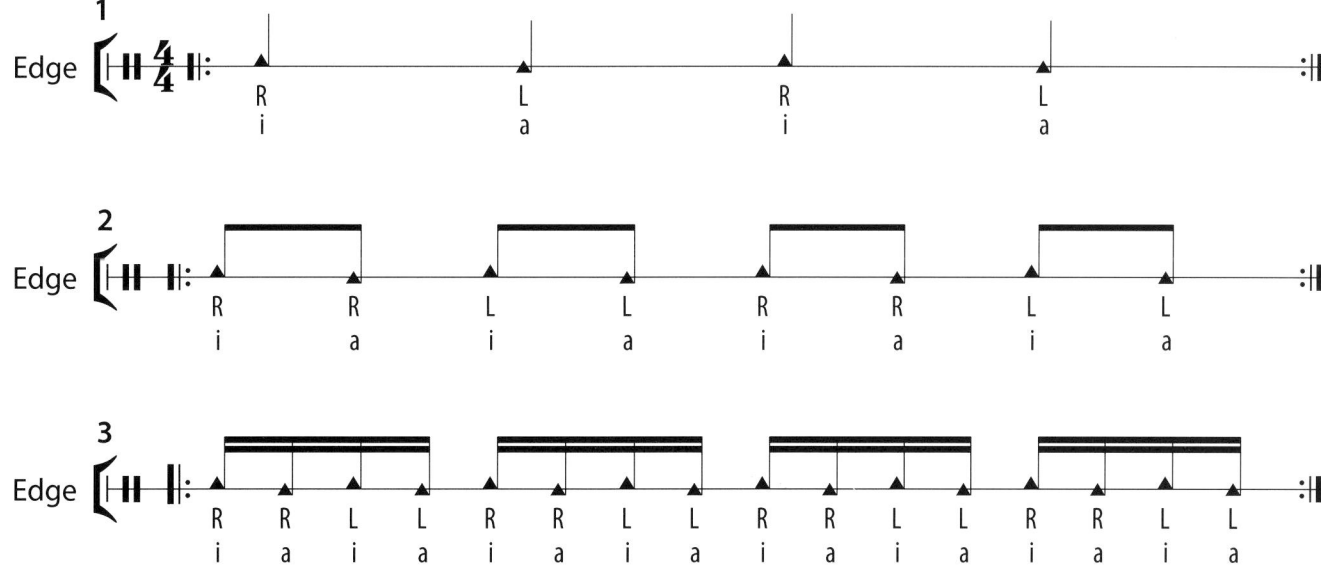

As soon as you have mastered this technique (*okay: you learn your whole life*), and the fingers start to 'run', begin with a **'call & response' game**. Give yourself a rhythm melody in common playing style, the example here is the *Son Clave* as the basic figure of Cuban music (*see p. 36*).

First, play the clave with **R L-stickings** on the cajón as a so-called **call**:

Split Hand: Son Clave 3/2 (Call)

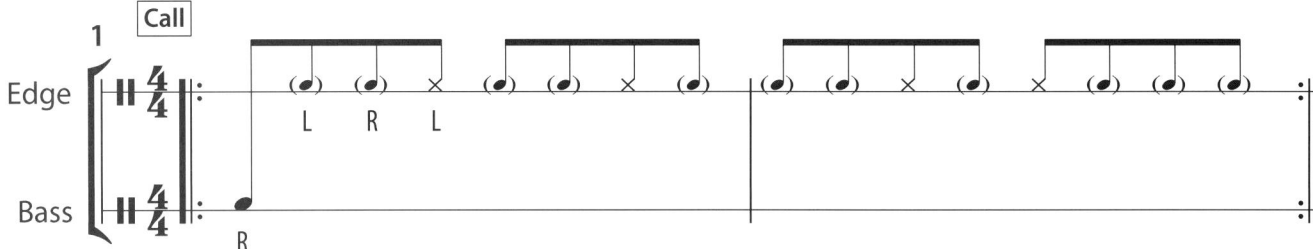

You build the accents of this rhythm melody into the double-fill strokes of the split-hand technique *on the edge of the cajón* by integrating them into the **R R L L**-sticking (**Response**).

Split Hand (Double strokes as response)

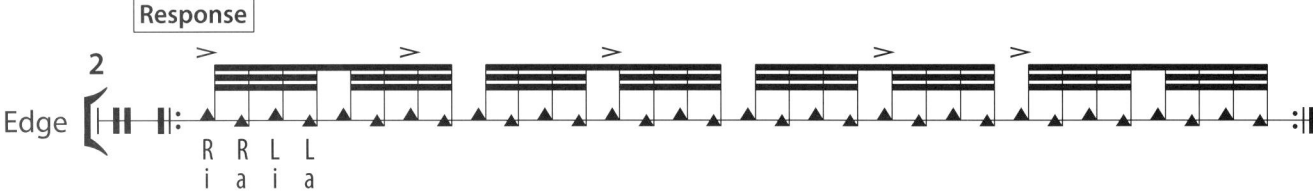

This *call and response* method is a very common practice to solo and to give the solo a common thread – here the accents of the *Son Clave 3/2*. Below are some more *basic traditional patterns* and their implementation with the split hand.

Split Hand: Soca (SoulCalypso, originally from Trinidad Tobago)

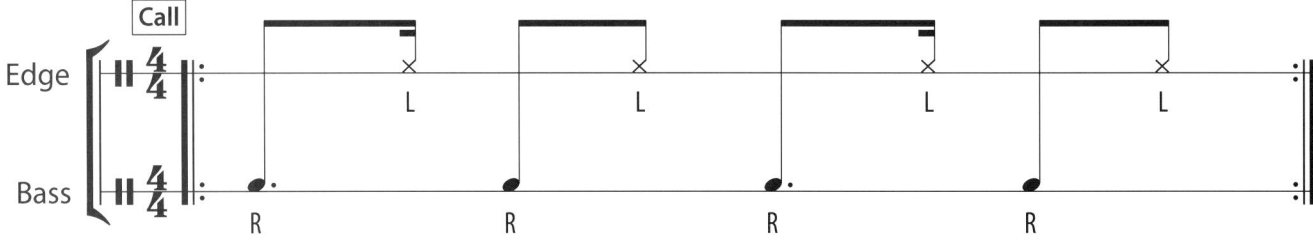

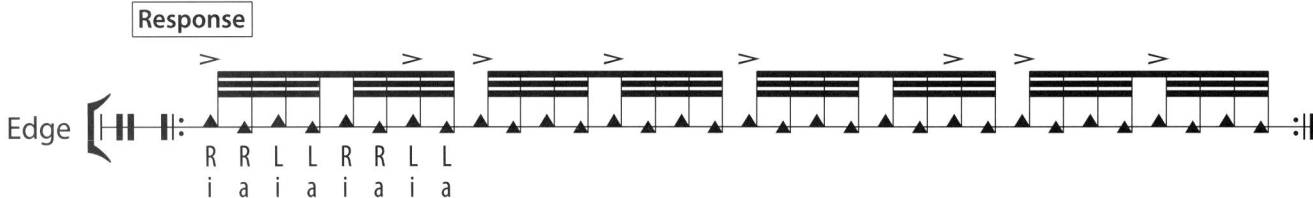

116

Split Hand: Maksum (original rhythm from Egypt played on the darabouka)

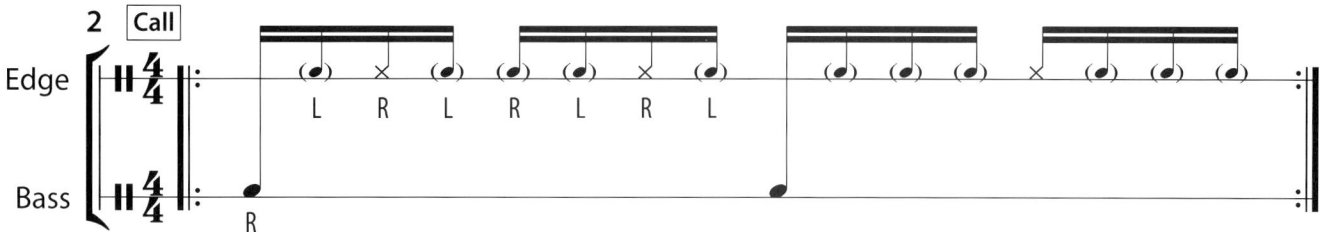

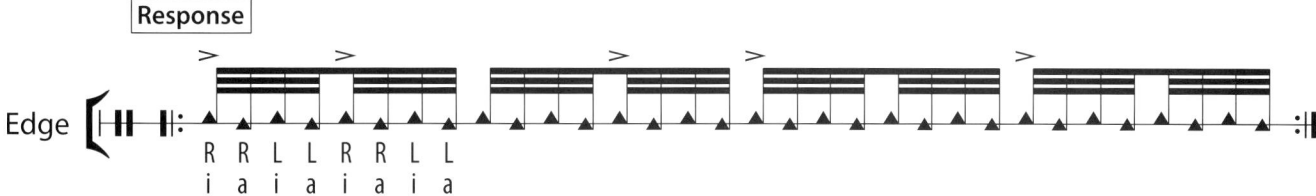

Split Hand: Samba Clave (originally from Brazil)

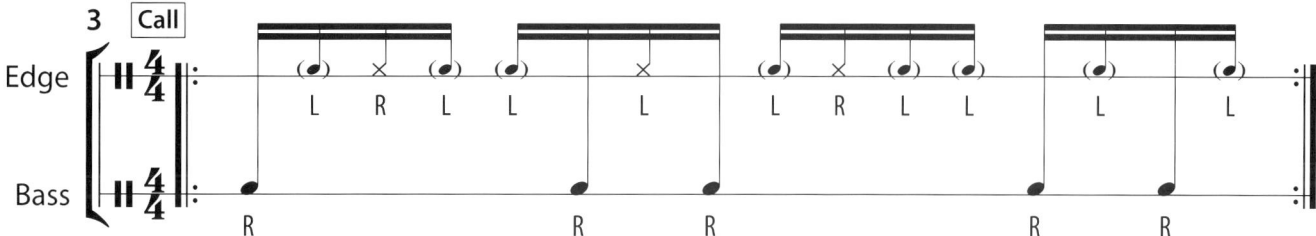

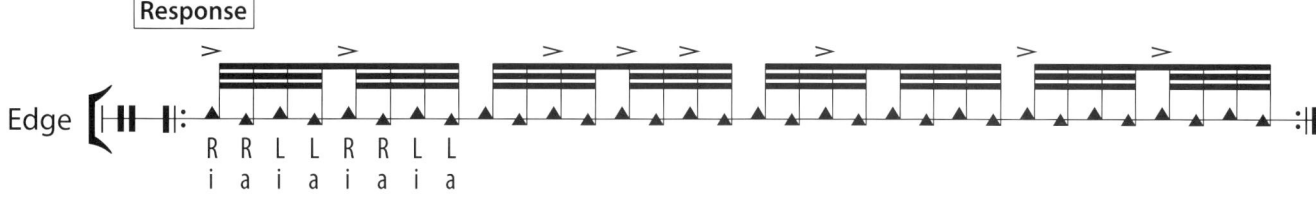

Split Hand: Bossa Clave (originally from Brazil)

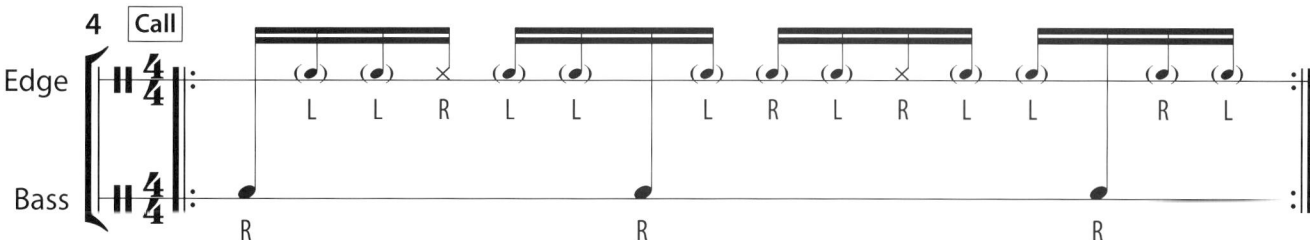

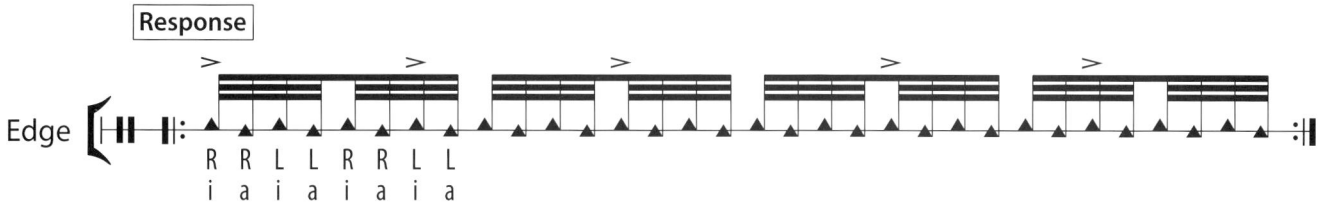

Split Hand: Ternary

Of course, the same *split-hand conception* works in a *ternary context*, i.e., *triplets* and *sixtuplets* and their adaptation into rhythms. Play the following three preliminary exercises first:

Split Hand: Preliminary exercises with short fingerrolls

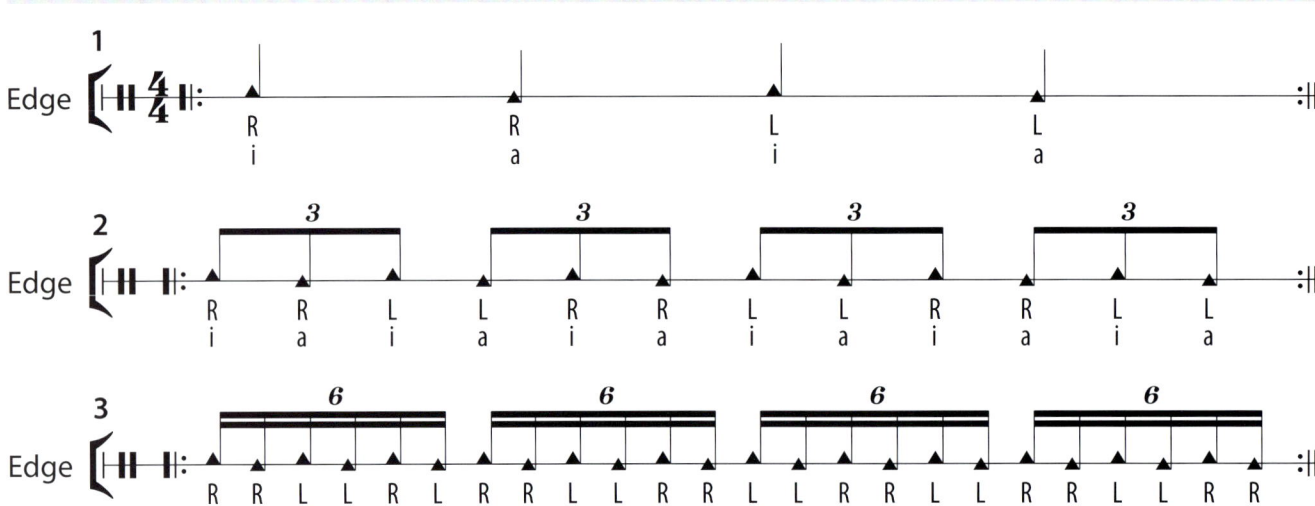

Split Hand: Ternary (Call & Response 1)

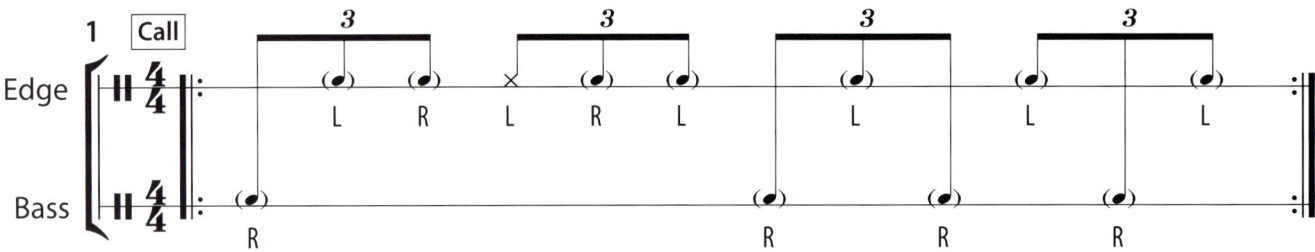

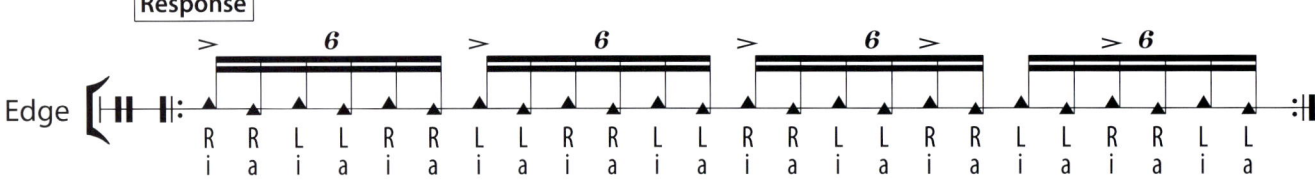

Split Hand: Ternary (Call & Response 2)

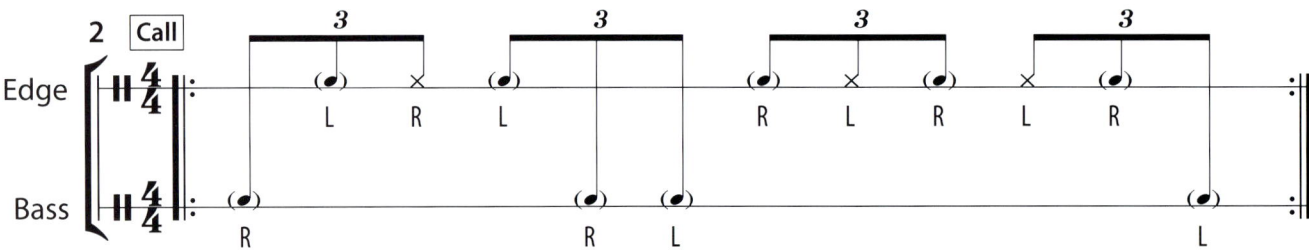

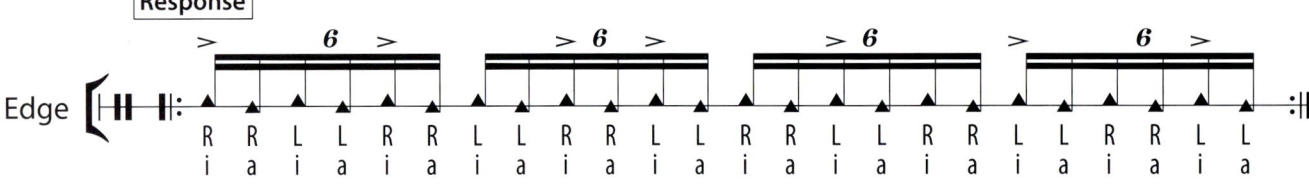

Now start with the **short rolls** that make your grooves sound special.

Step 1: First practice each note line separately.

Step 2: Then play both lines in succession.

In both steps, make sure the volume is even and the sequence is always the same:

First *index finger* (**i**), then *ring finger* (**a**).

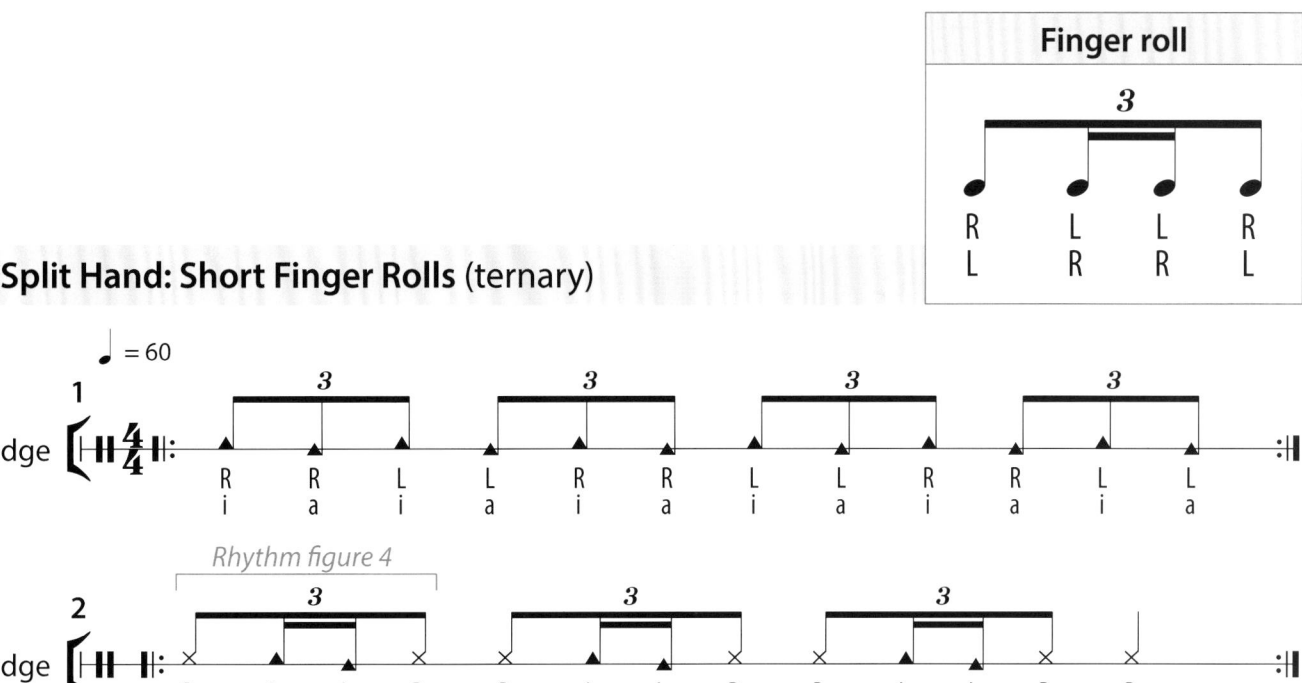

Split Hand: Short Finger Rolls (ternary)

Transfer the same to five strokes, called **5-stroke rolls**:

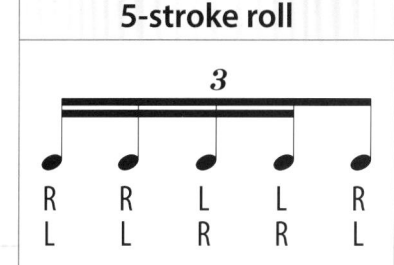

Split Hand: 5-Stroke Rolls (ternary)

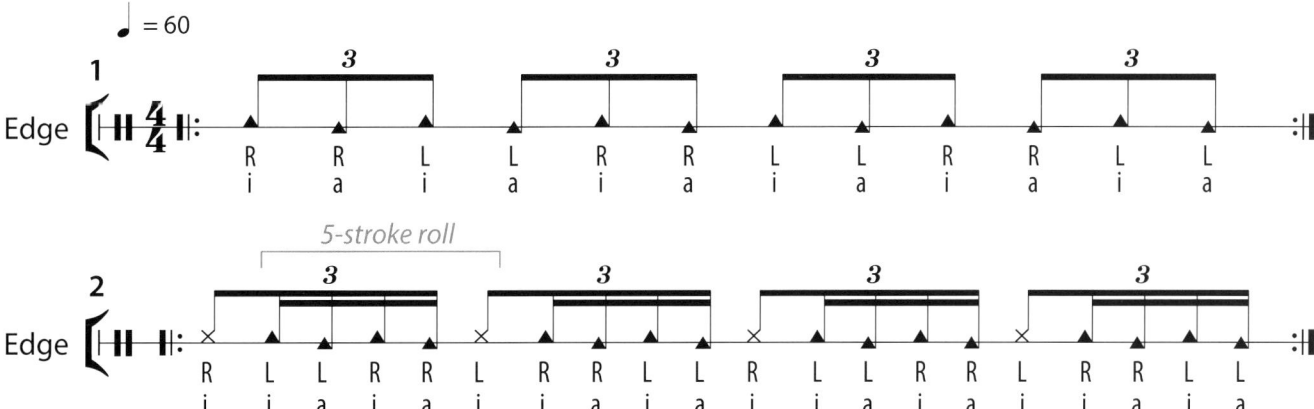

119

And with seven strokes, the so-called **7-stroke rolls**:

Split Hand: 7-Stroke Rolls (binary)

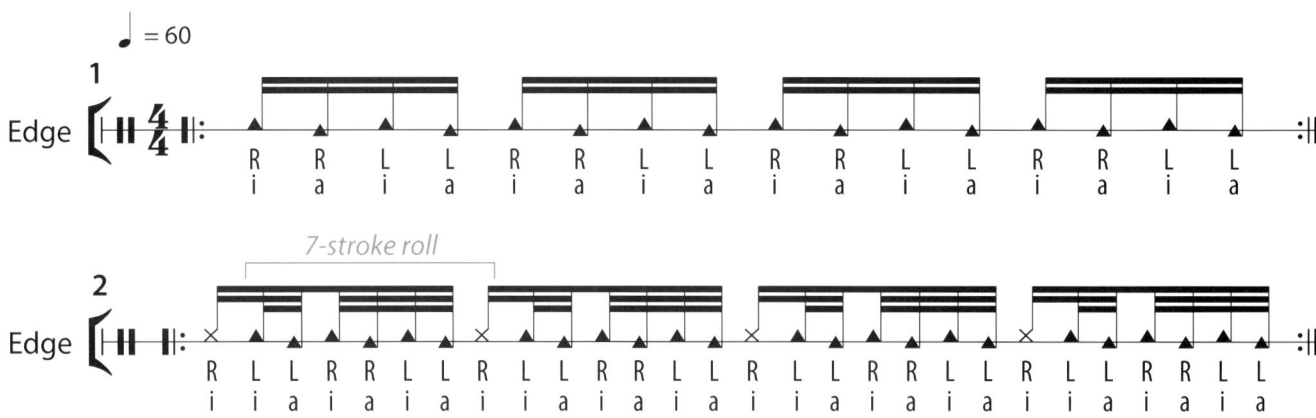

Now you incorporate these rolls into grooves:

Split-Hand grooves using rolls

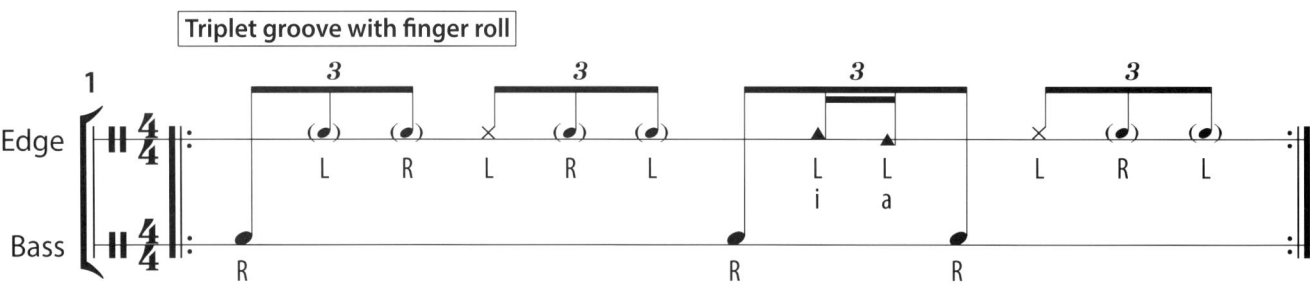

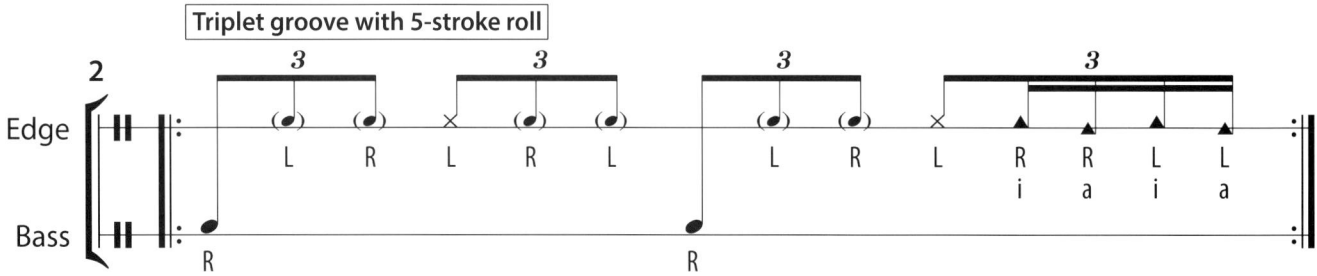

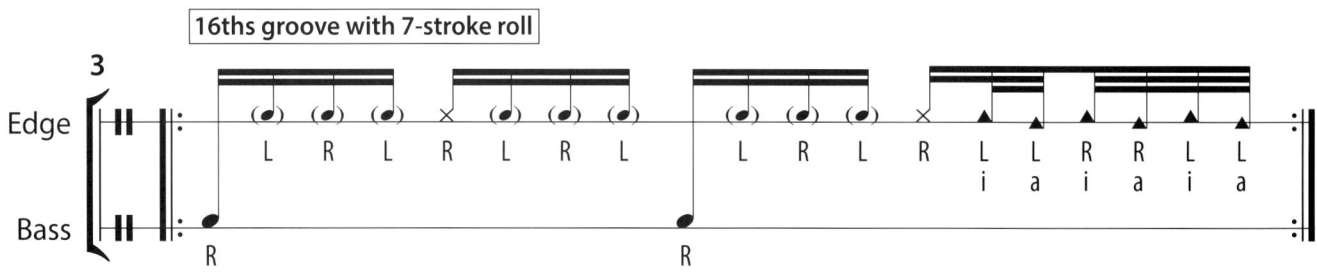

120

Combinations of Floating and Split Hand

Now it's time to *mix it up*!

Combine floating hand and split hand technique. There are no limits to your creativity. I have chosen the tonally largest distance for the following exercises, i.e.:

The *leading hand* plays **floating hand** in the bass, while the other hand contrasts finely, at the outermost edge with the **split hand.**

Preliminary combination exercises

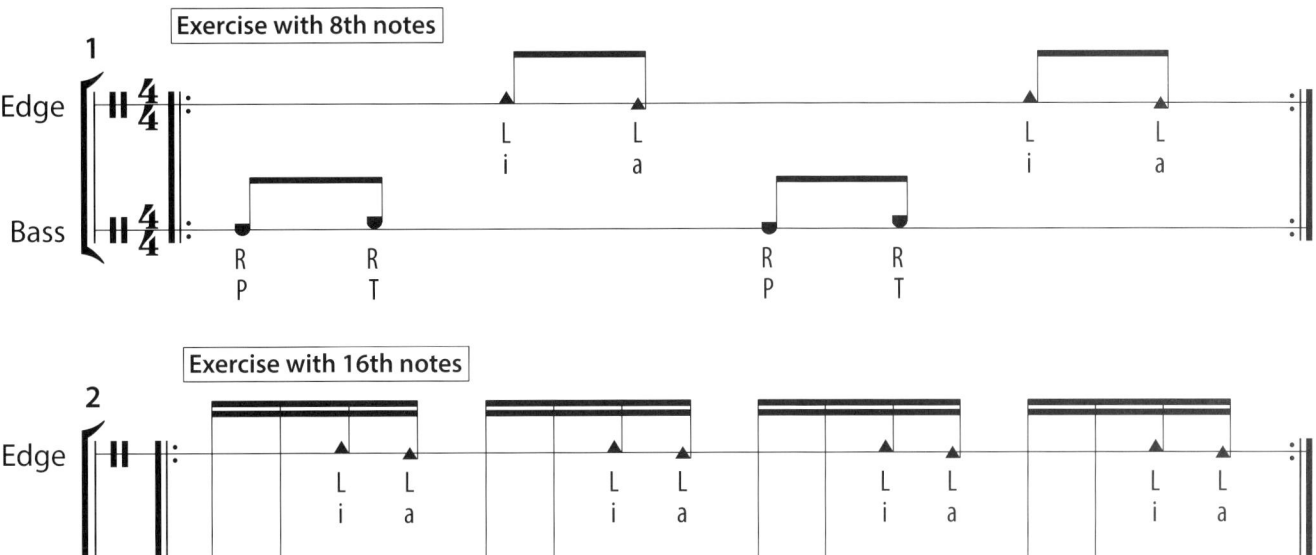

And again, the use of **short rolls** in a groove:

Online video 61

Grooves using Floating/Split-Hand combinations

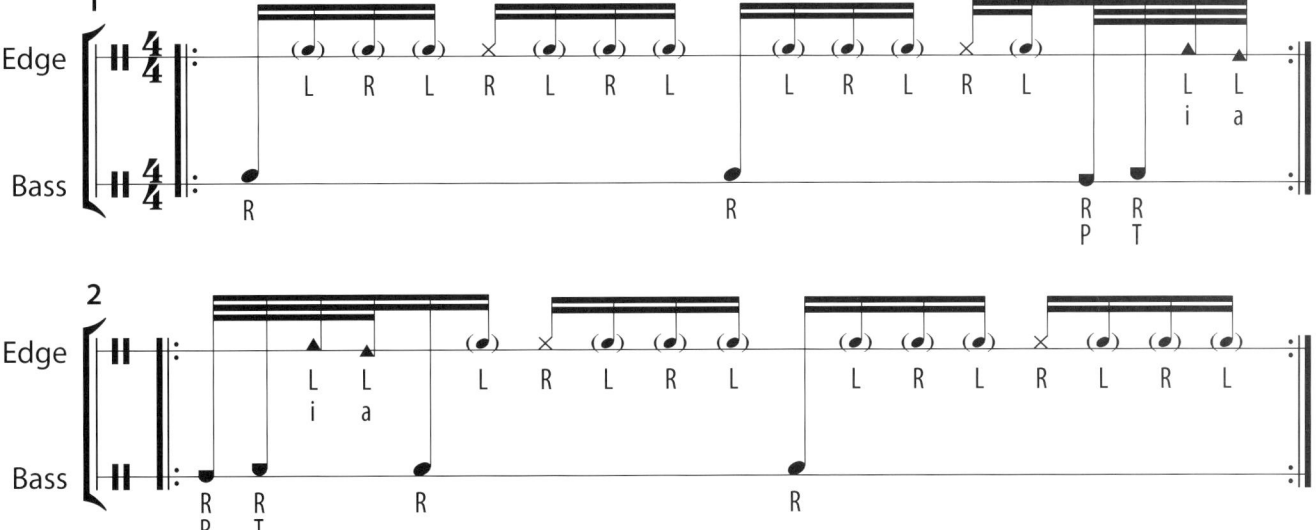

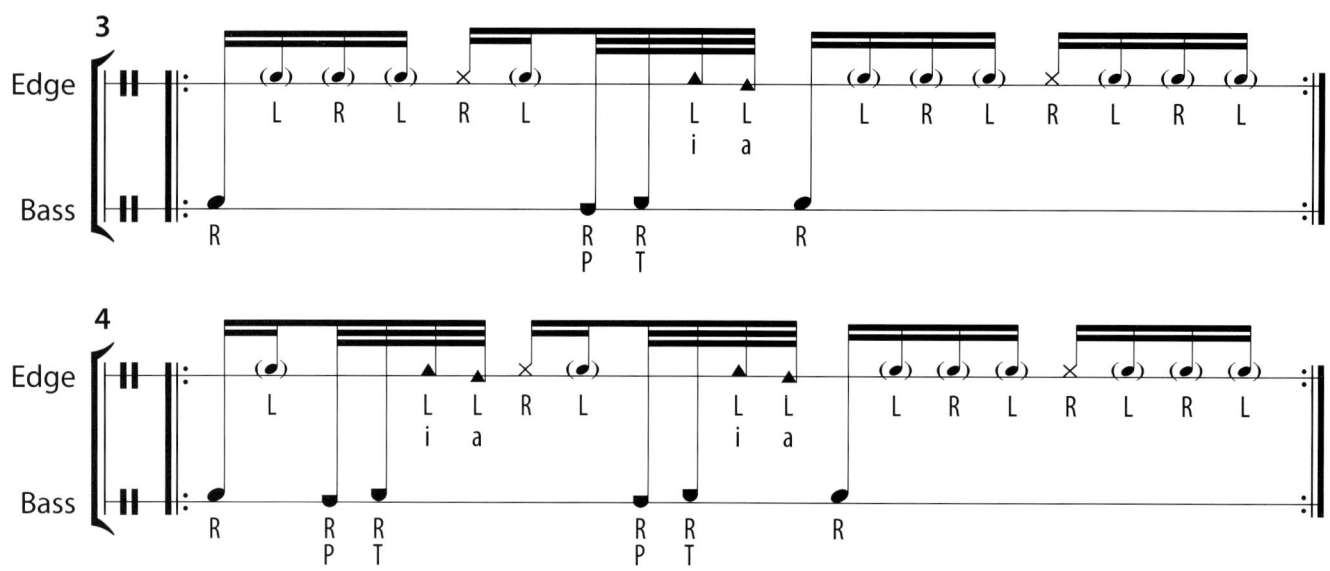

And again as *Samba basic pattern* with Floating Hand and Split Hand:

Samba basic pattern using Floating/Split combinations

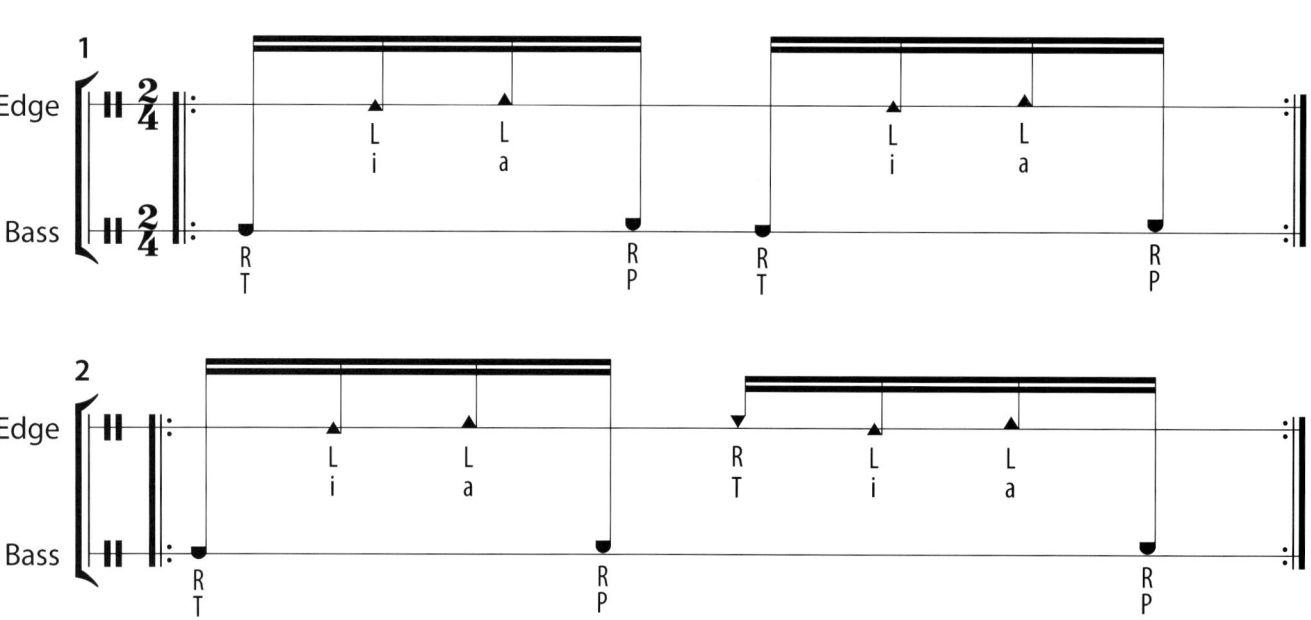

Phrasing

As a rhythmist, phrasing means:

1. I want to express myself individually on the instrument, to develop a personality that can be heard and that distinguishes me from other musicians.

2. I want to play authentic rhythms from all over the world, so that every listener recognizes: 'This is a samba, this is a hip hop groove, this is reggae, funk, R&B' etc.

This will be a life long learning process that will require listening to a variety of music and attempting to play along even if, at first, you fail miserably. That's the only way I learned to phrase. I'd like to explain this to you using a simple method.

Binary and ternary phrasing

Start with a *binary*, i.e. straight eighth-note figure at the *edge of the cajón*.

Sticking: hand-to-hand, tempo = 60 bpm.

8th-notes pattern (binary)

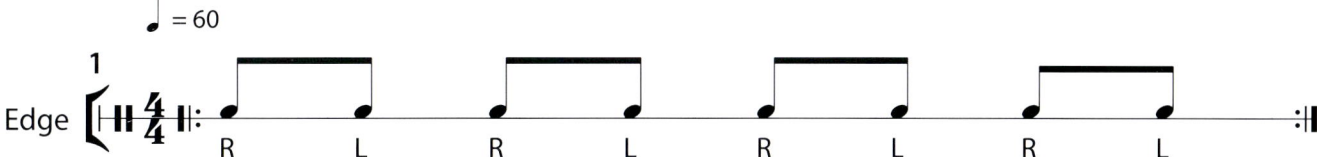

With the *second exercise*, you play the same eighth-note sequence *ternary in the shuffle feel* (*see also p. 77*). The sticking is still **R L** or **L R**, but the pattern 'bounces':

8th-notes pattern (ternary in shuffle feel)

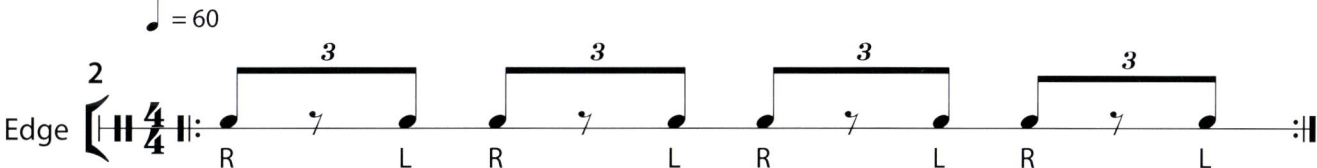

123

> **IMPORTANT:**
> *On the video I play the binary pattern first and then the ternary one.*
> *This sets the two corner points ... binary – ternary.*

Country becomes Gospel

This also works when applied to bass and edge:

The *first groove* is a **classic country** that is played *binary*.

Online video 62

Country groove (binary)

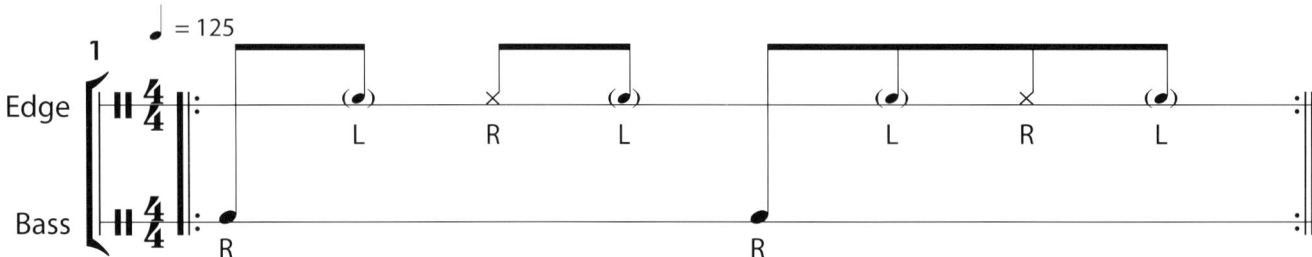

If you take over hand stickings, movement, and pulse and play the same pattern *ternary*, you get a *gospel* with a wonderful 'swing feel'.

Gospel groove (ternary in swing feel)

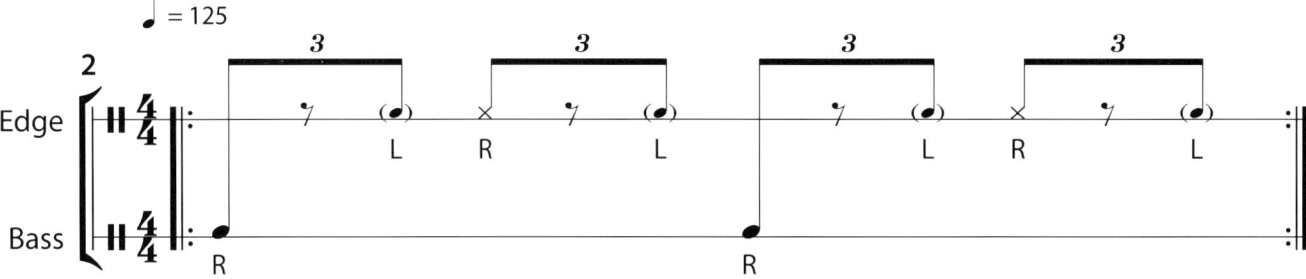

This concept: the same figure, the same movement (bass and edge) and the same stickings, but changing phrasing (*binary – ternary*) gives you a multitude of possibilities and also means that you have to master a rhythm in its playing style, but you can always use it twice and thus serve very different styles ...

124

... for example:

Online video 63

Medium Rock becomes Hip Hop

Medium Rock (binary)

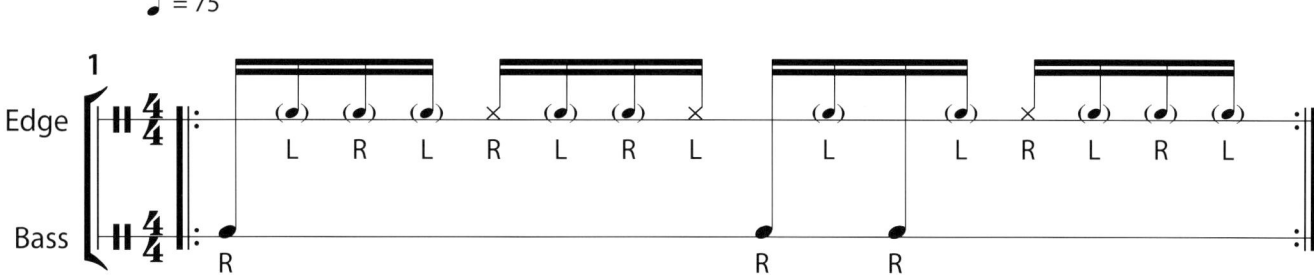

Hip Hop (ternary)

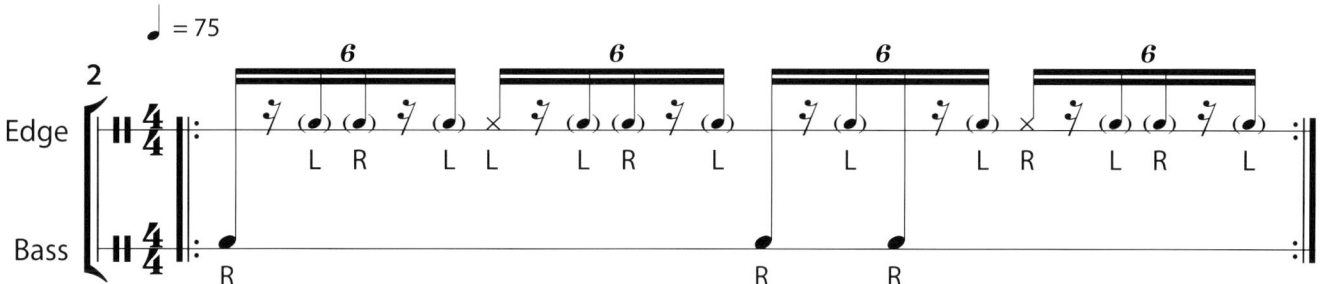

Son Clave 3/2 becomes New Orleans

Online video 64

Son Clave 3/2 (binary)

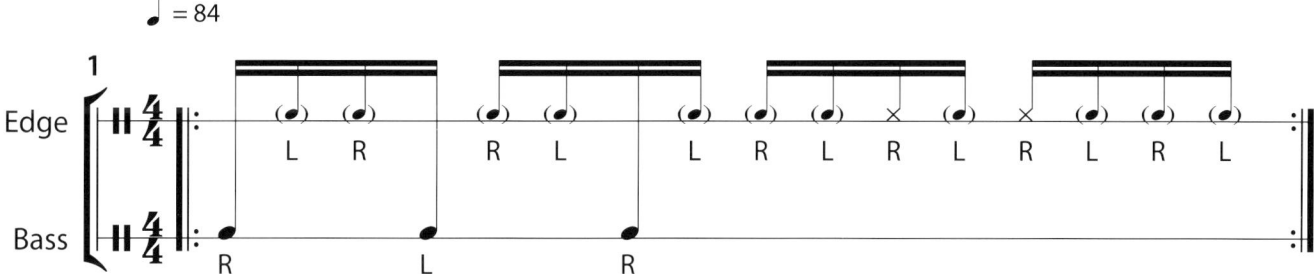

New Orleans (ternary)

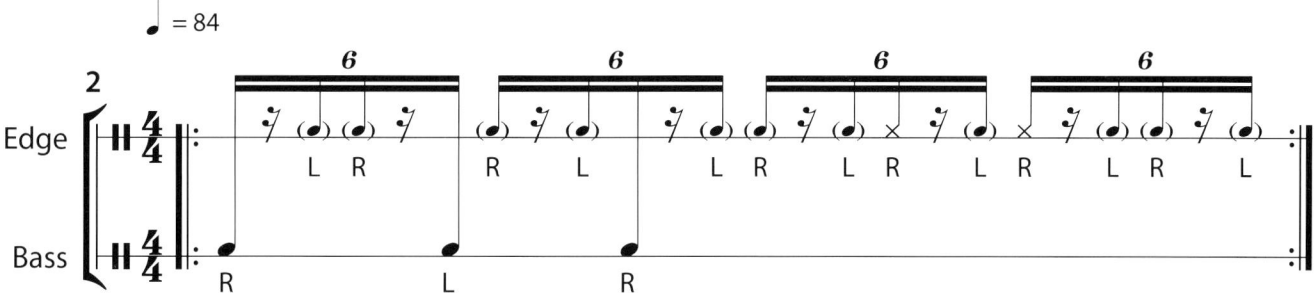

Online video 65

IMPORTANT:
Now it's getting more nuanced and I advise you to watch the video first where I start with the binary rhythm, then become more and more ternary until I finally end up in the shuffle.

This 'gray area' between binary and ternary playing is what we need in order to play, for example, authentic Brazilian music. Here it is no longer a matter of '2' (binary), but not yet of '3' (ternary).

I would like to illustrate this with the example of the *surdo*, the bass drum pattern in bossa and samba (*see p. 85*):

Your *leading hand* plays the upbeat bass, i.e. the beat on the pulse is always slightly louder (*see accent mark*) than the one on the fourth sixteenth note, just like the *heartbeat*.

Surdo Bass pattern (binary)

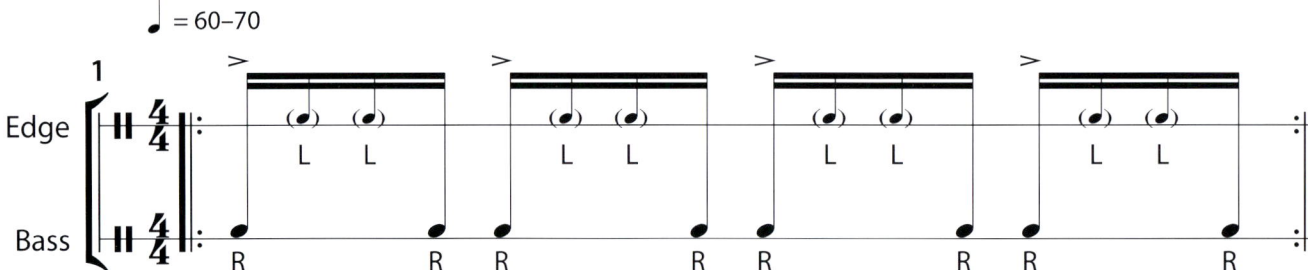

Now we interpret the pattern *ternary*, that is, as a *shuffle*:

Surdo Bass pattern (ternary in shuffle feel)

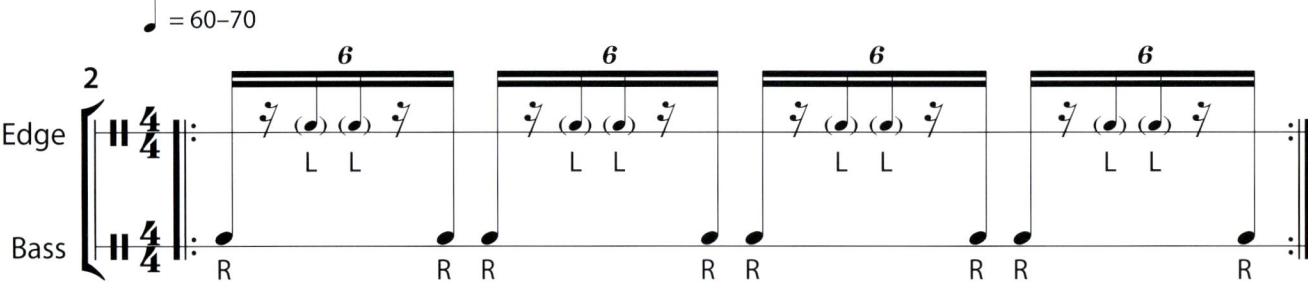

The authentic pattern of bossa and samba that needs to be created lies somewhere in between. So it's a matter of *feeling*, which can't be precisely represented in words or in notes. This is one of the main reasons for the decision to offer you **videos** complementary to this book. They not only show clearly how to play, but they also convey via the ear how the patterns and grooves are supposed to sound.

Online video 65

What we can only learn to a certain extent, will certainly improve as a result if we get to know the music we want to play. Listening is very important – not only in relation to the videos of this book.

You will always have styles and phrasings in your repertoire that you can utilize and build as your vocabulary on the instrument. However, you should also always deal with music that is difficult for you and whose rhythms and phrasing are not so easy to learn. This will help you expand your repertoire and find new ways of musical expression.

The following *playlist* provides a list of titles and albums that will help expand your musical repertoire – and thus also your rhythmic vocabulary. Here is a selection of such songs to play along with, which will give you a feel for the respective styles.

Playlist as listening recommendations

Cuban Style

album	title	artist(s)
El Rumbero del Piano	Café Pas d`Histoires	Eddie Palmieri
Pasado Presente	Si Te Contara Mambo	Guillermo Rubalcaba
The Best of Los Van Van	Que Tiene Vav Van Soy Normal, Natural	Los Van Van
Ruben Blades Y son de Solar LIVE	Todos Vuelven La Cancion del Final del Mundo	Ruben Blades
La sesion cubana	Nena	Zucchero
Tributo Tropical a los Beatles	Day Tripper Hey Jude	Various Artists
Rhythms del mundo classics	Because the Night One Step too Far	Various Artists

Brazilian Style

album	title	artist(s)
Brasil Acoustico	Favela	Jards Macale
Samba Mania Nacional Vol.1	E Preciso Muito Amor Brincadeira Tem hora Porta Aberta Meu Drama/Amei demais	Ze Carlos Sapatos Various Artists Eduardo
Nova Bossa/Red Hot on Verve	Agua de beber The Girl from Ipanema Corcovado Mas Que Nada	Astrud Gilberto & Antonio C. Jobim Astrud Gilberto & Antonio C. Jobim Stan Getz & Antonio C. Jobim Tamba Trio
Brazil Classics 2:O Samba	S.P.C.	Zeca Pagodinho
Nova Bossa/Red Hot on Verve	Mas Que Nada A Deusa Dos Orixás Formosa Quem me Guia	Tamba Trio Clara Nunes Ciro Monteiro Almir Guineto

Peruvian Style

album	title	artist(s)
Best of Susana Baca	Valentin Maria Lando	Susana Baca
30 Años Eva Ayllón	Obertura Raices de festejo	Eva Ayllón

Spanish Flamenco

album	title	artist(s)
Ciudad de las ideas	Ojos de la alhambra Ciudad de las ideas	Vicente Amigo
Solo Compas – Solea por Bulerias	Solea Por Bulerias	Grupo de Juana Amaya
El Mal Querer	Malamente Pienso en tu mirar	Rosalia
En Hispanoamerica	Tico Tico	Paco de Lucia
Fuente y caudal	Entre dos aguas	Paco de Lucia
Best of Gipsy Kings	Bamboleo Volare	Gipsy Kings

African Style

album	title	artist(s)
Guide (Wommat)	Leaving (Dem) Generations (Diamond)	Youssou N`Dour
Rhythmen der Malinke	Kassa Mendiani	Famadou Konate

Pop / Hip Hop / Funk / R & B / Blues

album	title	artist(s)
Thriller	Billie Jean Beat It	Michael Jackson
Elephunk	Where is the Love Shut Up	Black Eyed Peas
Curtain Call	Stan Lose Yourself	Eminem
In Between Dreams	Never Know	Jack Johnson
Good Things	I Need a Dollar	Aloe Blacc
Eterno Agosto	Sofia	Alvaro Soler
Back to Black	Valerie	Amy Winehouse
This Is the Life	This is the life	Amy MacDonald
FIA	FIA	Davido
The Writing`s on the Wall	Say My Name	Destiny`s Child
Creole Moon	Imitation of Love Now That You Got Me	Dr. John
The Raw & The Cooked	Good Thing	Fine Young Cannibals
The Best of James Brown	Papa`s Got a Brandnew Bag Funky Drummer	James Brown
Greatest Hits	Mexico How Sweet It Is	James Taylor

APPENDIX

Microphones

The following pictures show you different ways to amplify your cajón with a microphone.

Live situation

It is recommended to amplify the cajón with a *clip microphone* (here e.g. *AKG C 419*), which is attached on the back in the sound hole.

Studio situation

In the studio you use *two microphones* to achieve a differentiated sound and to reproduce the full frequency spectrum of your instrument.

You record the **bass frequencies** through the sound hole, here with a *dynamic* microphone, the *AKG D 112*, which is especially suitable for the bass range.

For the *mid and high frequencies*, I recommend a *condenser microphone* placed in front of your cajón, here an *AKG C 414* with a large diaphragm. The sound of both microphones is mixed, because you have recorded on two channels.

In a live situation you mic up your cajón at the sound hole.

Micro at the sound hole for the bass frequencies ...

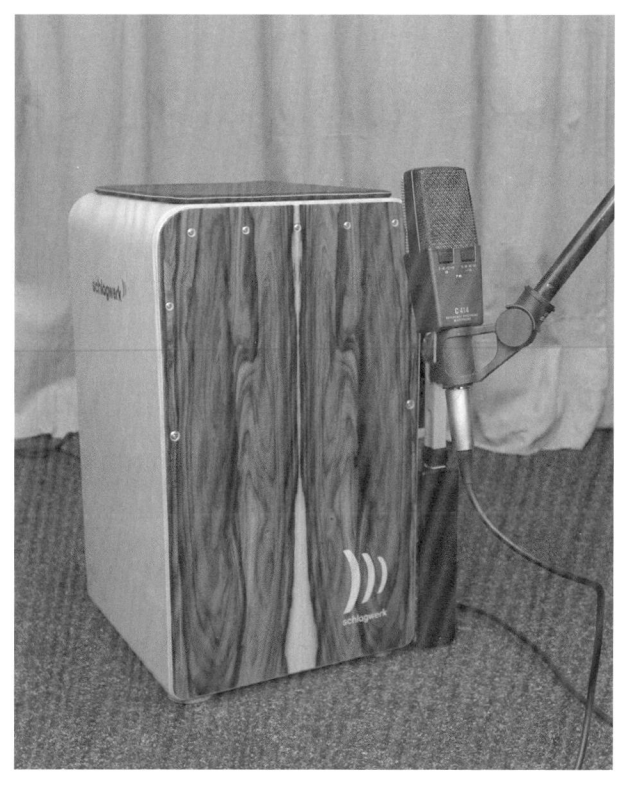

... Micro in front of the cajón for medium and high frequencies.

List of CD Play-Alongs

demo track	play-along	title	style	bpm	page(s)	time
1	2	Viva la Juventud	Son Clave – Cuba	$\quarternote = 105$	37	01:17
3	4	Barka Kapuut	Kalamatianos – Greece	$\eighthnote = 100$	47	01:49
5	6	Al Blue	Shuffle / Fast Blues	$\quarternote = 125$	48–51, 76, 77, 80	01:55
7	8	Am I going with you?	Pop	$\quarternote = 90$	26, 27, 28, 55–57, 72	01:29
9	10	Remember Boozoo	Zydeco	$\quarternote = 97$	58	01:14
11	12	One Old Melody	Singer/Songwriter Pop	$\quarternote = 102$	62, 64	02:19
13	14	Bem Vindo A Lapa	Latin Pop	$\quarternote = 81$	73, 86–89	01:41
15	16	Nao posso dancar	Forró	$\quarternote = 99$	83, 84	01:41
17	18	Diario Roubado	Samba Reggae	$\quarternote = 87$	90	01:24
19	20	In the Trap	Trap Music	$\quarternote = 93$	95	01:35
21	22	At the Right Moment	Trip Hop	$\quarternote = 75$	97	01:41
23	24	Kleine Baggy	Lounge	$\quarternote = 120$	98	01:17
25	26	Lorien	Kuduro	$\quarternote = 125$	99	01:40
27	28	Tano River	Kuduro variations (polyrhythm.)	$\quarternote = 115$	101	01:11
29	30	Sara	Kuduro shuffle	$\quarternote = 92$	101	01:08
31	32	Move Out and Scream	Reggaeton	$\quarternote = 96$	102	01:23
33	34	Berghain	Moombahton	$\quarternote = 109$	103	01:40
35	36	Nine Miles	Dub	$\quarternote = 138$	103	01:23

Play-Along Downloads

All play-alongs are compositions written by Peter Philipzen.

List of Videos